MW01514939

National Academy of Arbitra
2015 Skills Enhancement Workshop
Four Seasons Hotel Denver
Denver, CO
October 23, 2015
1:00 pm – 5:00 pm

Binder Index

Tab 1 – Agenda

Tab 2 – Presenter Bios

Tab 3 – Reference Materials

Tab 4 – *Babcock & Wilcox Construction Co.*, Decision

Tab 5 – GC 15-02, *Babcock & Wilcox* Memo, with attachments

Tab 6 – Deferral flow charts

Tab 7 – GC 15-04, Report of the General Counsel Concerning Rules

Tab 8 – Hypothetical Fact Pattern and Questions

Tab 9 – Answer Key for Hypothetical, with citations

National Academy of Arbitrators
2015 Skills Enhancement Workshop
Four Seasons Hotel Denver
Denver, CO
October 23, 2015
1:00 pm – 5:00 pm

AGENDA

I. Welcome and Introduction **1:00 p.m. to 1:10 p.m.**

Plenary session – Jennifer Abruzzo and John Doyle – 1:10 p.m. to 1:50 p.m.

II. Discussion *Babcock & Wilcox*
   a. Why the Change
   b. The New Standard for the Board to Defer – what is expected of arbitrators
   c. What's covered by the new standard and what isn't (8(a)(1) and/or (3) vs. 8(a)(5))

III. Overview of Material to Be Covered
   a. Protected Activity under Section 7
   b. Interference with Protected Activity
   c. Discipline and Discharge under 8(a)(1) and/or 8(a)(3) Theories
   d. Remedial Scheme

Workshops (3 groups) 1:50 p.m. to 2:50 p.m.

Small Group Presentations and Discussions led and moderated by Jennifer Abruzzo, John Doyle, Kelly Selvidge, Leticia Peña, Julia Durkin, Todd Saveland, and Kristyn Myers covering the following topics:

IV. What activity is "protected" by the Act under Section 7 –
   a. Classic Union activity
      i. Advocating for a Union
      ii. Membership in a Union
      iii. Holding Union office
      iv. Filing grievances
      v. Asserting contractual rights
   b. Internal Union activity
      i. Running for Union office
      ii. Campaigning for/supporting candidates for Union officer or ballot initiatives
      iii. Dissenting from/criticizing the Union's decisions courses of action
      iv. Pursuing Internal Union appeals
   c. Refraining from Union activity
      i. Resisting unionization
      ii. Choosing to be a nonmember
      iii. Choosing not to pay dues

    iv. *Beck* objections in connection with representation fees

    v. Efforts to decertify a Union

   d. Concerted Activity for Mutual Aid and Protection

    i. "With or on the authority of other employees"

    ii. Pertaining to Terms and Conditions of Employment

    iii. Conduct which May Lose the Protection of the Act

   e. Where the Act's Protection May Be Lost

    i. Disloyalty/disparagement

    ii. Intermittent strikes, partial strikes, strikes in violation of a no-strike clause

    iii. Discussion of *NLRB v. Local Union No. 1229, IBEW (Jefferson Standard Broadcasting),* 346 U.S. 464 (1953)

Break: 2:50 p.m. to 3:00 p.m.

Plenary Session: 3:00 p.m. – 4:00 p.m. John Doyle and Matt Lomax presentation covering the following topics:

V. Non-Disciplinary Types Of "Interference" With Section 7 Rights

  a. Granting Benefits (Note: May Also Violate Section 8(A)(3))

  b. Withholding Benefits (Note: May Also Violate Section 8(A)(3))

  c. Onerous Assignments/Working Conditions

  d. Surveillance

  e. Interrogation

  f. Solicitation Of Grievances

  g. More Stringent Enforcement Of Rules

  h. Threats

  i. Promising Benefits

  j. Creating Impression Of Surveillance

  k. Other Coercive Statements

  l. *Weingarten* Rights

  m. Analysis Of Employer Rules

VI. Defenses to Allegations of Non-Disciplinary Interference with Employee Rights

  a. Past Practice

  b. Business Reasons

  c. Isolated - De Minimis

  d. Subsequent Neutralizing Statements

  e. Joking Or Ambiguous

  f. Opinion

VII. Assessing Disciplines/Discharge Alleged to Be Improperly Motivated

  a. *The Continental Group*

  b. *Wright Line*

  c. *Atlantic Steel*
  d. *Clear Pine Mouldings*
  e. *Burnup and Sims*

VIII. NLRA Remedial Scheme
  a. Notice to Employees
  b. Cease and Desist Order
  c. Revocation of Unlawful Rules
  d. Expungement of Disciplines/Discharge
  e. Reinstatement
  f. Backpay

Workshop groups (3 groups) 4:00 p.m. to 4:50 p.m.

Group workshops led by John Doyle, Leticia Peña, Kelly Selvidge, Julia Durkin, Todd Saveland, and Kristyn Myers where participants will use supplied fact scenarios for issue-spotting exercise and moderated group discussion of how to apply the principles discussed during the training in practice.

4:50 p.m. to 5:00 p.m. Awarding of Certificates of Training

INSTRUCTOR BIOS

Jennifer Abruzzo - Ms. Abruzzo is the Deputy General Counsel of the National Labor Relations Board. She assists the General Counsel with overall oversight of multiple headquarters divisions and the 26 Regional Offices of the NLRB. Ms. Abruzzo left private practice and began working for the NLRB in 1995 as a field attorney in the Miami Office. She was promoted to the positions of Supervisory Field Attorney and Deputy Regional Attorney before moving to the NLRB's Division of Operations-Management in Washington, DC in January 2006. In February 2011, she joined former Acting General Counsel Solomon in the Office of the General Counsel, and she was named Deputy General Counsel to General Counsel Richard F. Griffin, Jr. in November 2013.

John Doyle – Mr. Doyle is a Deputy Assistant General Counsel in the Division of Operations-Management of the Office of the General Counsel in Washington, DC. He assists the General Counsel in managing the Agency's Regional Offices and provides programmatic support for the national enforcement and administration of the National Labor Relations Act. A graduate of Colgate University and Fordham University School of Law, Mr. Doyle joined the NLRB's Region 10 Offices in 1995, working first in the Atlanta, Georgia Regional Office and later in the Birmingham, Alabama Resident Office. In 2011, Mr. Doyle was promoted to Deputy Regional Attorney in the NLRB's Region 5 Office in Baltimore, Maryland, before assuming his current duties in 2014.

Julia Durkin – Ms. Durkin is a Field Attorney in Region 27, Denver. She earned a B.A. in Business Administration at the University of Mary Washington, graduating with honors. Julia earned her J.D. from Catholic University Columbus School of Law, graduating cum laude. Julia Durkin joined the Agency in 2010.

Matthew S. Lomax – Mr. Lomax is a Supervisory Field Examiner with Region 27 of the NLRB. He began working for the Agency in 1997 in Region 14, St. Louis after graduating from Truman State University in Missouri with a B.S. degree in Justice Systems. He earned an M.B.A. from Webster University in St. Louis in 2008. In 2011, he was promoted to his current position as Supervisory Field Examiner, in which position he is responsible for processing unfair labor practice and representation cases.

Kristyn Myers – Ms. Myers is a Field Attorney in Region 27, Denver. She graduated from the University of Colorado in 1997 with a B.A. in American History. She attended law school at Hamline University in St. Paul, Minnesota. After graduating from law school in 2002, she served a one-year clerkship for Justices Gilbert and Anderson at the Minnesota Supreme Court. Kristyn began her career with the NLRB in 2003 as a field attorney in Region 18, Minneapolis, and in 2009 she transferred to Region 27, Denver, Colorado.

Leticia Peña – Ms. Peña is the Deputy Regional Attorney for Region 27 of the National Labor Relations Board (Denver, Colorado). She is a graduate of the University of Colorado. Following graduation from Antioch Law School in 1983, Ms. Peña entered the private practice of law. She joined the NLRB in 1990 as a Field Attorney in the San Francisco Regional Office (Region 20) and subsequently transferred to the Denver Regional Office. In 2002, she was promoted to Supervisory Attorney in the Denver Regional Office, and in 2011 to the Deputy Regional Attorney position. Since April of 2015 she has been serving as Acting Regional Attorney for Region 27, with overall responsibility for the Region's legal work. Ms. Peña has been a Contributing Editor, *The Developing Labor Law,* from 2000 through the present and has taught various courses at the University of Denver, Sturm College of Law.

Jose R. Rojas - Mr. Rojas has been a Field Attorney in Region 27, Denver since October 2012. He earned his B.A. in Sociology at the University of California, Santa Cruz, and he earned his J.D. from University of California, Hastings College of the Law.

Todd Saveland – Mr. Saveland is a Field Attorney with Region 27 of the NLRB. Mr. Saveland joined the Agency in 2003 as a Field Examiner working in the Boston Regional Office, where he investigated hundreds unfair labor practice cases and dozens of representation petitions, before transferring to the Denver Regional office in 2007. While working full-time, Mr. Saveland attended law school part-time, earning with a Juris Doctor degree from the University of Denver in 2010. He became a Field Attorney in 2011. Mr. Saveland also holds a B.A. from Carleton University, Ottawa, Ontario, graduating with Honors, and a Master of Industrial Relations from Queen's University, Kingston, Ontario.

Kelly A. Selvidge – Ms. Selvidge is the Assistant to the Regional Director in NLRB Region 27, Denver. A career NLRB employee, she began working for the Agency in 1984 in Region 31, Los Angeles while still a student at the University of California Los Angeles (UCLA). She graduated from UCLA with a B.A. degree in Political Science in 1985. After graduation, she worked as a Field Examiner in the Agency's field office in Brooklyn, New York from 1985 until 1990, when she transferred to the downtown Los Angeles Regional office (Region 21). She served as a Supervisory Field Examiner in Region 21 from 1992 until her 2006 promotion to her current position.

REFERENCE MATERIALS WITH CASE LAW CITATION

I.   Welcome and Introduction 1:00 p.m. to 1:10 p.m

II.   Discussion *Babcock & Wilcox*
        a. Why the Change
        b. The New Standard for the Board to Defer – what is expected of arbitrators
        c. What's covered by the new standard and what isn't (8(a)(1) and/or (3) vs. 8(a)(5))

III.   Overview of Material to Be Covered
        a. Protected Activity under Section 7
        b. Interference with Protected Activity
        c. Discipline and Discharge under Section 8(a)(1) and (3) Theories
        d. Remedial Scheme

IV.   **What activity is "protected" by the Act under Section 7 -**

Section 7 states: Employees shall have the right to self-organization, to form, join, or assist labor organizations, to bargain collectively through representatives of their own choosing, and to engage in other concerted activities for the purpose of collective bargaining or other mutual aid or protection, and shall also have the right to refrain from any or all such activities …

Forming, joining, or assisting labor organizations (unions) is the type of Section 7 activity that many people think of first. This workshop will touch briefly on classic "union activity," and a few less classical varieties of protected union activities. Then it will turn to the broader, and sometimes more challenging concept to understand, of concerted activity for mutual aid and protection.

a. Union activity

The following are classic types of activities protected by Section 7 of the Act and an employer cannot discipline or otherwise discriminate against employees for engaging in such protected activities.

        i.   Advocating for a Union
        ii. Membership in a Union
        iii. Holding Union office
        iv. Filing grievances
        v.   Asserting contractual rights (see *NLRB v. City Disposal Systems, Inc.*, 465 US 822 (1984))

b. Internal Union activity

The Board has held activities within a union to be within Section 7's protections as well. This includes:

    i. Running for Union office

    ii. Campaigning for/supporting candidates for Union officer or ballot initiatives

    iii. Dissenting from/criticizing the Union's decisions courses of action

    iv. Pursuing Internal Union appeals

c. Refraining from Union activity

    i. Resisting unionization – Employees have the same right to campaign against a union organizing effort or union representation matters as for. Usually issues will arise if an employer treats opponents of the union differently than supporters. It is a violation for union representatives to tell represented employees that the union will not represent nonmember employees notwithstanding that the Union does in fact represent such employees. *Letter Carriers Local 233 (U.S. Postal Service)*, 311 NLRB 541 (1993)

    ii. Choosing to be a nonmember - (In *NLRB v. General Motors Corporation*, 373 U.S. 734, 742-43 (1963), the Supreme Court held that the term "member" requires <u>only</u> the payment of periodic dues and fees as opposed to full membership.)

    iii. Choosing not to pay dues - In *Communications Workers of America (CWA) v. Beck*, 487 U.S. 735, 762-63 (1988), the Supreme Court held that employees who are required to pay union dues and fees pursuant to a union security clause may only be charged for representational activities; that is, costs related to collective bargaining, contract administration, and grievance adjustment.

    iv. Efforts to decertify a Union afford employees and even supervisors who are included in the bargaining unit by agreement of the parties are afforded Section 7 protections from adverse action by either the employer or the union but the decertification effort must be started by the bargaining unit employee. See, e.g. *SKC Electric, Inc.*, 350 NLRB 857 (2007) (Board found RD Petitioner was an agent of the employer for purposes of soliciting decertification signatures because an employer official told him to do so)

d. Concerted Activity for Mutual Aid and Protection

The Board's decision in *Meyers Industries* is the seminal case for assessing whether conduct is protected by Section 7 of the Act as "concerted activity for mutual aid and protection." *Meyers Industries*, 268 NLRB 493 (1984) (Meyers I), remanded sub nom. *Prill v. NLRB*, 755 F.2d 941 (D.C. Cir.), cert.denied, 474 U.S. 948 (1985), reaffd., 281 NLRB 882 (1986) (*Meyers II*), enfd. sub nom. *Prill v. NLRB*, 835 F.2d 1481 (D.C. Cir. 1987), cert. denied, 487 U.S. 1205 (1988).

i. "With or on the authority of other employees"

Under the *Meyers* test, "to be concerted, individual employee activity must be engaged in with, or on the authority of other employees, and not solely by and on behalf of the employee himself." 268 NLRB at 497; 281 NLRB at 885.

Here are some examples of where this test is met:

a.   Authorization is not required to be explicit. "… an employee need not be expressly 'appointed' or 'nominated' as spokesman in order for his or her actions to be found concerted."

   Midland Hilton & Towers, 324 NLRB 1141, 1141 (1997)

b.   Authorization need not be subject-specific. Although two employees each advanced somewhat different complaints (cancellation of health insurance vs. failure to increase wages to compensate for cancellation), they were united in protesting the loss of benefits generally. The Board found their joint protest concerted.

   Hahner, Foreman & Harness, Inc., 343 NLRB 1423, 1424 (2004)

c.   Authorization may be implied if shown to be a "logical outgrowth" of prior discussions among employees. "We will find that an individual is acting on the authority of other employees where the evidence supports a finding that the concerns expressed by the individual employee are a logical outgrowth of the concerns expressed by the group."

   Amelio's, 301 NLRB 182, 183, fn. 4 (1991)

d.   An individual employee's call, on her own initiative, to the Department of Labor questioning her employer's holiday pay practices was concerted activity because she and two fellow employees earlier had brought the matter of holiday overtime compensation to a manager's attention.

   Every Woman's Place, 282 NLRB 413, 413 (1986), enfd. mem. 833 F.2d 1012 (6th Cir. 1987)

e.   In *Salisbury Hotel*, 283 NLRB 685, 686-687 (1987), even without evidence that employees agreed to act together, there was agreement among them that the lunch-hour policy should be taken up with management, and this was enough to make concerted a single employee's call to Dept. of Labor.

See also *Mike Yurosek & Son, Inc.*, 306 NLRB 1037, 1038 (1992), affd. 310 NLRB 831 (1993), enfd. 53 F.3d 261 (9th Cir. 1995); and *Boese Hilburn Electric Service Co.*, 313 NLRB 372, 373 (1993)

On the other hand, here are some examples where the standard was not met:

Examples of Activity found NOT Concerted

a.   *Oakes Machine Corp.*, 288 NLRB 456, 457 (1988) (employee's act of complaining to a state agency about allegedly unsafe working conditions not within Section 7 because it was not done in concert with other employees).

b.   *D.A. Collins Refractories*, 272 NLRB 931, 932 (1984) (employee not engaged in concerted activity when he filed individual unemployment compensation claim).

c.   *Capital Times Co.*, 234 NLRB 309 (1978) (employee cannot engage in concerted activity with supervisor or other non-employee).

d.   *Adelphi Institute Inc.*, 287 NLRB 1073 (1988) (inquiry by employee just placed on probation to another employee as to whether that employee had ever been on probation, held not concerted but rather individual action since employee was not initiating, inducing, or preparing for group action).

e.   *Goodyear Tire & Rubber Co.*, 269 NLRB 881 (1984) (employee's refusal to perform an assignment based on his belief that the equipment was unsafe held not concerted where employee acted alone and no other employee had complained).

f.   *United Parcel Service, Inc.*, 311 NLRB 974, 975 (1993) (false, intimidating, and coercive circumstances under which employee conducted investigation at another employer's place of business sufficiently egregious to cause employee to lose any protection he would otherwise be entitled to under the Act); see also, *Newark Morning Ledger*, 316 NLRB 1268, 1271 (1995).

g.   *House of Raeford Farms, Inc.*, 325 NLRB 463 (1998) (no violation where employees left work early and were not engaged in concerted protected activities – employees not free to set their own terms and conditions of employment).

ii. Pertaining to Terms and Conditions of Employment

Besides the requirement of concert, the Board requires that the matter pertain to a term or condition of employment, and involve a collective, rather than an individual goal. As an example:

a. Employees' reports to a state health department of excessive heat in a nursing home reflecting concerns about patients were not protected—no direct relationship to the employee's working conditions.

Waters of Orchard Park, 341 NLRB 642, 642-645 (2004)

b. Employees' activities will not be protected if those activities are aimed at influencing such matters as a change in management hierarchy, or the direction, scope or business management of an entity, or changes in employer practices or policies, if those matters bear no real relationship to employees' working conditions. See *Damon House, Inc.*, 270 NLRB 143, 143 (1984)

Some common forms of PROTECTED activity concerning working conditions are:

a. Petitions and group complaints made to employer
b. Concerted complaints to state and federal agencies
c. Complaints to Employer's customer

iii. Conduct which may Lose the Protection of the Act

Although ordinarily employees may engage in Section 7 activity with immunity from retribution, certain conduct can render the activity unprotected:

a. If the conduct amounts to disloyalty, defamation, disparagement of the product, or the employee engages in a malicious falsehood.

In *NLRB v. Local Union. No. 1229, IBEW (Jefferson Standard)*, 346 US 464, 471-472 (1953), the Court held that a television station lawfully discharged technician employees for "detrimental disloyalty" because they had prepared and distributed a leaflet to the public which strongly disparaged the quality of the station's broadcasting. In that case, the employees were not on strike, the leaflet did not refer to the union or a labor dispute, and the leaflet did not seek support or sympathy for the technicians. Id. at 476-477.

In general, communications are protected where 1) the communication indicates that it is related to an ongoing labor dispute and 2) the communication "is not so disloyal, reckless or maliciously untrue as to lose the Act's protection."

Found protected:

- *Endicott Interconnect Technologies, Inc.*, 345 NLRB 448, 451-452 (2005) (employee's comments in a newspaper article and internet posting referred to labor dispute and were protected despite remarks that that layoffs had left "gaping holes" in company's "critical knowledge base," and statements that company was "being tanked" by management, and that they would put company "into the dirt"), enf. denied, 453 F.3d 532 (D.C. Cir. 2006);

- *Community Hospital of Roanoke Valley*, 220 NLRB 217, 222-223 (1975) (statements by nurses regarding pay levels on television broadcast related to employees' efforts to improve wages and working conditions, protected), enfd. 538 F.2d 607 (4th Cir. 1976);

- *Emarco, Inc.*, 284 NLRB 832, 832-834 (1987) (employees' remarks that employer-subcontractor was not paying its bills, was unable to finish the job, and was "no damn good" and a "son-of-bitch," made in response to general contractor's questions about the cause of a strike against employer-subcontractor, protected).

Found Not protected:

- *Mountain Shadows Golf Resort*, 330 NLRB 1238, 1238-1239, 1241 (2000) (flyer distributed outside city council chambers unprotected; flyer made no reference to a labor dispute, its purpose and origin were undisclosed, and flyer was highly critical of company's management, and suggested that company be replaced by a competitor), affd. 338 NLRB 581 (2002), review denied, 86 Fed. Appx. 305 (9th Cir. 2004);

- *American Arbitration Association, Inc.*, 233 NLRB 71, 74-75 (1977) (employee engaged in unprotected disloyal conduct by using confidential files and sending a questionnaire to the employer's clients that ridiculed the employer's business operations);

- *Fire House Restaurant*, 220 NLRB 818, 824-825 (1975) (employees engaged in unprotected disloyal conduct when they criticized the quality of food served in the employer's restaurant).

b.   If the conduct constitutes a partial, intermittent, or sporadic strike where for example, employees work a partial day or choose which tasks to perform, or a strike in violation of an express or implied no-strike clause

     i.   *DaimlerChrysler Corp.*, 344 NLRB 1324, 1324-1326 (2005) (employee's email advocating a slowdown was unprotected)

     ii.   *Audubon Health Care Center*, 268 NLRB 135, 135-136 (1983) (nurses' aides who refused to work in one section while agreeing to work in another section, engaged in an unprotected partial strike)

iii. Employer's may discipline employees for instigating or participating in a strike or slowdown that is contrary to the collective-bargaining agreement. *Midwest Precision Castings Co.*, 244 NLRB 597, 599 (1979) (respondent did not violate the Act by disciplining union steward for inducing employee participation in an unauthorized illegal work slowdown in direct violation of contractual no-strike, no slowdown clause);

Moreover, under *Teamsters v. Lucas Flour Co.*, 369 US 95 (1962), a no-strike clause is implied during the term of collective-bargaining agreement that provides a grievance/arbitration procedure as the exclusive method for resolving disputes.

iv. *Chrysler Corp.*, 232 NLRB 466, 474 (1977), affd. mem. 125 LRRM 3063 (D.C. Cir. 1979) (Mere participation in or active leadership of an unauthorized work stoppage "is in and of itself sufficient grounds for removal.").

v. *Metropolitan Edison Co. v. NLRB*, 460 U.S. 693, 699 fn. 6 (1983) ("[E]mployees who instigate or provide leadership for unprotected strikes may be subject to more severe discipline than other employees.").

c. Misuse of Confidential Information

In *Asheville School, Incorporated,* 347 NLRB 877, 877 & fn. 2 (2006) the Board stated in adopting the judge's finding that the Respondent's discharge of the charging party did not violate Sec. 8 (a) (1), that it was unnecessary to pass on whether her conversations with other employees were concerted under Sec. 7. The Board found, in agreement with the judge, that under the circumstances presented, the charging party's disclosure of confidential wage and salary information was not protected. In balancing the respondent's interest in confidentiality with the charging party's interest in disclosure, the Board noted that the record established that the charging party, as respondent's payroll accountant, possessed special custody of wage and salary personnel records on respondent's behalf, that respondent treated the information in these records as confidential, and that the charging party was aware that her established job duties, which she breached, required that she maintain the confidentiality of this information. See *Clinton Corn Processing Co.*, 253 NLRB 622, 623-625 (1980) (discharge of payroll clerk lawful where she disclosed confidential wage and salary information); see also *Cook County College Teachers Local 1600*, 331 NLRB 118, 120 (2000); *International Business Machines Corp.*, 265 NLRB 638, 638 (1982).

V. Non-disciplinary Types of "Interference" with Section 7 Rights

Section 8(a)(1) of the Act provides that it shall be an unfair labor practice for an employer "to interfere with, restrain, or coerce employees in the exercise of the rights guaranteed in section 7." The Board applies an objective standard, assessing whether conduct reasonably tends to interfere with employee rights. Thus, actual coercion is not necessary and the finding of a Section 8(a)(1) violation:

> "does not depend on the respondent's motive or the success or failure of the coercion, but depends instead on whether the respondent engaged in conduct that may reasonably tend to interfere with the free exercise of rights under the Act."

Naomi Knitting Plant, 328 NLRB 1279, 1280 (1999), citing *Williamhouse of California, Inc.*, 317 NLRB 699, 713 (1995).

a. GRANTING BENEFITS (Note: may also violate Section 8(a)(3))

1. In finding a grant of benefits unlawful, Board does not rely on any presumption that benefits granted are unlawful, rather it draws an inference of improper motivation and interference with employee free choice from all the evidence presented and from respondent's failure to establish a legitimate reason for the timing of the benefit. *Holly Farms Corp.*, 311 NLRB 273, 274 (1993) (granting wage increase *unlawful* where wage increase was unscheduled, contrary to employer's policy, addressed a primary concern of certain employees and the size, timing, and applicability of the increase entirely at respondents' discretion).

2. *Great Lakes Warehouse Corp.*, 330 NLRB 807 (2000) (Offer of supervisory position).

b. WITHOLDING BENEFITS (Note: may also violate Section 8(a)(3))

1. It is well established that as a general rule an employer must grant benefits "as he would if a union were not in the picture". An exception to this rule exists for employers whose pattern of granting wage increases has been haphazard. In order to fall within that exception, an employer, among other things, must not seek to put the onus for delaying the wage increase on the union.

c. ONEROUS ASSIGNMENTS/WORKING CONDITIONS

1. New and more onerous working conditions, *Marcus Management, Inc.*, 292 NLRB 251 (1989); announcement of "crackdown", *Treanor Moving & Storage Company, Inc.*, 311 NLRB 371 (1993); "gag order" imposed on union supporter.

2. Assignment of additional work because of union activities and restricting movement of union supporters in plant. *Fieldcrest Cannon, Inc.*, 318 NLRB 470, 498-499, 504-507 (1995).

d. SURVEILLANCE

1. Observation of open activity

    a. Where employees are conducting their activities openly on or near company premises, open observation of such activities by an employer is not unlawful. *Roadway Package System*, 302 NLRB 961 (1991)

    b. Posting a guard with binoculars, constitutes more than ordinary or casual observation of public union activity and is unlawful. *Sands Hotel & Casino,* 306 NLRB 172 (1992) (no evidence the respondent's conduct was based on safety or property concerns) cf. *McGraw Edison*, 259 NLRB 702, 716 (1981) (employer had reason to anticipate violence so no violation to post security guards).

    c. Conduct deemed lawful under principle that management officials may observe public union conduct so long as officials do not "do something out of the ordinary." *Eddyleon Chocolate Co.,* 301 NLRB 887, 888 (1991). Compare, *Villa Maria Nursing and Rehabilitation Center, Inc.*, 335 NLRB 1345, 1353 (2001) where increase in number of security guards and time spent watching activities of union organizers went beyond "mere observation" and was deemed unlawful.

2. Photographing and Videotaping

    a. Absent proper justification, photographing employees engaged in protected concerted activities constitutes unlawful surveillance because it has a tendency to intimidate employees and interfere with exercise of Section 7 rights. Photographing in the mere belief that something "might" happen is not a sufficient justification. *F.W. Woolworth Co.*, 310 NLRB 1197 (1993); see also, *National Steel and Shipbuilding Co.*, 324 NLRB 499 (1997) (peaceful union rallies); *Labor Ready, Inc.*, 327 NLRB 1055 (1999), (employer videotapes of workers employed by temporary service in waiting room waiting for assignments unlawful).

    b. *Ordman's Park & Shop*, 292 NLRB 953, 956 (1989) (no violation to photograph non-employee union reps who picketed on sidewalk and distributed handbills; no photography of any employees and no evidence of coercion of employees; employer wanted to secure evidence of alleged trespassing activities, citing *Roadway Express, Inc.*, 271 NLRB 1238 (1984). See also, *Town and Country Supermarkets*, 340 NLRB 1410, 1414 – 1415 (2004) (employer privileged to photograph and videotape employees where employer had reasonable basis to anticipate misconduct/unlawful union conduct that justified such conduct).

c. *Washington Fruit and Produce Co.*, 343 NLRB 1215, 1216-1218 (2004)(videotaping employees during union rally found lawful under *National Steel and Shipbuilding Co.,* 324 NLRB 499 (1997), where employer had legitimate safety and trespassing concerns. Here, union held large rally outside building without giving employer advance notice of intent, duration of rally, size or purpose. Over 100 people demonstrated, many of them nor recognizable by employer).

e. INTERROGATION

1. <u>TEST</u>: Interrogation of employees is not unlawful per se. In determining whether or not an interrogation violates Section 8(a)(1) of the Act, the Board looks at **whether, under all the circumstances, the interrogation reasonably tends to interfere with, restrain, or coerce employees** in the exercise of their Section 7 rights. *Rossmore House*, 269 NLRB 1176, 1177 (1984), *Emery Worldwide*, 309 NLRB 185, 186 (1992).

2. *Sunnyvale Medical Clinic*, 277 NLRB 1217 (1985) (applied totality of circumstances test to interrogation, even though not an open and active union supporter; areas of inquiry in test are: background, the nature of information sought, identity of the questioner, and the place an method of interrogation; no violation found where: employee was not open union supporter but was not intent on keeping her support for the union hidden from the employer; no history of employer hostility towards or discrimination against union supporters; nature of the questions was general and non-threatening; employee and supervisor had a friendly relationship and conversation was casual and amicable).

3. *Los Angeles Airport Hilton Hotel and Towers*, 354 NLRB No. 17 (2009), incorporated by reference 355 NLRB No. 122 (2010) (interrogation of employee about attendance at union meeting unlawful, as was another interrogation that occurred in context of warning being given for participating in protected concerted activity. However, interrogation of employee about what employee would do in event of strike not unlawful where employee had initiated conversation).

4. *Westwood Health Care Center d/b/a Medcare Associates*, 330 NLRB 935, 939 (2000) (in analyzing questioning of employees, Board followed totality of circumstances set forth in *Rossmore House* and so-called "*Bourne*" factors, so named because they were first set out in *Bourne v. NLRB*, 332 F.2d 47, 48 (2d Cir. 1964). Those factors are: (1) The background, i.e. is there a history of employer hostility and discrimination? (2) The nature of the information sought, e.g., did the interrogator appear to be seeking information on which to base taking action against individual employees? (3) The identity of the questioner, i.e. how high was he in the company hierarchy? (4) Place and method of interrogation, e.g. was employee called from work to the boss's office? Was there an atmosphere of unnatural formality? (5) Truthfulness of the reply. Board held factors are not to be mechanically applied in each case, nor does a determination require strict evaluation of each factor, rather, they are useful indicia that serve as starting point for assessing the "totality of the circumstances"; where there has been several incidents of interrogation, each incident does not require a formalistic application of the "*Bourne*" factors to each of the separate incidents alleged unlawful, but will take into account all those incidents rather than consider them in isolation.

5. *Gardner Engineering*, 313 NLRB 755 (1994), (questioning of an employee regarding the union sentiments of others is unlawful).

f. SOLICITATION OF GRIEVANCES

1. *Manorcare Health Services-Easton*, 356 NLRB No. 39 (2010) (a past practice of soliciting grievances does not immunize an employer from Board sanction for soliciting grievances and promising to remedy them for the purpose of discouraging unionization. "[I]t is not the solicitation of grievances itself that is coercive and violative of Section 8(a)(1), but the promise to correct grievances … that is unlawful." *Uarco, Inc.*, 216 NLRB 1, 2 (1974)).

2. When an employer institutes a new practice of soliciting employee grievances during a union organizational campaign, "there is a compelling inference that he is implicitly promising to correct those inequities he discovers as a result of his inquiries and likewise urging on his employees that the combined program of inquiry and correction will make union representation unnecessary." *Embassy Suites Resort*, 309 NLRB 1313, 1316 (1992), citing *Reliance Electric Co.*, 191 NLRB 44, 46 (1971).

3. *Ichikoh Mfg.*, 312 NLRB 1022, 1024 (1993) (in absence of any evidence that respondent has a past practice and policy of soliciting employee grievances, employer, after soliciting from employees their concerns, implicitly promised to remedy several grievances in violation of 8(a)(1), including working on a new employee handbook).

g. MORE STRINGENT ENFORCEMENT OF RULES

1. *Fleming Companies, Inc.*, 336 NLRB 192 (2001)

h. THREATS

1. Discipline

2. Discharge

3. Layoff

4. Changes in Terms and Conditions of Employment

    a. *KEZI, Inc.*, 300 NLRB 594 (1990) (no violation by circulating a memorandum to employees telling them that employer planned to implement a 401K pension plan that excludes coverage of employees who are members of a collective-bargaining unit for which retirement benefits were the subject of good-faith bargaining).

5. Unspecified Reprisals

   a. *Valerie Manor, Inc.*, 351 NLRB 1306 (2007) (threat of unspecified reprisals).

   b. *Paul Mueller Co.*, 332 NLRB 312 (2000) (threatening two strikers with closer supervision because of union activity).

   c. *Yale New Haven Hospital*, 309 NLRB 363, 368 (1992) (supervisor unlawfully threatened employee with reprisal by telling an employee that if he did not stop protected activities he would "talk" to him again; implies that the talk will not be mere conversation but will concern the employment of the offending employee).

   d. *Cox Fire Protection*, 308 NLRB 793 (1992) (owner's statement that "this isn't a threat, but I want to kick your ass", held unlawful as employees could reasonably fear that the owner was clearly disposed to unfavorably exercising his authority as an employer against any employee involved in the protected activity; fact that the owner did not elaborate on his metaphor by specifically mentioning "forms of retaliation" does not significantly lessen the ominous nature of the statement coming from a company owner whose control over the employees' job security was virtually total).

   e. *Leather Center, Inc.*, 308 NLRB 16 (1992) (production manager's statement to employee that he knew she was talking to employees about the union and that she should be careful, unlawful, as remarks constitute a veiled threat of possible repercussions because of her suspected union activities).

6. Implied Threats

   a. *Double D Construction Group, Inc.*, 339 NLRB 303 (2003) – shaking finger and saying "...remember your bills..." threatened job security and thus violated Section 8(a)(1).

   b. *Equipment Trucking Co., Inc.*, 336 NLRB 277 (2001) (statement, if you don't like it, find another job, implied threat of discharge).

i. Promising Benefits

1. *Fabric Warehouse*, 294 NLRB 189 (1989) (violation where respondent did not merely compare the benefits it currently provided its union employees with those provided its nonunion employees or simply promise to maintain the status quo if there were no union; respondent told the employees they *would receive* a certain package of benefits that combined some of the best elements of both the union and the nonunion benefits it currently provided its employees, thus offering them a better set of benefits than either their own or the nonunion employees' current benefits; respondent also told employees that these benefits were better than the benefits they currently received and that they had to decide whether they wanted to go nonunion by a certain date).

j. Creating impression of surveillance

1. TEST: *Register Guard*, 344 NLRB 1142, 1144 (2005) (test is whether the employee would reasonably assume from the statement that their union activities had been placed under surveillance." *Flexsteel Industries,* 311 NLRB 257, 257 (1993).

2. The Board does not require employees to keep their activities secret before an employer can be found to have created an unlawful impression of surveillance. Nor has the Board held that the smallness of a plant will preclude the finding that the employer created an impression of surveillance. Board does not require that an employer's words on their face reveal the employer acquired its knowledge of the employee's activities by unlawful means. *United Charter Service*, 306 NLRB 150, 151 (1992).

k. OTHER COERCIVE STATEMENTS

1. Union supporter should quit

    a. *Medco Health Solutions Of Las Vegas, Inc.*, 357 NLRB No. 25 (2011) (respondent's statement that, if employee could not support the respondent's policies, there were other jobs out there and perhaps "this wasn't the place for him" was an implied threat in violation of 8(a)(1)).

    b. *McDaniel Ford, Inc.*, 322 NLRB 956 (1997) (statement to employees engaged in protected concerted activities that if they were unhappy, they should look for jobs somewhere else; threat violated 8(a)(1)).

    c. *Stoody Co.*, 312 NLRB 1175, 1181 (1993) (statement to employee that those who were "so nitpicking" as to complain about detrimental action taken unilaterally by the employer should seek other employment; such statements convey the message that complaints about working conditions and continued employment are incompatible and implicitly threaten discharge to those who would voice them).

2. Union supporter disloyal

    a. *House Calls, Inc.*, 304 NLRB 311, 313 (1991) (owner stating to employees that they were ingrates who were hitting him when he was down, equated union activity with disloyalty in violation of 8(a)(1)).

    b. *Dauman Pallet, Inc.*, 314 NLRB 185, fn. 7 (1994) (co-owner's statement that employee who had joined other employees in a strike had "betrayed" him and "stabbed him the back").

3. Disparaging union supporters or union

    a. *Wal-Mart Stores, Inc.*, 350 NLRB 879, 880 (2007) (although Section 8(c) provides that "[t]he expressing of views, argument, or opinion" are not unlawful if "such expression contains no threat of reprisal or force or promise of benefit," supervisor's conduct was not merely the expression of personal opinion, but both disparaged employee for engaging in protected activities and suggested that his protected activity was incompatible with continued employment; respondent violated 8(a)(1) by disparaging employee's union activity and inviting him to quit).

    b. *Circuit-Wise, Inc.*, 306 NLRB 766, 788 (1992) (supervisor's moderately obscene comments questioning the masculinity of the union, merely amounted to name calling and did not rise to the level of actions violative).

    c. *Mademoiselle Knitwear*, 297 NLRB 272 (1989) (calling union "crooks", not violative).

    d. *Domsey Trading Corp.*, 310 NLRB 777, 793 (1993) (employer's conduct on picket line of making racial, ethnic, sexual slurs and gross vulgarities directed against the employees and union representatives in the presence of employees, unlawful).

4. Stating that Protected Activity is the Reason for the Discipline

    a. *Publix Super Markets, Inc.*, 347 NLRB 1434, 1435 (2006) (supervisor's threats to discipline and/or discharge employees for engaging in concerted activity of serving as witnesses for co-worker, violated 8(a)(1)).

    b. *Black Magic Resources*, 312 NLRB 667, fn. 3 (1993), 317 NLRB 721 (1995) (telling employee he would not have been discharged if he had not filed a grievance, violated 8(a)(1)).

c. *Teledyne Advanced Materials*, 332 NLRB 539 (2000) (telling employees not to talk about union and that they could be written up if caught talking about the union violative).

I. The Basics of Weingarten Rights

1. Right to Union Representation in Investigatory Interview

- In a unionized setting, an employee has a right to union representation in an *investigatory* interview with the employer when the employee *reasonably believes* the interview may result in discipline and the employee *requests* representation.

ii. Union Representative Participation

- The union representative has a right to participate in the interview, although the participation is subject to some limitations.

iii. Employer Options

- Once the employee requests representation, the employer has three options: (1) grant the request; (2) discontinue the interview; or (3) give the employee the option to continue without representation or to end the interview.

2. When Do *Weingarten* Rights Apply?

Overview

A. *Weingarten* rights apply when these four elements are present:

i. The employee is *represented* by a union

ii. The interview is *investigatory*

iii. The employee *reasonably believes* discipline might result

iv. The employee *requests* representation

B. Further, a collective-bargaining agreement may provide an employee a right to union representation in other situations.

> Example

> i.   A contract may require the employer, rather than the employee, to call in the steward whenever an employee receives discipline.

> ii. However, in that case, a failure to have a steward present would be a contractual violation and not a violation of Section 8(a)(1) of the Act.

A. Representation by a Union

> *Weingarten* rights apply only to employees represented by a union.

> *IBM Corp.*, 341 NLRB 1288 (2004)

B. Interview Is Investigatory

1. Investigation of misconduct

    a. *Weingarten* rights generally apply to an interview when an employer investigates an employee's alleged misconduct, such as theft, fraud, or altercations with another employee.

        i.   Examples

             • Specifically, in *J. Weingarten, Inc.,* 202 NLRB 446 (1973), the Board found sales clerk Collins was entitled to a representative when the employer questioned her about placing only $1 in the cash register when the box of chicken cost $2.98.

             • Where the employer did not allow a representative when conducting a criminal investigation of security police officers making unauthorized purchases under a uniform allowance program, a *Weingarten* violation was found.

               Postal Service, 241 NLRB 141 (1979)

             • A *Weingarten* violation was also found where the employer did not allow the employee to have a representative and the investigation involved alleged adulteration of gasoline, an obvious form of dishonesty.

               Exxon Co., 223 NLRB 203 (1976)

- When employees were interviewed following a fight between employees, a *Weingarten* violation was found.

  Potter Electric Signal Co., 237 NLRB 1289 (1978), enfd. in relevant part 600 F.2d 120 (8th Cir. 1979)

2. Decision to discipline

   a. If Decision Is Final – Not Investigatory

      i. *Weingarten* does *not* apply where the meeting is held solely for the purpose of informing an employee of, and acting upon, a previously made disciplinary decision.

         Baton Rouge Water Works Co., 246 NLRB 995, 997 (1979)

      ii. *Example*

         - In *Airco Alloys*, 249 NLRB 524 (1980), the "conversation" appeared to be voluntary because it occurred after the employer told the employee that he was being terminated and the employee was not asked any questions by the employer. Instead, the employee attempted to explain his performance and the Board found no *Weingarten* violation.

   b. If Decision Is Not Final – Investigatory

      i. *Weingarten* rights apply if an employer informed an employee of a disciplinary action and then sought facts or evidence in support of that action, or attempted to have the employee admit his alleged wrongdoing or sign a statement to that effect. *Baton Rouge Water Works Co.*, supra.

         See also *Brunswick Electric Membership Corp.*, 308 NLRB 361, 396-400 (1992)

      ii. *Example*

         - In *ITT Lighting Fixtures*, 261 NLRB 229 (1982), enfd. in relevant part, 719 F.2d 851 (6th Cir. 1983), the employer claimed it made the decision to suspend before an interview and thus there was no *Weingarten* violation. The Board disagreed because:

            o During the interview the employer did not tell the employee that it had made a decision

            o The employee was questioned about why he left work early

            o The employee was not suspended until after the second meeting

- In *Beverly Farm Foundation,* 323 NLRB 787, 794 (1997), the employer unlawfully denied an employee's *Weingarten* rights where:

    o The employee requested a representative

    o The discipline to be imposed was not pre-determined by the employer because the internal review committee, whose members were authorized to investigate violations of an abuse and neglect policy, could question the employee about the incident and the employee could present his version of the events.

- In *Henry Ford Health System,* 320 NLRB 1153, 1154 (1996), the Board found that *Weingarten* rights apply when an employer's disciplinary action is not final and binding until it is reviewed by a grievance council.

    o The council's proceedings were investigatory because they included testimony from the grievant and other witnesses and review of documents.

C. Employee Reasonably Believes Interview May be Leading to Discipline

1. Objective standards

    a. *Weingarten* rights apply when an employee's request for representation is based on a reasonable belief, in light of all the circumstances, that discipline may ensue.

    b. The "reasonable grounds" for fearing disciplinary action will be measured by objective standards under all circumstances of the case; hence, the employee's motivation will not be probed.

    > *Weingarten,* 420 U.S. at 257, fn. 5 (1975), citing the Board in *Quality Mfg.,* 195 NLRB 197, 198 (1972)

    > See also *Roy H. Park Broadcasting,* 255 NLRB 229, 232 (1981); *Consolidated Edison Co.,* 323 NLRB 910 (1997)

D. Employee Requests Representation

1. Who makes the request

a. *Weingarten* rights arise only when an employee requests representation inasmuch as the employee may forgo his guaranteed right and voluntarily participate in an interview unaccompanied by a union representative.

Weingarten, 420 U.S. at 257

i. A request for representation must be made by the employee involved, not a union official.

- In *Appalachian Power Company,* 253 NLRB 931, 933 (1980), a steward's statements that he was present at a meeting as the shop steward did not invoke *Weingarten* protections because the employee involved, not the steward, had an immediate stake in the outcome of the disciplinary process and had the right to determine whether union assistance was more or less advantageous to his interests.

ii. An employer is not required to offer union representation; it must be requested by the employee.

Montgomery Ward & Co., 269 NLRB 904, 905 (1984) (employer is not required to volunteer representative; fear or confusion on part of employee does not obviate requirement that employee must request representation before *Weingarten* protections come into play), citing *Weingarten,* 420 U.S. at 257; *Coca-Cola Bottling Co. of Los Angeles,* 227 NLRB 1276 (1977)

2. To whom the request is made

a. The employee's request for union representation is valid if:

i. Made to the interviewer during or prior to the interview

Lennox Industries, supra; *Amoco Oil Co.,* 278 NLRB 1, 8 (1986)

OR

ii. Communicated by another person to the person conducting the interview prior to the interview. *Consolidated Freightways Corp.,* 264 NLRB 541, 542 (1982).

M. ANALYSIS OF EMPLOYER RULES

1. The Board has recognized that determining the lawfulness of an employer's work rules requires balancing competing interests. Resolution of the issue presented by contested rules of conduct involves "working out an adjustment

between the undisputed right of self-organization assured to employees under the Wagner Act and the equally undisputed right of employers to maintain discipline in their establishments. ... Opportunity to organize and proper discipline are both essential elements in a balanced society." *Lafayette Park Hotel*, 326 NLRB 824 (1998), citing *Republic Aviation v. NLRB*, 324 U.S. 793, 797-798 (1945).

2. In *Lafayette Park Hotel*, the Board held an employer may violate Section 8(a)(1) through the mere maintenance of certain work rules even in the absence of enforcement. The appropriate inquiry is: **whether the rule in question "would reasonably tend to chill employees in the exercise of their Section 7 rights."**

3. In *Lutheran Heritage Village-Livonia,* 343 NLRB 646 (2004), the Board refined the standard and found that mere maintenance of a work rule may violate 8(a)(1) if the rule has a chilling effect on Section 7 activity. This includes (1) rules that explicitly restrict protected concerted activity and (2) rules that do not explicitly prohibit Section 7 activity if:

    a. employees would reasonably construe the rule's language to prohibit Section 7 activity;

    b. the rule was promulgated in response to union or other Section 7 activity; or

    c. the rule was actually applied to restrict the exercise of Section 7 rights

4. The Board cautions against "reading particular phrases in isolation," and will not find a violation simply because a rule could conceivably be read to restrict Section 7 activity. *Lutheran Heritage* at 646-647. See also *Palms Hotel and Casino*, 344 NLRB 351, 355-356 (2005) ("We are simply unwilling to engage in such speculation in order to condemn as unlawful a facially neutral work rule that is not aimed at Section 7 activity and was neither adopted in response to such activity nor enforced against it.") The rule must be given a reasonable reading and we must not presume improper interference with employee rights. The potentially violative phrases must be considered in the proper context. Compare *Flex Frac Logistics, LLC*, 358 NLRB No. 127, slip op. at 3 (2012); *The Roomstore*, 357 NLRB No. 143, slip op. at 1 n.3, 1617 (2011); *Wilshire at Lakewood*, 343 NLRB 141, 144 (2004).

5. Some additional circumstances to consider are:

    a. Does the rule address legitimate business concerns?

    b. Is the rule ambiguous as written?

    c. Has the Employer exhibited antiunion animus?

d. Has the Employer by other action led employees to believe the rule prohibits Section 7 activity?

6. Rules that are ambiguous as to their application to Section 7 activity, and that contain no limiting language or context that would clarify to employees that the rule does not restrict Section 7 rights, are unlawful. *Claremont Resort and Spa*, 344 NLRB 832, 836 (2005) (rule proscribing "negative conversations" about managers that was contained in a list of policies regarding working conditions, with no further clarification or examples, was unlawful because of its potential chilling effect on protected activity.) *Norris/O'Bannon*, 307 NLRB 1236, 1245 (1992), quoting *Paceco*, 237 NLRB 399 fn. 8 (1978) ("Where ambiguities appear in employee work rules promulgated by an employer, the ambiguity must be resolved against the promulgator of the rule rather than the employees who are required to obey it."). Board precedent holds the mere maintenance of an ambiguous or overly broad rule is unlawful because it tends to inhibit employees from engaging in otherwise protected activity. *Ingram Book Co.*, 315 NLRB 515, 516 (1994); *J. C. Penney Co.*, 266 NLRB 1223, 1224 (1983).

7. In contrast, rules that clarify and restrict their scope by including examples of clearly illegal or unprotected conduct, such that they could not reasonably be construed to cover protected activity, are not unlawful. *Tradesman Intl.*, 338 NLRB 460, 460-462 (2002) (prohibition against "disloyal, disruptive, competitive, or damaging conduct" would not be reasonably construed to cover protected activity, given the rule's focus on other clearly illegal or egregious activity and the absence of any application against protected activity.)

Memorandum GC 15-04

1. Issued March 18, 2015 to provide guidance to employers preparing or reviewing their handbooks and other rules.

2. Divided into two parts:

    a. Comparisons of rules found unlawful with rules found lawful and explanations.

        i. Confidentiality
        ii. Employee conduct
        iii. Company logos, copyrights, and trademarks
        iv. Photography and recording
        v. Leaving work
        vi. Conflict of interest

b. Handbook rules from a settled unfair labor practice charge against Wendy's International LLC. Sets forth Wendy's rules initially found unlawful with Wendy's modified rules, adopted pursuant to a settlement agreement, which the Office of the General Counsel does not believe violate the Act.

Purple Communications, 361 NLRB No. 126 (2014)

1. A Board majority overruled *Register Guard,* 351 NLRB 1110 (2007), which held that employees have no statutory right to use their employer's email system for Section 7 purposes.

2. In *Purple,* the majority concluded that an employer that gives its employees access to its email system must presumptively permit the employees to use the email system for statutorily protected communications during nonworking time.

3. An employer can rebut the presumption by showing that special circumstances make its restrictions necessary to maintain production and discipline.

4. The decision applies only to email, only to employees who use their employer's email system for work, and only to employees' nonworking time. Employers may still monitor email use for legitimate management reasons and tell employees that they have no expectation of privacy when they use the email system.

5. The Board may expand the holding of *Purple* to other forms of electronic communications.

No-solicitation rules / No-distribution rules

1. *Stoddard-Quirk Manufacturing Co.*, 138 NLRB 615 (1962) (rules prohibiting *distribution* of literature are presumed valid unless they extend to activities during non-working time and in non-working area; the right of employees to *solicit* on plant premises must be afforded subject only to the restriction that it be on nonworking time). Distribution of literature may be prohibited even in non-working areas if an employer establishes a business justification for such a rule.

2. *Our Way, Inc.*, 268 NLRB 394 (1983) (rules against solicitation or distribution of literature during "working time" are presumptively lawful, and will not be condemned as ambiguous merely because the term "working time" is not defined; rules using "working time" are valid because that term connotes periods when employees are performing actual job duties, periods which do not include employees' own time such as lunch and break periods; rules using the term "working hours" connotes from beginning of shift to the end and are presumptively invalid).

3. Any rule that requires employees to secure permission from their employer as a precondition to engaging in protected concerted activity on an employee's free time and in nonwork areas is unlawful. *Brunswick Corp.*, 282 NLRB 794, 795 (1987); *Cardinal Home Products, Inc.*, 338 NLRB 1004, 1005-1006 (2003) (two overly broad no solicitation/no distribution rules; Board rejected employer's contention that rules were not enforced; held mere maintenance of overly broad rules was bad.)

4. Although a rule may be presumptively lawful on its face, such rule may still violate 8(a)(1) if the *timing* of the promulgation of the rule indicates an unlawful motive. Timing by itself is not presumed to be unlawful; rather, upon a showing of timing, the burden is on the employer to explain the timing.

5. Board has held that lawful rule prohibiting distribution of literature in work areas does not apply to mixed use area. The concerns for protecting the production process do not rise to the same level when an employer compromises a work area by permitting non-work use of it. *Transcon Lines*, 235 NLRB 1163, 1165 (1978), *Rockingham Sleepwear*, 188 NLRB 698, 701(1971); *United Parcel Service*, 327 NLRB 317 (1998), *Meijer , Inc., v. NLRB*, 463 F.3d 534 (2006)(in order to constitute work area in which solicitation may be banned, area must be integral, not merely incidental to employer's main function.

6. Discriminatory enforcement

    a. A presumptively valid rule may violate the Act if it is applied in a disparate fashion; *Lawson Co.*, 267 NLRB 463, 473 (1983); *St. Vincent's Hospital*, 265 NLRB 38 (1982), *Sandusky Mall*, 329 NLRB 618, 620 (1999).

    b. A no-solicitation rule will not be unlawful merely because it allows charitable solicitations as an exception to the general rule. Narrow exception found to otherwise nondiscriminatory, valid no-solicitation policy for small number of isolated beneficent acts. *Hammary Mfg. Corp.*, 265 NLRB 57 (1982). Cf., *Albertson's Inc.*, 332 NLRB 1132, 1135-1136, fn, 12 and 13, (2000) (employer allowed charitable, civic and educational groups to solicit in and around property on various occasions but denied nonemployee union representatives the same right).

    c. *Funk Mfg. Co.*, 301 NLRB 111, 113 (1991) (disparate enforcement of no solicitation rule unlawful).

    d. *Emergency One, Inc.*, 306 NLRB 800 (1992) (respondent unlawfully restricted conversation about union matters during work time, while permitting conversations about other nonwork matters); see also, *ITT Industries, Inc.*, 331 NLRB 4 (2000).

7. Health care setting

   a. *Beth Israel Hospital v. NLRB*, 437 U.S. 483 (1987) (employer rules which prohibit employees' solicitation in health care facilities in areas other than immediate patient care areas are presumptively invalid).

   b. *Health Care & Retirement Corp.*, 310 NLRB 1002, 1005 (1993) (rule stating that "soliciting or distributing written materials during working time or in any work area or resident care area is not permitted" was overly broad and violative; Consistent with *Beth Israel Hospital*, Board's policy requires that an employer's "ban on employee solicitation be limited to immediate patient care areas").

   c. *Eastern Maine Medical Center*, 253 NLRB 224 (1980) (violation to prohibit non-work time solicitation in work areas, including second floor lobby, which are not immediate patient care areas).

8. Retail Industry

   a. Employers in the retail industry may prohibit solicitation by employees in the sales area even on their non-work time because such solicitation may disrupt a retail store's business. See *J.C. Penney Co.*, 266 NLRB 1223 (1983).

   b. The Board has treated gambling casinos as akin to retail stores. Employers who operate gambling casinos may prohibit employees from soliciting in the casino's gambling areas and adjacent aisles and corridors frequented by customers. See *Double Eagle Hotel & Casino*, 341 NLRB 112 (2004).

   c. In cases involving hotels, the Board has recognized that a hotel has some customer service areas that are not easily identifiable. A hotel employer's interest in customer service, however, does not entitle it to designate all public areas of its facility, including parking lots, sidewalks, and public restrooms, to be guest service areas and thereby permit an employer to prohibit employee solicitation at any time. See *Crowne Plaza Hotel*, 352 NLRB 382 (2008).

9. No-Talking Rules

   a. Analyzed under a different standard than no-solicitation rules. An employer can prohibit employees from talking about a union or about their terms and conditions of employment during times when they are supposed to be working if that prohibition also extends to other subjects not associated or connected with the employees' work tasks. See *Scripps Memorial Hospital Encinitas*, 347 NLRB 52 (2006).

Access Rules

1. Access for employees

   a. *Hillhaven Highland House*, 336 NLRB 646 (2001), held: (1) under Section 7 of the Act, offsite employees (in contrast to nonemployee union organizers) have a non-derivative access right, for Section 7 purposes, to their employer's facilities; (2) that an employer may well have heightened private property right concerns when offsite (as opposed to onsite) employees seek access to its property to exercise their Section 7 rights; but (3) that, on balance, the Section 7 organizational rights of offsite employees entitle them to access to the outside, nonworking areas of the employer's property, except where justified by business reasons, which may involve considerations not applicable to access by off-duty, onsite employees.

   b. The test for determining the right to access for off-duty, on site employees is spelled out in *Tri-County Medical Center*, 222 NLRB 1089 (1976). A rule prohibiting access to off-duty employees would be valid only if it:
      i. limits access solely to the interior of the facility and other working areas,
      ii. is clearly disseminated to all employees, and
      iii. applies to off-duty employees seeking access to the plant for any purposes, not just union activity.

   c. A rule denying off-duty employees access to parking lots, gates, and other outside nonworking areas is invalid unless sufficiently justified by business reasons.

   d. The test for determining the right to access for offsite visiting employees is, except where justified by business reasons, an employer rule that denies off duty employees entry to outside nonworking areas of the employer's facility is invalid.

2. Access for non-employees

   a. *NLRB v. Babcock & Wilcox Co.*, 351 U.S. 105 (Need to accommodate both Section 7 "rights" and "property" rights – balancing test – nonemployee distribution of union literature in parking lot permitted because no other reasonable alternative channels of communication).

b. *Lechmere, Inc. v. NLRB*, 502 US 527, (1992) (Supreme Court rejected the Board's Jean Country test which had protected some trespassory activity by nonemployees. Held that an employer who prohibits all nonemployee solicitation on its property may lawfully prohibit protected activity by nonemployees on the same property except in the rare case where "the inaccessibility of employees makes ineffective the reasonable attempts by nonemployees to communicate with them through the usual channels." Only when reasonable access is infeasible then it becomes appropriate to balance Section 7 and private property rights. Exception is a narrow one and does not apply wherever non-trespassory access to employees may be cumbersome or less-than ideally effective, but only where the location of a plant or the living quarters of the employees placed the employees beyond the reach of reasonable union efforts to communicate with them. Classic examples are logging camps, mountain resort hotels. Union's burden is a heavy one - not satisfied by mere conjecture or expression of doubts concerning the effectiveness of non-trespassory means of communication. Fact employees live in large metropolitan area does not in itself render them inaccessible).

c. *K-Mart Corp.*, 313 NLRB 50, 58 (1993) (employer violated 8(a)(1) by causing police to remove nonemployee handbillers, while permitting the Salvation Army and a religious organization to solicit in front of the store on the same day).

d. *Great Scot, Inc.*, 309 NLRB 548 (1992), (employer violated 8(a)(1) by asking nonemployee "area standards" handbillers to leave and by asking police to remove handbillers from store's property, because employer routinely allowed other organizations, both commercial and nonprofit, to use its parking lot for activity unrelated to its store, including at least six different civic organizations).

e. *Sandusky Mall*, 329 NLRB 618 (1999) (Employer allowed distribution of materials by some charities but refused to allow the union to distribute information protesting the employer's use of non-union workers at one of its stores; 8(a)(1) violation found).

3. Solicitation by nonemployee organizers

   1. *Farm Fresh, Inc.*, 326 NLRB 997 (1998), (Board found that *Lechmere* effectively overruled *Montgomery Ward & Co.*, 288 NLRB 126, 127 (1988) (which had prohibited employer refusals to allow non-disruptive union solicitation of off-duty employees inside a public snackbar/cafeteria located on the employer's premises. No violation found because there was no showing of disparate application of no solicitation rule).

4. Employer Must Have Sufficient Property Interest to Control Access

1. Burden on party claiming property interest to establish it, *Giant Food Stores, Inc.*, 295 NLRB 330, 332, fn. 8 (1989).

2. Easement only granted right to use, not control, state owned property - state law governs breadth of easement; thus, employer not privileged to deny access to nonemployee organizers - *Johnson & Hardin Co.*, 305 NLRB 690 (1991).

3. *TNT Technologies Ltd. d/b/a Ambrose Electric*, 330 NLRB 78(1999) (Respondent could not bar union from jobsites to which it lacked the right to control access where no threat to safety or job performance).

Rules Prohibiting Discussion of Wages/Working Conditions

1. *Automatic Screw Products Co.*, 306 NLRB 1072 (1992), (respondent violated 8(a)(1) by promulgating and maintaining rule prohibiting employees from discussing their salaries and also by disciplining an employee for violating that rule); *Koronis Parts*, 324 NLRB 675 (1997).

2. *Leather Center Inc.*, 312 NLRB 521, 527 (1993) (rule or policy barring employees from any discussion of wages, unlawful); *Lockheed Martin Astronautics*, 330 NLRB 422, 423 (2000) (discussion of working conditions not protected where no showing of intent to make common cause or seek concerted action).

3. *Desert Palace Inc. d/b/a Caesar's Palace*, 336 NLRB 271 (2001) (instruction to employees not to discuss ongoing drug investigation not violative).

Social Media Rules

1. The General Counsel has three reports concerning social media cases (OM 12-59 on May 30, 2012, OM 12-31 on January 24, 2012, and OM 11-74 on August 18, 2011). The memos explain that to determine whether the various rules could reasonably chill Section 7 protected activity in violation of Section 8(a)(1), we apply the principles in *Lafayette* and *Lutheran*.

2. An employer's admonition that no employee should ever be pressured to 'friend" or otherwise connect with a co-employee via social media cannot be reasonably read to restrict Section 7 activity. The rule was sufficiently specific in its prohibition against pressuring co-employees and clearly applies only to harassing conduct. It could not reasonably be interpreted to apply more broadly to restrict employees from attempting to "friend" or otherwise contact their colleagues for the purpose of engaging in protected activity.

3. Rule prohibiting employees from revealing personal information regarding co-workers was unduly broad and could reasonably be interpreted as restraining Section 7 activity. A rule that precludes employees from discussing terms and conditions of employment, or sharing information about themselves or their fellow employees with each other or with non-employees violates Section 8(a)(1).

4. Rule stating that no post may violate privacy or confidential rights of any person or entity provided no definition or guidance as to what the Employer considered to be private and confidential. Rule could reasonably be interpreted as prohibiting protected employee discussions of wages and other terms and conditions of employment and is therefore overbroad and unlawful, particularly, where the Employer applied it as such.

5. A requirement that employees "identify himself/herself" when posting comments about the Company is unlawfully overbroad. The rule would require employees to self-identify whenever discussing terms and conditions of employment with one another or with third parties such as labor organizations. The Board has recognized that requiring employees to publicly self-identify in order to participate in collective action would impose a significant burden on Section 7 rights. Thus, because this requirement could chill employees' protected communications for fear of identification and subsequent retaliation, it is unlawful.

6. Rule's broad prohibition against referring to the Company in postings that would "negatively impact the Company's reputation or brand" clearly encompasses concerted communications protesting the Employer's treatment of its employees. Indeed, there is nothing in the rule, or anywhere else in the employee handbook, that even arguably suggests to employees that communications protected by Section 7 are excluded. Moreover, an employee reading the rule would reasonably assume the employer would regard Section 7 statements, such as those critical of the Employer's labor policies or its treatment of employees, as negatively impacting its reputation or brand. Maintenance of this rule has a reasonable tendency to inhibit employees' protected activity in violation of Section 8(a)(1).

Bulletin Boards

1. *Register-Guard*, 351 NLRB 1110, 1118 (2007) (in order to be unlawful, discrimination must be along Section 7 lines. In other words, unlawful discrimination consists of disparate treatment of activities or communications of a similar character because of their union or other Section 7-protected status") (note – this aspect of *Register Guard* was not addressed in *Purple Communications*).

2. *Holly Farms Corp.*, 311 NLRB 273, 274 (1993) (employer violates the Act by discriminatorily prohibiting the posting of union notices on bulletin boards that are available for general use by employees).

3. *Honeywell, Inc.*, 262 NLRB 1402 (1982) (there is no statutory right for employees to use the employer's bulletin boards; however, an employer cannot discriminatorily prohibit employees from posting union notices on bulletin boards that are available for general use by employees).

Rules Regarding Reporting Conduct of Union Advocates

1. *St. Francis Medical Center*, 340 NLRB 1370, 1382 (2003) (respondent's invitation to associates to report what they perceived as purely subjective harassment without regard to the lawfulness of the union activity complained of clearly violates the Act).

2. *Arcata Graphics*, 304 NLRB 541 (1991) (seriousness of conduct employer requests be reported is not determinative; issue is whether statement is so vague as to invite employees generally to inform on fellow workers who were engaged in union activity).

Rules Against Union Insignia

1. An employee's right to wear union insignia while at work generally is protected by Section 7 of the Act, and an employer may not interfere with that right absent a showing of special circumstances. *See Albertson's Inc.*, 351 NLRB 254, 256-257 (2007); *Albis Plastics*, 335 NLRB 923, 924 (2001) and cases cited therein. *Republic Aviation Corp. v. NLRB*, 324 U.S. 793 (1945) (right to wear union insignia at work has been long recognized).

2. Special circumstances include situations where display of union insignia might "jeopardize employee safety, damage machinery or products, exacerbate employee dissension, or unreasonably interfere with a public image that the employer has established, as part of its business plan, through appearance rules for its employees." *Bell-Atlantic-Pennsylvania*, 339 NLRB 1084, 1086 (2003), citing *Nordstrom, Inc.*, 264 NLRB at 700.

3. The Board has consistently held that customer exposure to union insignia, standing alone, is not a special circumstance which permits an employer to prohibit display of such insignia. *Meijer, Inc.*, 318 NLRB 50 (1995); *Nordstrom, Inc.*, 264 NLRB at 700. Nor is the requirement that employees wear a uniform a special circumstance justifying a button prohibition. *United Parcel Service*, 312 NLRB 596, 596-598 (1993). Finally, the fact that the prohibition applies to all buttons, not solely union buttons, is not a special circumstance. *Harrah's Club*, 143 NLRB 1356, 1356 (1963), *Floridan Hotel of Tampa*, 137 NLRB 1484 (1962).

4. *The Southern New England Telephone Co.*, 356 NLRB No. 118 (2011) (respondent failed to demonstrate "special circumstances" justifying the

prohibition of shirt because the shirt was not reasonably likely, under the circumstances, to cause fear or alarm among customers).

5. *Escanaba Paper Co.*, 314 NLRB 732 (1994), (employer violated 8(a)(1) by prohibiting employees from displaying buttons, T-shirts, and other items with messages pertaining to activities protected by Section 7 and by promulgating and maintaining progressive discipline for violating the prohibition; respondent failed to demonstrate that "special circumstances," such as violence, interference with training or production or threats thereof, existed; burden of showing special circumstances does not necessarily require an employer to wait for actual violence to occur; rather Board weighs the employees' right to engage in Section 7 related activities against the respondent's rights to maintain discipline and production; if there are threats of misconduct, employer could take steps against the specific persons who uttered threats; employees' right to protest working condition was not affected by the signing of contract with union).

6. The Board did find that special circumstances existed in a case involving employees who worked in a grocery store and wore shirts that said "Don't Cheat About the Meat!" The Board concluded that the shirts reasonably threatened to create concern among store customers that they may be cheated which raised the possibility of harm to the employer's customer relationships. *Pathmark Stores*, 342 NLRB 378, 379 (2004).

Defenses to 8(a)(1) Allegations

A. Past Practice

1. *Wal-Mart, Inc.*, 339 NLRB 1187, 1187-1188 (2003) (an employer cannot rely on past practice to justify solicitation of grievances where the employer "significantly alters its past manner and methods of solicitation").

2. *American Red Cross, Missouri-Illinois Blood Services Region*, 347 NLRB 347, 350-351 (2006) (employer did not violate 8(a)(1) by soliciting employees' grievances; employer's actions were consistent with its past practice of soliciting employee feedback).

B. Business Reasons

1. *Matanuska Elec. Ass'n, Inc.* 333 NLRB 964, 964 (2001), (employer did not violate 8(a)(1) by amending its bylaws to provide that a member of the local union that represents employees, as well as anyone who lives with and is financially interdependent with the union member, cannot become or remain a member of board of directors; even assuming amended bylaw restricts the Section 7 rights of employees, it does not violate the Act because it serves legitimate interest in ensuring that it has the undivided loyalty of those who direct its operations).

C. Isolated - de minimis

1. *Sunnyside Home Care Project, Inc.*, 308 NLRB 346, 348 (1992) (sole violation found was a threat to discharge an employee because she intended to engage in a strike; such a violation is not de minimis); *Golub Corp.*, 338 NLRB 515, 516 (2002) (an explicit threat of suspension is by no means a "de minimis" matter, certainly not to the threatened employee).

2. *Morton's IGA Foodliner*, 237 NLRB 667 (1978) (single instance of interrogation sufficient to find violation)

D. Subsequent Neutralizing Statements

1. *Passavant Memorial Area Hospital*, 237 NLRB 138 (1978) (repudiation must be timely, unambiguous, specific in nature to the coercive conduct, and free from other proscribed illegal conduct. There must be adequate publication of the repudiation to the employees involved and there must be no proscribed conduct after the publication. Repudiation should give assurances to employees that, in the future, their employer will not interfere with their Section 7 rights).

E. Joking or Ambiguous

1. *Chinese Daily News*, 346 NLRB 906, 932 (2006), (although manager made the remark intending it as a joke, it is appropriate to consider whether or not the remark under all the circumstances, from the employees' perspective and irrespective of the speaker's intent, reasonably could be expected to chill employees' Section 7 rights).

2. *Suburban Electrical Engineers/Contractors, Inc.*, 351 NLRB 1, 2 (2007) (manager's comment was devoid of any express or implicit references to adverse employment consequences for employee; the incident occurred in an atmosphere of morning geniality as managers and employee walked from the parking lot into the Respondent's facility before going to a job; and the incident occurred in an atmosphere free of any other recent unfair labor practices).

3. *Selville Flexpack Corp.*, 288 NLRB 518, 534 (1988) (no violation when in course of supervising hanging of large plywood boards containing anti-union message, employer told employee that if it found out who started union he was going "to drop the boards on them." Remark made at beginning of campaign and in context free of unlawful statements. Employee admitted that official was kidding and that employee himself laughed).

F. Opinion

1. 8(c) provides that expressing of views, argument or opinion is not an unfair labor practice, if the expression contains no threat of reprisal or promise of benefit. In analyzing whether a statement is protected by 8(c) or violative of Section 7 rights, one must look to see whether statement constitutes unlawful threat of retaliation in response to protected activity.

2. *Rogers Electric, Inc*, 346 NLRB 508, 509-510 (2006) (remarks did not rise to the level of unlawful conduct. Comments amounted to nothing more than personal statement that formally contacting state government officials was not the best way to get matters changed. Statement amounts only to a personal opinion, protected by 8(c), that the employees do not need a union).

3. *Michigan Timber & Truss, Inc.*, 328 NLRB 459 (1999) (statement that company did not need or want a union not violative).

4. *Mid-South Drywall Co., Inc.*, 339 NLRB 480, 481 (2003) (the fact that the threat was couched in terms of personal opinion was not sufficient to neutralize its coerciveness; reasonable employee would tend to be coerced by the statement of opinion 8(a)(1)).

VI. Standards for Assessing Disciplines/Discharged Alleged to Be Improperly Motivated

    a. *The Continental Group,* 357 NLRB No. 39 (2011)

In *Double Eagle Hotel & Casino*, 341 NLRB 112 (2004), the Board had established that discipline imposed pursuant to an overbroad rule is unlawful per se. In *The Continental Group* the Board clarified the Double Eagle rule, stating that such discipline is unlawful where an employee violated the rule by (1) engaging in protected conduct or (2) engaging in conduct that otherwise implicates the concerns underlying Section 7 of the Act. Even in these circumstances, an employer will avoid liability if it can establish that the employee's conduct actually interfered with the employee's own work or that of other employees or otherwise actually interfered with the employer's operations, and that the interference, rather than the violation of the rule, was the reason for the discipline.

    b. *Wright Line, Inc.,* 251 NLRB 1098 (1980) enfd. 662 F.2d 899 (1st Cir. 1981) cert. denied 455 U.S. 989 (1982)

Wright Line is perhaps the most widely used standard for assessing whether an employer was justified in taking the disciplinary action it did. *Wright Line* provides for a burden shifting analysis consists of two prongs:

> First, we shall require that the General Counsel make a prima facie showing sufficient to support the inference that protected conduct was a "motivating factor" in the employer's decision. Once this is established, the burden will shift to the employer to demonstrate that the same action

would have taken place even in the absence of the protected conduct. Id. at 1098

Thus, if an employer can show that it has treated other employees who had not engaged in protected activities the same way it treated the employees who had engaged in protected activities near the time of disciplinary action was taken against them,

There has been some deviation as to the exact formulation of the elements and burdens under *Wright Line*. In *Midwest Terminals of Toledo International*, 362 NLRB No. 57, slip op. at 1, fn. 2 (2015), the Board explained there are three elements to a prima facie case: union activity by the employee, employer knowledge of the activity, and antiunion animus by the employer. Animus may, be inferred from circumstantial evidence, such as timing, disparate treatment, or shifting explanations for the conduct. E.g. *Shattuck Denn Mining Corp. v. NLRB*, 362 F.2d 466 (9th Cir. 1966). Once the prima facie case is established, the Board will conclude the action was unlawfully motivated unless the employer affirmatively establishes it would have taken the same action against the employee in any event. The employer cannot meet its burden, however, merely by showing that it had a legitimate reason for its action; rather, it must demonstrate that it would have taken the same action in the absence of the protected conduct. *Bruce Packing Co.*, 357 NLRB No. 93, slip op. at 3–4 (2011). If the employer's proffered reasons are pretextual (i.e., either false or not actually relied on), the employer fails by definition to show that it would have taken the same action for those reasons regardless of the protected conduct. *Metropolitan Transportation Services*, 351 NLRB 657, 659 (2007).

c. *Atlantic Steel Co.*, 245 NLRB 814 (1979)

While the Act protects an employee from repercussions when engaging in protected, concerted activity, the Board and Courts have recognized that the protection is not limitless. *Atlantic Steel Co.*, 245 NLRB 814 (1979), sets forth the factors to be considered in determining whether an employee's conduct loses the protection of the Act: (1) the place of the discussion, (2) subject matter of the discussion, (3) the nature of the employee's outburst, and (4) whether the outburst was, in any way, provoked by the employer's unfair labor practice. Generally, employees are permitted "some leeway for impulsive behavior" *Tampa Tribune*, 351 NLRB 1324, 1324-25 (2007), *enf. denied Media General Operations, Inc. v. N.L.R.B.*, 560 F.3d 181 (4th Cir. 2009). See also:

Kiewitt Power Constructors Co., 355 NLRB 708 (2010) (although intemperate, statement that things could "get ugly" and that supervisor "better bring [his] boxing gloves" were not unambiguous or "outright . . . threats of physical violence")

Thor Power Tool Co., 351 F.2d 584, 587 (7th Cir. 1965) (conduct protected even though employee called his manager a "horse's ass")

Wolkerstorfer Co., 305 NLRB 592, fn. 2 (1991)(An employee does not forfeit the protection of the Act unless his misconduct is "so violent" or "of such character as to render [the employee] unfit for further service.")

Severance Tool Industries, 301 NLRB 1166, 1169 (1991) (protection not lost because employee raised his voice at respondent's president and called him a "son of a bitch").

Atlantic Steel Factors:

    (1) <u>the place of the discussion</u>

NLRB v. Starbucks Corp., 679 F.3d 70 at 79 (2nd Cir. (2012)(Board observes distinction between outbursts where there was little if any risk other employees or customers heard the obscenities and those where risk was high)

Plaza Auto Ctr., Inc., 360 NLRB No. 117 (2014)(Board scrutinizes outbursts that occur in presence of statutory employees, not other managers, more strictly; held conduct was not menacing, physically aggressive, or belligerent)

Media General Operations, Inc. v. NLRB, 560 F.3d 181 at 187 (4th Cir. 2009) (In balancing *Atlantic Steel* factors, Board generally finds remarks made in private are less disruptive to workplace discipline than those in front of fellow employees)

Datwyler Rubber and Plastics, 350 NLRB 669, 670, 676 (2007) (employee's comments at group meeting that general manager "was a devil" and that "God would punish him and the Company for making the employees work seven days a week" held protected because comments occurred during employee meeting in non-work area where employees were free to raise work concerns)

Noble Metal Processing, Inc.. 346 NLRB 795, 800 (2006) (place of discussion weighs in favor of protection where outburst occurred during meeting held away from work area)

    (2) <u>subject matter of the discussion,</u>

Consumers Power Co., 282 NLRB 130, 132 (1986)("disputes over wages, hours, and working conditions are among the disputes most likely to engender ill feelings and strong responses")

Crown Central Petroleum, 177 NLRB No. 29 (during course of grievance meeting employee said management ordered overtime and management said they requested overtime. Primary issue was the veracity of management so it was protected for employee to imply management was lying).

    (3) <u>the nature of the employee's outburst,</u>

Plaza Auto Center, Inc., 360 NLRB No. 117 (2014)(employee raised his voice, stood up, pushed a chair, called the manager a "fucking crook," "stupid," "asshole," and said manager would "regret it" if he was fired, actions all held protected; Employer's testimony about his or her subjective fear is not determinative)

Severance Tool Industries, 301 NLRB 1166, 1170 (1991)(calling president "son of a bitch" not so opprobrious as to lose the protection of the Act where no threats of violence, actual insubordination or acts of violence)

United States Postal Service, 250 NLRB 4 fn 1 (1980)(obscenities uttered by employee as part of the *res gestae* of concerted protected activity generally not so egregious as to remove the protection of the Act and warrant the employee's discipline)

Farah Manufacturing Company, Inc., 202 NLRB 666 (1973)(refusal to lower one's voice during protected concerted activity is protected not insubordinate)

      (4) whether the outburst was, in any way, provoked by the employer's unfair labor practice.

Felix Industries, Inc., 339 NLRB 195, 196-197 (2003) adopted by 2004 WL 1498151 (D.C. Cir. 2004)(finding relevant that employer did not merely reject employee's request for contract payments, but expressed astonishment and anger that employee was even making an issue of the matter, thereby expressed hostility towards employee's choice to exercise his Section 7 rights)

Overnite Transportation Co., 343 NLRB 1431, 1437 (2004)(it was only after supervisor had refused to discuss issue that steward brought up the subject of whether supervisor had committed wartime atrocities.)

      d. *Clear Pine Mouldings*, 268 NLRB 1044 (1984), enfd. 765 F.2d 148 (9th Cir. 1985), cert. denied 474 U.S. 1105 (1986)

The Board has developed a more specific rule regarding a particular subset of protected concerted activity – picket line conduct. Recognizing that tensions can run especially high in these settings, and that retribution can beget retribution, the Board in *Clear Pine Mouldings* held that employers may deny reinstatement to employees who engage in physical threats, or verbal threats which have the effect of coercing or intimidating other employees. However, non-threatening, albeit uncivil, picket line conduct, is immune. Thus, vile language and gestures, when undertaken on the picket line, cannot form the basis for employer adverse action. E.g. *Airo Die Casting, Inc.,* 347 NLRB 810 (2006) (racial epithets, including use of "n" word, invalid basis to refuse to reinstate striker, if unaccompanied by threats of violence); *Nickell Moulding*, 317 NLRB 826, 827-828 (1995); *Calliope Designs, Inc.*, 297 NLRB 510, 521 (1989) (calling nonstriker a "prostitute" and "whore" insufficient basis to refuse to reinstate striker).

      e. *Burnup and Sims,* 379 U.S. 21, 23 (1964)

This framework applies when an employer honestly but mistakenly believes that an employee has engaged in misconduct during the course of activity protected by the Act, and discharges or disciplines the employee for the supposed misconduct. The steps of that analysis may be summarized as follows: When an employer discharges an employee for misconduct arising out of a protected activity, the employer has the burden of showing that it held an honest belief that the employee engaged in serious misconduct. Once the employer establishes that it had such an honest belief, the burden shifts to the General Counsel to affirmatively show that the misconduct did not in fact occur.

Remedial Scheme

VII. NLRB Remedial Scheme

The Board's standard remedies for violations of Section 8(a)(1) and (3) include:

a. Posting of a Notice to Employees, utilizing "clear laypersons' language" *Ishikawa Gaskets America, Inc.*, 337 NLRB 175, 176 (2001) enfd. 354 F. 3d 534 (6th Cir. 2004). This language reinforces' employees understanding of their statutory rights and remedies the damage done to them by unlawful conduct. If you are looking for sample language, whatever case provided substantive law on the violation will have a notice included in the Board decision

b. Cease and Desist Order; Board order's customarily direct charged parties to cease and desist from the unlawful conduct found to have occurred, or any "like or relate" interference with, restraint, or coercion of employees' Section 7 rights

c. Where the Board has determined that an employer rule violated the Act, it orders the employer to rescind the rule and advise employees in writing that it has done so. E.g. *Lutheran Heritage Village-Livonia*, 343 NLRB 646 (2004)

d. The Board also requires employers to expunge records of any unlawfully-issued disciplines or discharges from its files and advise the affected employees in writing that it has done so, and that the rescinded action will not be used against the employee in any way

e. The Board orders reinstatement of unlawfully-discharged employees to their former positions, without prejudice to their seniority and other rights previously enjoyed

f. The Board's backpay formula calculates lost earnings less interim earnings, plus interest and any added costs for search-for-work expenses or increased transportation costs. The Board also requires employers to pay any excess tax liability employees incur as a result of lump-sum payments, and to allocate social security withholdings to quarters for which the backpay payments correspond.

Babcock & Wilcox Construction Co., Inc. *and* Coletta Kim Beneli. Case 28-CA-022625

December 15, 2014

DECISION AND ORDER[1]

BY CHAIRMAN PEARCE AND MEMBERS MISCIMARRA, HIROZAWA, JOHNSON, AND SCHIFFER

In this case we consider whether to adhere to, modify, or abandon the Board's existing standard for deferring to arbitral decisions in cases involving alleged violations of Section 8(a)(3) and (1) of the National Labor Relations Act. The Board's standard for deferral is solely a matter for the Board's discretion. Section 10(a) of the Act expressly provides that the Board is not precluded from adjudicating unfair labor practice charges even though they might have been the subject of an arbitration proceeding and award, and the courts have uniformly so held. *International Harvester Co.*, 138 NLRB 923, 925926 (1962) (footnotes omitted), enfd. 327 F.2d 784 (7th Cir. 1964), cert. denied 377 U.S. 1003 (1964), cited with approval in *Carey v. Westinghouse Electric Corp.*, 375 U.S. 261, 271 (1964).

In its seminal decision in *Spielberg Mfg. Co.*, 112 NLRB 1080 (1955), the Board held that it would defer, as a matter of discretion, to arbitral decisions in cases in which the proceedings appear to have been fair and regular, all parties agreed to be bound, and the decision of the arbitrator is not clearly repugnant to the purposes and policies of the Act. Id. at 1082. The deferral doctrine announced in *Spielberg* was intended to reconcile the Board's obligation under Section 10(a) of the Act to prevent unfair labor practices with the Federal policy of encouraging the voluntary settlement of labor disputes. Thirty years later, in *Olin Corp.*, 268 NLRB 573 (1984), the Board adopted the current deferral standard, holding that deferral is appropriate where the contractual issue is "factually parallel" to the unfair labor practice issue, the arbitrator was presented generally with the facts relevant to resolving that issue and the award is not "clearly repugnant" to the Act.

The General Counsel contends that the current deferral standards, as explicated in *Olin*, are inadequate to ensure that employees' statutory rights are protected in the arbitral process. He urges the Board to adopt a more demanding standard in 8(a)(3) and (1) cases, specifically those alleging that employers have retaliated against employees for exercising their rights under Section 7 of the Act. Under the General Counsel's proposed standard, the Board would defer only if the statutory right was either incorporated in the collective-bargaining agreement or presented to the arbitrator by the parties, and if the arbitrator "correctly enunciated the applicable statutory principles and applied them in deciding the issue."[2] Under the General Counsel's proposed standard, the party *favoring* deferral would have the burden of showing that those criteria were met. On such a showing, if the proceedings appeared to have been fair and regular, and all parties agreed to be bound, the Board would defer unless the award was "clearly repugnant" to the Act, as under the current standard. See GC Memorandum 11–05 at 6–7 (January 20, 2011).

On February 7, 2014, the Board invited the parties and interested amici to file briefs addressing the following questions.

1. Should the Board adhere to, modify, or abandon its existing standard for postarbitral deferral under *Spielberg Mfg. Co.*, 112 NLRB 1080 (1955), and *Olin Corp.*, 268 NLRB 573 (1984)?

2. If the Board modifies the existing standard, should the Board adopt the standard outlined by the General Counsel in GC Memorandum 11–05 (January 20, 2011) or would some other modification of the existing standard be more appropriate: e.g., shifting the burden of proof, redefining "repugnant to the Act," or reformulating the test for determining whether the arbitrator "adequately considered" the unfair labor practice issue?

3. If the Board modifies its existing post-arbitral deferral standard, would consequent changes need to be made to the Board's standards for determining whether to defer a case to arbitration under *Collyer Insulated Wire*, 192 NLRB 837 (1971); *United Technologies Corp.*, 268 NLRB 557 (1984); and *Dubo Mfg. Corp.*, 142 NLRB 431 (1963)?

4. If the Board modifies its existing postarbitral deferral standard, would consequent changes need to be made to the Board's standards for determining whether

---

[1] On April 9, 2012, Administrative Law Judge Jay R. Pollack issued the attached decision. The General Counsel filed exceptions and a supporting brief; the Respondent filed an answering brief; and the General Counsel filed a reply brief.

The National Labor Relations Board has considered the decision and the record in light of the exceptions and briefs, and has decided to affirm the judge's rulings, findings, and conclusions and to adopt the recommended Order.

[2] The General Counsel does not contend that the standard should be changed for cases involving alleged violations of Sec. 8(a)(5), which address the employer's duty to bargain in good faith. Accordingly, our decision does not address the standard for deferral in 8(a)(5) cases.

to defer to prearbitral grievance settlements under *Alpha Beta*, 273 NLRB 1546 (1985), review denied sub nom. *Mahon v. NLRB*, 808 F.2d 1342 (9th Cir. 1987); and *Postal Service*, 300 NLRB 196 (1990)?

The Board also invited the parties and amici to submit empirical and other evidence bearing on those questions.[3]

After careful consideration, we agree with the General Counsel that the existing deferral standard does not adequately balance the protection of employees' rights under the Act and the national policy of encouraging arbitration of disputes arising over the application or interpretation of a collective-bargaining agreement. The current standard creates excessive risk that the Board will defer when an arbitrator has not adequately considered the statutory issue,[4] or when it is impossible to tell whether he or she has done so. The result is that employees are effectively deprived of their Section 7 rights if disciplinary actions that are, in fact, unlawful employer reprisals for union or protected concerted activity are upheld in arbitration.[5] Accordingly, we have decided to modify our standard for postarbitral deferral in 8(a)(3) and (1) cases, but not precisely along the lines suggested by the General Counsel.

We agree that the burden of proving that deferral is appropriate is properly placed on the party urging deferral. We also agree that deferral is appropriate only when the arbitrator has been explicitly authorized to decide the statutory issue, either in the collective-bargaining agreement or by agreement of the parties in the particular case. We believe, however, that the General Counsel's proposal that deferral is warranted only if the arbitrator "correctly enunciated the applicable statutory principles and applied them in deciding the issue" would set an unrealistically high standard for deferral. Our modified standard, by contrast, will require that the proponent of deferral demonstrate that the parties presented the statutory

issue to the arbitrator, the arbitrator considered the statutory issue or was prevented from doing so by the party opposing deferral, and Board law reasonably permits the award. On such a showing, the Board will defer.[6] Our reasons follow.

I. DISCUSSION

A. Statutory Background

Before turning to the specific questions presented here, we examine the statutory background of today's case. We begin by recognizing two well-established premises of American labor law, both of which derive from the policy of the Act, set forth in Section 1, to "encourag[e] the practice and procedure of collective bargaining." The first is that this system of free and robust collective bargaining cannot exist if employees who seek to participate in it can be disciplined or discharged for doing so. Recognizing this obvious truth, in Section 1 of the Act, Congress declared it to be the policy of the United States to eliminate the causes of certain substantial obstructions to the free flow of commerce and to mitigate and eliminate these obstructions when they have occurred . . . by protecting the exercise by workers of full freedom of association, self-organization, and designation of representatives of their own choosing, for the purpose of negotiating the terms and conditions of their employment or other mutual aid or protection. 29 U.S.C. §151.

To further that policy, Congress enacted Section 7 of the Act, which declares that "[e]mployees shall have the right to self-organization, to form, join, or assist labor organizations, to bargain collectively through representatives of their own choosing, and to engage in other concerted activities for the purpose of collective bargaining or other mutual aid or protection," 29 U.S.C. §157. To

---

[3] Briefs were received from the General Counsel, the Respondent, and amici American Federation of Labor-Congress of Industrial Organizations (AFL–CIO), U.S. Chamber of Commerce (Chamber), National Association of Manufacturers (NAM), Council on Labor Law Equality (COLLE), United States Postal Service (USPS), Association for Union Democracy (AUD), United Nurses Associations of California/ Union of Health Care Professionals (UNAC/ UHCP), Realty Advisory Board on Labor Relations (RAB) and League of Voluntary Hospitals and Nursing Homes (LVH), National Elevator Bargaining Association (NEBA), and the law firm Weinberg, Roger & Rosenfeld.

[4] We use the term "statutory issue" interchangeably with, and as shorthand for, "unfair labor practice issue." In his dissent, Member Miscimarra objects to this usage. For the reasons discussed below, we find no merit in his position.

[5] We do not suggest that the current standard constitutes an impermissible construction of the Act. We simply conclude, for the reasons discussed below, that our modified standard will more effectively protect employees' exercise of their Sec. 7 rights while continuing to effectuate the national policy favoring the private resolution of workplace disputes through arbitration.

[6] As Member Johnson observes in his dissent, most reviewing courts have either explicitly or implicitly endorsed the current deferral standard, although as the authors of a leading labor law text have observed, "with varying degrees of enthusiasm." Thus, as the authors point out,

> Some courts have expressly endorsed the *Olin* criteria and have held that the Board must be consistent in adhering to them; others have endorsed those criteria, essentially by way of dictum, while upholding the Board's decision not to defer because of noncompliance with those criteria; and some courts of appeals [have] extended the *Olin* reasoning and criteria to apply to grievance settlements between the union and the employer in advance of the arbitration step in the collective agreement. Other courts have expressly reserved judgment on whether the *Olin* doctrine represents a proper exercise of the Board's discretion. [] One court of appeals, the Eleventh Circuit, has flatly rejected the Board's decision in *Olin*."

Robert A. Gorman & Matthew W. Finkin, *Basic Text on Labor Law* 1028 (2d ed. 2004) (citations omitted). To the extent the courts have approved *Olin* as a *permissible* exercise of the Board's discretion, we do not disagree. But neither the Board nor any court has held that the current standard is *compelled* by anything in the language or purpose of the Act.

ensure that employees are free to exercise their Section 7 rights without fear of reprisal, Congress enacted Section 8(a)(1), which provides, as relevant here, that it is unlawful for employers to "interfere with, restrain, or coerce employees in the exercise of the rights guaranteed in Section 7," and Section 8(a)(3), which provides that it is unlawful for employers to discriminate against employees "to encourage or discourage membership in any labor organization." 29 U.S.C. §§158(a)(1), 158(a)(3).

Congress created the National Labor Relations Board as the sole entity charged with administering the Act and preventing unfair labor practices. Section 10(a) of the Act explicitly provides that

> The Board is empowered . . . to prevent any person from engaging in any unfair labor practice [listed in section 8] affecting commerce. *This power shall not be affected by any other means of adjustment or prevention that has been or may be established by agreement, law, or otherwise....*

29 U.S.C. §160(a) (emphasis added). Thus, Congress explicitly empowered the Board to protect employees' statutory rights, even if other entities might also be authorized to do so in other proceedings.

Significantly, the Board performs this function in the public interest and not in vindication of private rights. *Robinson Freight Lines*, 117 NLRB 1483, 1485 (1957) (footnote omitted), enfd. 251 F.2d 639 (6th Cir. 1958). As the Supreme Court observed long ago, "The Board as a public agency acting in the public interest, not any private person or group, not any employee or group of employees, is chosen as the instrument to assure protection from the . . . unfair conduct in order to remove obstructions to interstate commerce." *Amalgamated Utility Workers v. Consolidated Edison Co.*, 309 U.S. 261, 265 (1940). A fundamental premise, then, underlying our decision today is that enforcement by the Board of the public rights embodied in the Act is an essential aspect of the statutory scheme designed by Congress to promote industrial peace and stability.

The second premise underlying our decision is the central role of arbitration in promoting industrial peace and stability.[7] Section 1 of the Act declares it to be "the policy of the United States to eliminate the causes of certain substantial obstructions to the free flow of commerce and to mitigate and eliminate these obstructions when they

have occurred by encouraging the practice and procedure of collective bargaining . . . ." Through collective bargaining, representatives of employers and employees attempt to reach an agreement that will govern their workplace relationships. Even when the parties are successful in reaching such an agreement, however, they recognize that not every contingency can be anticipated and that disputes may arise over the interpretation of particular aspects of the agreement, including those concerning discipline and discharge. Accordingly, and to avoid having to resolve those disputes by recourse to economic weapons such as strikes and lockouts, the parties typically include in collective-bargaining agreements a grievance procedure through which their representatives attempt to reach a satisfactory resolution. When such attempts fail, the agreement generally provides for a neutral arbitrator or arbitral board to render a final decision that is binding on the parties. Arbitration is a process that has been freely chosen by the parties through collective bargaining as a means for obtaining a final resolution of disputes. Indeed, Congress stated in Section 203(d) of the Labor-Management Relations Act that "[f]inal adjustment by a method agreed upon by the parties is declared to be the desirable method for settlement of grievance disputes arising over the application or interpretation of an existing collective-bargaining agreement." 29 U.S.C. §173(d).

As important as arbitration is to the effective functioning of labor-management relations, however, given Congress' specific statutory direction in Section 10(a), the Board need not automatically defer to arbitral decisions when the matter has also been alleged as a violation of the Act. Rather, deferral is a matter of discretion. As the Board held long ago,

> There is no question that the Board is not precluded from adjudicating unfair labor practice charges even though they might have been the subject of an arbitration proceeding and award. Section 10(a) of the Act expressly makes this plain, and the courts have uniformly so held.

International Harvester Co., 138 NLRB 923, 925–926 (1962) (footnotes omitted), enfd. 327 F.2d 784 (7th Cir. 1964), cert. denied 377 U.S. 1003 (1964), cited with approval in *Carey v. Westinghouse Electric Corp.*, 375 U.S. 261, 271 (1964). Recognizing the discretionary nature of the Board's deferral policy, the D.C. Circuit has remarked, "Sec. 203(d) reads most naturally as a general policy statement in favor of private dispute resolution, not as any kind of limitation on Board authority." *Hammontree v. NLRB*, 925 F.2d 1486, 1493 (D.C. Cir. 1991). The court also stated that "Sec. 203(d) represents a quintessential delegation to the Board, not this court, to

---

[7] *United Steelworkers v. Warrior & Gulf Navigation Co.*, 363 U.S. 574, 578 fn. 4 (1960) (observing that "[a] major factor in achieving industrial peace is the inclusion of a provision for arbitration of grievances in the collective bargaining agreement" and "[c]omplete effectuation of the federal policy is achieved when the agreement contains both an arbitration provision for all unresolved grievances and an absolute prohibition of strikes").

formulate a deferment policy that accommodates all of its varying statutory responsibilities." Id.at fn. 12.

In sum, deferral is solely a matter of the Board's statutory discretion to resolve alleged unfair labor practices where in its judgment its intervention is necessary to protect the public rights defined in the Act. Concomitantly, the Board may withhold its authority to adjudicate alleged unfair labor practices where in its judgment Federal labor policy would be best served by deferring to an arbitral decision involving the same subject matter.[8] As discussed further below, the discretionary aspect of the Board's deferral policy is particularly significant in 8(a)(3) and (1) cases such as this, where employees' contractual rights, implicated in the grievance, are separate from their rights under the Act.

B. A Brief History of Postarbitral Deferral

The Board's postarbitral deferral policy has traveled a long and winding road.[9] The Board began almost 60 years ago, as an exercise of discretion, to defer in what it deemed appropriate circumstances to arbitral decisions involving alleged unfair labor practices. In its 1955 *Spielberg* decision, the Board announced that it would defer if the proceedings appeared to have been fair and regular, all parties had agreed to be bound, and the arbitrator's decision was "not clearly repugnant to the purposes and policies of the Act." 112 NLRB at 1082. After some years of experience applying *Spielberg*, the Board held it improper to defer when the arbitrator had not considered the unfair labor practice issue, explaining that "[w]e cannot, in giving effect to arbitration agreements, neglect our function of protecting the rights of employees granted by our Act." *Raytheon Co.*, 140 NLRB 883, 886 (1963), enf. denied 326 F.2d 471 (1st Cir. 1964). The *Raytheon* rule was extended in *Airco Industrial Gases*, 195 NLRB 676, 677 (1972), to cases where the arbitration award gave no indication whether the arbitrator ruled on the unfair labor practice issue. Id. at 677. Then, in *Yourga Trucking*, the Board held that the party urging deferral bore the burden of showing that the deferral standards were met. 197 NLRB 928, 928 (1972).

---

[8] Because of the discretionary character of the Board's deferral to arbitration, the Supreme Court's decisions in such cases as *14 Penn Plaza LLC v. Pyett*, 556 U.S. 247 (2009), and *Gilmer v. Interstate/Johnson Lane Corp.*, 500 U.S. 20 (1991), are not controlling here. In any event, those cases address whether parties may be contractually required to arbitrate certain statutory claims, not (as here) whether and when an administrative agency exclusively charged with administering a statute should exercise its statutory discretion to defer to an arbitral decision disposing of such claims.

[9] See Gorman & Finkin, supra, *Basic Text on Labor Law* §31.2 (tracing "tortuous history" of Board's deferral doctrine).

Two years later, however, the Board abruptly reversed course, citing concern that under the existing standard, parties would withhold evidence relevant to the unfair labor practice issue in arbitral proceedings in an attempt to have the Board decide the issue. *Electronic Reproduction Service Corp.*, 213 NLRB 758, 761 (1974). To avoid such piecemeal litigation, the Board held that it would defer to arbitral awards unless the party opposing deferral could show that special circumstances prevented that party from having a full and fair opportunity to present evidence relevant to the statutory issue.

Six years later, the Board overruled *Electronic Reproduction Service*, and returned to the principles laid down in *Raytheon*, *Airco*, and *Yourga Trucking*. *Suburban Motor Freight, Inc.*, 247 NLRB 146, 146–147 (1980). In *Suburban Motor Freight*, the Board ruled that it would "give no deference to an arbitration award which bears no indication that the arbitrator ruled on the statutory issue of discrimination in determining the propriety of an employer's disciplinary actions." Id. The Board also returned to the previous burden of proof allocations, under which the party seeking deferral was required to show that the standards for deferral had been met. Id.

Four years later, however, the Board in *Olin* overruled *Suburban Motor Freight* and held that it would find that an arbitrator has adequately considered the unfair labor practice if: (1) the contractual and unfair labor practice issues were factually parallel, and (2) the arbitrator was generally presented with the facts relevant to resolving the unfair labor practice. 268 NLRB at 574, 575. The Board also placed the burden on the party opposing deferral to demonstrate that the standards for deferral had *not* been met. Id.

C. The New Standard for Postarbitral Deferral

Having carefully considered the arguments of the parties and amici, we are persuaded that the existing deferral standard does not adequately protect employees' exercise of their rights under Section 7. In practice, the standard adopted in *Olin* amounts to a conclusive presumption that the arbitrator "adequately considered" the statutory issue if the arbitrator was merely presented with facts relevant to both an alleged contract violation and an alleged unfair labor practice. The presumption is theoretically rebuttable, but, as indicated above, the burden is on the party opposing deferral to show that the conditions for deferral are not met. In many, if not most arbitral proceedings, the parties do not file written briefs; there is no transcript of proceedings; and decisions often are summarily stated. In such situations, it is virtually impossible to prove that the statutory issue was *not* considered. For example, in *Airborne Freight Corp.*, 343 NLRB 580, 581 (2004), the Board deferred the 8(a)(3) discharge allegation even though the record did not show what arguments and evidence were presented in the grievance proceeding, because the General Counsel was unable to show that the statutory issues were *not* presented to the grievance panel. In our view, deferral in such circumstances amounts to abdication of the Board's duty to ensure that employees' Section 7 rights are protected.

Accordingly, we have decided to modify our deferral standard as follows. If the arbitration procedures appear to have been fair and regular, and if the parties agreed to be bound,[10] the Board will defer to an arbitral decision if the party urging deferral shows that: (1) the arbitrator was explicitly authorized to decide the unfair labor practice issue; (2) the arbitrator was presented with and considered the statutory issue, or was prevented from doing so by the party opposing deferral; and (3) Board law reasonably permits the award. This modified framework is intended to rectify the deficiencies in the current deferral standard in a way that provides greater protection of employees' statutory rights while, at the same time, furthering the policy of peaceful resolution of labor disputes through collective bargaining. Thus, as discussed below, this approach will enable us to determine whether the arbitrator has actually resolved the unfair labor practice issue in a manner consistent with the Act, without placing an undue burden on unions, employers, arbitrators, or the arbitration system itself.

1. The arbitrator must be explicitly authorized to decide the statutory issue

Arbitration is a consensual matter. The Supreme Court has expressly held that "arbitration is a matter of contract and a party cannot be required to submit to arbitration any dispute which he has not agreed so to submit." *Steelworkers v. Warrior & Gulf Navigation Co.*, supra, 363 U.S. at 582 . See also *Gateway Coal Co. v. United Mine Workers*, 414 U.S. 368, 374 (1974) ("The law compels a party to submit his grievance to arbitration only if he has contracted to do so."). Further, Section 203(d)'s endorsement of arbitration as "the desirable method for settlement of grievance disputes" is confined to disputes *"arising over the application or interpretation of an existing collective-bargaining agreement"*

(emphasis added).[11] We agree with the General Counsel, then, that the Board should not defer to an arbitrator's decision unless the arbitrator was specifically authorized to decide the unfair labor practice issue. The proponent of deferral can make this showing by demonstrating that the specific statutory right at issue was incorporated in the collective-bargaining agreement. If the right was not incorporated in the contract, the proponent must show that the parties explicitly authorized the arbitrator to decide the statutory issue.

2. The arbitrator must have been presented with and considered the statutory issue, or have been prevented from doing so by the party opposing deferral

Under the current deferral standard, an arbitrator will be found to have adequately considered the unfair labor practice issue if it and the contractual issue are "factually parallel" and if the arbitrator was "presented generally" with the facts relevant to resolving the statutory issue. *Olin*, 268 NLRB at 574. As discussed above, this amounts to a presumption that if an arbitrator is presented in some fashion with facts relevant to both an alleged contract violation and an alleged unfair labor practice, the arbitrator necessarily was presented with, and decided, the latter allegation in the course of deciding the former. We have repeatedly seen the shortcomings of that presumption, as this case illustrates.

Charging Party Coletta Kim Beneli was a union steward at the Respondent's workplace. She received a 3-day suspension without pay, assertedly for failing to fill out a safety form and for eating a pastry during a safety meeting. On the same day, she was summarily fired, ostensibly for using profanity in response to receiving the suspension. There is evidence to suggest, however, that Beneli's profane outburst was provoked by the Respondent's own wrongful actions and that the Respondent may have seized on Beneli's outburst as a pretext for getting rid of an assertive union steward. In this regard, the record establishes that shortly before her discharge, Beneli challenged several actions by the Respondent as violative of the parties' collective-bargaining agreement. The rec-

---

[10] These traditional requirements, articulated in *Spielberg*, 112 NLRB at 1082, are not in controversy and need no further explanation.

Amicus AUD suggests that in some cases, notably those involving union dissidents, union officials may be more closely aligned with management than with the grievant. In such circumstances, AUD contends that the Board should not defer where the charging party's position vis-à-vis the union is such that an objective observer would infer an adverse relationship. We think that AUD's concern can be effectively addressed when the Board is considering whether arbitral proceedings have been fair and regular.

[11] As explained in the leading treatise on labor arbitration:

Beginning with its *Enterprise Wheel* decision [*United Steelworkers of America v. Enterprise Wheel & Car Corp.*, 363 U.S. 593, 597 (1960)], the U.S. Supreme Court limited the arbitrator's role in rights disputes to interpretation and application of the collective bargaining agreement. The Court held that although an arbitrator could look outside the contract for guidance, "he does not sit to dispense his own brand of industrial justice," and the arbitrator's award is therefore legitimate only insofar as it "draws its essence" from the collective bargaining agreement.

Frank Elkouri & Edna Elkouri, *How Arbitration Works*, 143 (5th ed. 1997).

ord further establishes that only a few hours before suspending Beneli, the Respondent's project manager told the Union's assistant business manager that he wanted to discharge Beneli because she was raising contractual issues and trying to tell the Respondent what it was supposed to pay employees.

The Union grieved the discharge, contending that it violated the contractual prohibitions against retaliating against employees for engaging in union activity and against termination except for cause. The case was arbitrated before the contractual Grievance Review Subcommittee. But although the Union specifically argued that Beneli was fired for certain of her steward activities, in violation of the Act and Board decisions, there is nothing in the Subcommittee's decision to indicate whether it gave consideration to any of those matters or to the facts summarized above. The decision states only that Beneli's termination for using profanity did not violate the contractual prohibition against termination without just cause; it fails even to mention the statutory issue or the contractual prohibition against retaliation for union activity. In denying the grievance, the Subcommittee may have considered the statutory issue, or it may not have; there is simply no way to tell.

The Subcommittee's decision would appear to qualify for deferral under the current standard, even though it is impossible to determine whether the Subcommittee considered the statutory issue. As the judge found, it is conceded that the proceedings were fair and regular, and that all parties agreed to be bound by the panel's decision. Further, under *Olin*, the Subcommittee would be deemed to have "adequately considered" the unfair labor practice issue—whether Beneli was discharged for her steward activities—even if it actually did not consider that issue at all, because it was "factually parallel" to the contractual issue—discharging Beneli for the use of profanity—and the Subcommittee was "presented generally" with the facts relevant to resolving the statutory issue. Additionally, the absence of any evidence that the statutory issue was considered presents no impediment to deferral under the current standard because the General Counsel has the burden to show that the statutory issue was *not* considered. See, e.g., *Airborne Freight Corp.*, 343 NLRB at 581. Finally, the decision to deny Beneli's grievance was not found to be repugnant to the Act, because it was susceptible to an interpretation consistent with the Act.

This case is not an isolated example of the uncertainties that exist under the current standard. See, e.g., *Andersen Sand & Gravel Co.*, 277 NLRB 1204 (1985) (deferral appropriate even absent evidence that arbitral panel either considered or resolved unfair labor practice issue);

Airborne Freight Corp., 343 NLRB at 581 (deferral of 8(a)(3) discharge allegation appropriate, even though the record did not show what arguments and evidence were presented in the grievance proceeding, because the General Counsel was unable to show that the statutory issues were *not* presented to the grievance panel). Nor is there any way of knowing how many cases are never brought to the Board because the General Counsel or the party who would challenge deferral correctly assumes that, under our current standard, the Board would defer. Thus, the standards established in *Olin* may impede access to the Board's remedial processes and leave employees without any forum for the vindication of their statutory rights.

We are no longer willing to countenance such results. In our view, the Board does not fulfill its role under Section 10(a) as the only entity statutorily charged with protecting employees' Section 7 rights by deferring to decisions that do not indicate whether the arbitrator has even considered those rights. As the Ninth Circuit put it, "The Board cannot properly exercise its discretion in deferring to an arbitration decision when it is ignorant of the . . . basis for the [arbitral panel's] decision." *Stephenson v. NLRB*, 550 F.2d 535, 541 (9th Cir. 1977). The Board exercises its power to prevent unfair labor practices in the public interest and not simply in vindication of private rights. *Robinson Freight Lines*, 117 NLRB at 1485. Similarly, the Eleventh Circuit has stated: "By presuming, until proven otherwise, that all arbitration proceedings confront and decide every possible unfair labor practice issue, *Olin Corp.* gives away too much of the Board's responsibility under the NLRA." *Taylor v. NLRB*, 786 F.2d 1516, 1521–1522 (11th Cir. 1986). It is the policy of the Act to ensure—that is, for the Board to ensure—that employees may engage in union and other protected concerted activities to improve their lot in the workplace without fear of retribution; otherwise, the Act's policy of encouraging collective bargaining would soon be a dead letter. In our opinion, deferral under circumstances such as those presented here serves neither the public interest in protecting the exercise of employees' Section 7 rights nor, ultimately, the public interest in promoting industrial peace.

Accordingly, we shall defer to arbitral decisions only where the party urging deferral demonstrates that the arbitrator has actually considered the unfair labor practice issue, or that although the statutory issue is incorporated in the collective-bargaining agreement, the party opposing deferral has acted affirmatively to prevent the proponent of deferral from placing the statutory issue before the arbitrator.[12] We emphasize, however, that we are not returning to the rule of *Electronic Reproduction Services*, wherein the Board held that in the absence of "unusual circumstances" it would defer to arbitral awards dealing with discharge or discipline so long as there was an *opportunity* to present the statutory issue to the arbitrator, even where the record did not disclose whether the arbitrator had considered, or been presented with, the unfair labor practice issue involved.[13]

We shall find that the arbitrator has actually considered the statutory issue when the arbitrator has identified that issue and at least generally explained why he or she finds that the facts presented either do or do not support the unfair labor practice allegation. We stress that an arbitrator will not be required to have engaged in a detailed exegesis of Board law in order to meet this standard. We recognize that many arbitrators, as well as many union and employer representatives who appear in arbitral proceedings, are not attorneys trained in labor law matters. An important and attractive feature of the grievance-arbitration system is that it is less formal, less structured, and in most circumstances less costly than litigation. We do not intend to upset this system by adopting a deferral standard that would be all but impossible for participants lacking legal training to meet. In short, we do not seek to turn arbitrators into administrative law judges, or human resources representatives and shop stewards into labor lawyers. Accordingly, we decline to adopt the General Counsel's position that deferral is warranted only if the arbitrator "correctly enunciated the applicable statutory principles and applied them in deciding the issue." We think that meeting the standard announced today will be well within the capabilities of arbitrators and union and management representatives.

The Respondent and several amici oppose any standard that would encourage unions to withhold evidence concerning unfair labor practice issues in arbitration proceedings in order to defeat deferral. The new standard provides no such encouragement. Under our standard, either party can raise the statutory issue before the arbitrator; thus, an employer normally can ensure that the issue receives the arbitrator's consideration by raising it even if the union does not.[14] Indeed, both parties will normally be motivated to ensure that the unfair labor practice issue is presented to the arbitrator, in order to avoid unnecessary litigation, increased costs, and unwarranted delay in resolving the dispute.[15] Under the standard announced today, if the unfair labor practice issue is placed before an arbitrator and a party has evidence supporting its statutory claim but fails to introduce it in the arbitral proceeding, the Board will assess whether Board law reasonably permits the arbitrator's award in light of the evidence that was presented. Thus, a party would gain nothing by withholding evidence supporting its statutory claim. In such circumstances, if the other requirements for deferral are met, the fact that the arbitrator might have reached a different decision on the basis of the withheld evidence will not preclude deferral.

3. Board law must reasonably permit the award

If the previous requirements are met, deferral normally will be appropriate if the party urging deferral shows that Board law reasonably permits the arbitral award. By this, we mean that the arbitrator's decision must constitute a reasonable application of the statutory principles that would govern the Board's decision, if the case were presented to it, to the facts of the case. The arbitrator, of course, need not reach the same result the Board would reach, only a result that a decision maker reasonably applying the Act could reach.[16] In deciding whether to defer, the Board will not engage in the equivalent of de novo review of the arbitrator's decision.

This standard is more closely aligned with the Board's responsibilities under Section 10(a). Under the current standard, the Board will defer if the party opposing deferral fails to show that the award is "clearly repugnant to

---

[12] We do not expect to be confronted often with the latter circumstance. As discussed below, the employer will typically be able to present the statutory issue to the arbitrator even if the union fails or refuses to do so. We include this provision in the revised standard to ensure that deferral is not precluded if that is not the case.

[13] Member Johnson is thus correct in concluding that the Board would not defer under the new standards merely because a union had an opportunity to present the statutory issue to an arbitrator, but failed to do so. However, the new standard is no different from the current standard in this respect. *Olin*, 268 NLRB at 575 fn. 10 ("We do not resurrect that part of *Electronic Reproduction* which required no more than an "opportunity" to present the unfair labor practice issue to the arbitrator to warrant deferral."). See also *Hendrickson Bros., Inc.*, 272 NLRB 438, 439–440 (1984), enfd. mem. 762 F.2d 990 (2d Cir. 1985), overruled on other grounds *Don Chavas LLC d/b/a Tortillas Don Chavas*, 361 NLRB No. 10, slip op. at 5 fn. 31 (2014).

[14] Both NEBA and USPS oppose any change in the deferral standard that would require an employer to raise the unfair labor practice if the union failed to do so. However, satisfying the requirement that the statutory issue be placed before the arbitrator should not be especially onerous; in most cases informing the arbitrator of the unfair labor practice allegation in a pending charge would suffice.

[15] It is not apparent why a party would deliberately sabotage its own case before an arbitrator who is likely in a position to afford that party the relief it seeks, simply in order to have its case decided by the Board, perhaps much later and with no guarantee of success.

[16] An arbitrator need not necessarily provide the exact remedy the Board would have imposed. For example, the Board might defer to an award that allowed the respondent to deduct unemployment compensation from backpay, contrary to the Board's policy. The absence of any effective remedy, however, would preclude deferral. See, e.g., *Joseph Magnin Co.*, 257 NLRB 656, 656 fn. 1, enfd. 704 F.2d 1457 (9th Cir. 1983), cert. denied 465 U.S. 1012 (1984).

the Act," i.e., "palpably wrong" or "not susceptible to an interpretation consistent with the Act." *Olin*, 268 NLRB at 574 (fn. omitted). The effect of this standard has been to require deferral unless there is no conceivable reading of the facts in a given case that would support the arbitrator's decision. Thus, in a case such as this one involving an alleged 8(a)(3) discharge, the Board would routinely defer to an arbitrator's decision denying the grievance, even if there was considerable evidence of retaliatory motive. Notwithstanding a possibly rapid resolution of the workplace dispute and the avoidance of duplicative litigation before the Board, such an approach fails to ensure that employees' statutory rights are adequately protected. The overriding aim of deferral is not to resolve disputes quickly or to reduce the Board's caseload, although those are worthwhile aspects of the policy. The point, rather, is to give effect to the parties' voluntarily chosen process for resolving workplace disputes, *provided* that process leads to decisions that adequately protect employees' statutory rights. Our new standard is more likely to achieve this goal.

Contrary to the Respondent and several amici, adopting this standard will not necessarily reduce significantly the incidence of deferral in practice. As stated above, we are not seeking to turn arbitrators into administrative law judges, and we do not propose to review their decisions as though they were. All we require is a showing that the arbitrator's decision is one that a decision maker reasonably applying the Act could reach. Moreover, this should not be a difficult standard to meet. For example, as COLLE, NAM, NEBA, and our dissenting colleagues have argued, most collective-bargaining agreements contain provisions prohibiting discipline and discharge except for "just cause," and arbitrators are well versed in applying those principles. Thus, an arbitrator typically should understand that retaliation for the exercise of employees' Section 7 rights can never constitute "just cause," and the award would have to reflect that reasonable application of Board law.

We will not simply assume, however, merely from the fact that an arbitrator upheld a discharge under a "just cause" analysis, that the arbitrator understood the statutory issue and had considered (but found unpersuasive) evidence tending to show unlawful motive. Experience teaches that no such assumption is warranted. There have been numerous instances in which the Board declined to defer, even under the current standard, to arbitral decisions that upheld discipline or discharges under a "just cause" analysis *for conduct protected by the Act.* See, e.g., *Mobil Oil Exploration & Producing, U.S.*, 325 NLRB 176, 177–179 (1997), enfd. 200 F.3d 230 (5th Cir. 1999); *Garland Coal & Mining Co.*, 276 NLRB 963,

964–965 (1985) (finding in each case that the arbitrator's decision was "repugnant to the Act"); see also *Cone Mills Corp.*, 298 NLRB 661, 666–667 (1990).[17] As two leading scholars observe, "an arbitrator applying the 'just cause' provision in the contract—and sustaining the discharge—may well depart from the standards that the NLRB would apply" because they are "issues of legal characterization, in light of the policies of the NLRA, and are therefore not likely to have been precisely addressed by the arbitrator."[18]

Member Miscimarra rejects this approach. He advances instead a novel theory based on the provision in Section 10(c) of the Act and its legislative history that "[n]o order of the Board shall require the reinstatement of any individual as an employee who has been suspended or discharged, or the payment to him of any backpay, if such individual was suspended or discharged for cause." 29 U.S.C. §160(c). He contends that this provision, and its legislative history, *"makes 'cause' the relevant statutory issue* in all cases involving discharges and suspensions alleged to violate the Act (emphasis in original)." He further asserts that in enacting Section 10(c), Congress required that the Board's General Counsel prove that an allegedly unlawful suspension or discharge was not "for cause," and that deferral is appropriate unless the General Counsel can make that showing. Member Miscimarra claims that our decision today inappropriately treats "cause" as somehow "inferior to a more rigorous and exacting 'unfair labor practice' or 'statutory' issue." There is no merit to any of these assertions.

In cases in which discipline or discharge is alleged to violate the Act, the Board has long employed the two-stage causation analysis first announced in *Wright Line*, 251 NLRB 1083 (1980), enfd. on other grounds 662 F.2d 899 (1st Cir. 1981), cert. denied 455 U.S. 989 (1982), and approved by the Supreme Court in *NLRB v. Transportation Management Corp.*, 462 U.S. 393, 402–403 (1983). Under that analysis, the General Counsel first must prove, by a preponderance of the evidence, that the employee's protected conduct was a motivating factor in the employer's decision to discipline or discharge him.

---

[17] These decisions also illustrate why it is appropriate to require a showing that the unfair labor practice issue was presented to the arbitrator and that the arbitrator explained why the facts presented either support or fail to support the statutory allegation. Because it was clear in each case what facts were presented to the arbitrator and what the basis for the arbitrator's decision was, the Board could easily discern that the arbitrator's decision was not subject to an interpretation consistent with the Act. Had either the factual record or the arbitrator's reasoning been less fully developed in any of these cases, it might have been impossible for the party opposing deferral to show that the award was "palpably wrong."

[18] Gorman & Finkin, *Basic Text on Labor Law*, supra, §31.5 at 1037.

If the General Counsel fails to make that showing, there is no violation of the Act, regardless of whether the employer's action was for "cause"—e.g., incompetence, insubordination, or excessive absenteeism—or for some other reason. But if the General Counsel does carry his initial burden, the burden then shifts to the employer to prove, also by a preponderance of the evidence, that it would have taken the same action for other reasons (whether or not based on "cause" or "just cause"), regardless of the employee's protected activity. 251 NLRB at 1089. Thus, the employer need not assert 'just cause" for its decision, but if it does, it must prove not only that just cause existed, but that it would have taken the same action *even absent the protected conduct*. Under *Wright Line*, then (contrary to our colleague), the Board may find a violation even if the employer shows the existence of "cause" for its action.

The Supreme Court's decision in *Transportation Management* undermines Member Miscimarra's Section 10(c) argument not only by endorsing the *Wright Line* standard, but in two additional ways. First, the Court observed that the legislative history of Section 10(c) indicates that Congressional drafters simply assumed that discharges were *either* "for cause" *or* in retaliation for protected activity; they were "not thinking of the mixed motive" situation found in some discipline and discharge cases. [19] The Court remarked that the "for cause" proviso to Section 10(c)

> was sparked by a concern over the Board's perceived practice of inferring from the fact that someone was active in a union that he was fired because of antiunion animus even though the worker had been guilty of gross misconduct. . . . [It] thus has little to do with the situation in which the Board has soundly concluded that the employer had an antiunion animus and that such feelings played a role in a worker's discharge.

Id. at 402 fn. 6. Second, the Court specifically rejected the argument that the General Counsel must show that the employer would *not* have taken the same action, regardless of the protected activity: "Section 10(c) places the burden on the General Counsel only to prove the unfair labor practice, not to disprove an affirmative defense." Id. at 401 fn. 6. Thus, the Court implicitly rejected our colleague's contention that Congress meant to require the General Counsel to prove that the employer's action was not for "cause." In sum, Member Miscimarra is mistaken in asserting that "cause" is "the relevant stat-

utory issue" in all discipline and discharge cases under the Act and that deferral is appropriate wherever "cause" is shown. [20]

Member Miscimarra's chief concern seems to be that the Board will routinely refuse to defer in cases in which the arbitrator has determined that "cause" existed for discipline or a discharge. He asserts that under the new standard, "the Board must independently redecide *every* case in which an arbitrator determines only that 'cause' existed for a suspension or discharge." (Emphasis in original.) These fears are unfounded. As indicated above, if an arbitrator's decision can fairly be read as finding that discipline or discharge was for "cause" *and not for protected activity*, the decision would satisfy the part of the deferral standard requiring that Board law reasonably permit the award. Moreover, our new deferral standard will be applied only to the tiny fraction of arbitration decisions that come before the Board and that involve discipline or discharge alleged to be in retaliation for employee activity specifically protected by the Act. And such a case comes before the Board only after: (1) unfair labor practice charges are filed with the Board's regional office alleging violations of Section 8(a)(3) or (1) (the Board cannot proceed sua sponte); (2) an investigation is conducted and the Regional Director finds the unfair labor practice allegations meritorious; (3) the dispute is not settled by the parties; (4) the General Counsel issues a complaint;[21] (5) an administrative law judge issues a decision and order in the case; and (6) one or more parties file exceptions with the Board. In practice, only a small percentage of cases in which unfair labor practice

---

[19] See, for example, Senator Taft's statement: "If a man is discharged for cause, he cannot be reinstated. If he is discharged for union activity, he must be reinstated." 93 Cong. Rec. 6677, reprinted in 2 NLRB, Legislative History of the Labor Management Relations Act, 1947 at 1593.

[20] We also reject our colleague's view that placing the burden of proof on the party seeking deferral in a *Wright Line* case is somehow inconsistent with Sec. 10(c). There is a basic distinction, of course, between the standard for deferral and the standard for finding a violation of the Act. Where the Board chooses not to defer to an arbitrator's decision, the General Counsel is still required to prove a violation of the Act under applicable law. As explained, we disagree both with our colleague's interpretation of *Transportation Management* and with his view that Sec. 10(c), which limits the Board's remedial authority when a suspension or discharge is "for cause," somehow constrains the Board's discretion with respect to deferral. Sec. 10(c) clearly contemplates that the Board will determine whether an employer's action is "for cause" within the meaning of the statute. Its terms in no way suggest that the Board must always accept an arbitrator's "for cause" determination (where there is one)—and Sec. 10(a) refutes any such suggestion.

[21] The General Counsel's decision whether to issue complaints in unfair labor practice cases is final and unreviewable. See Sec. 3(d) of the Act; *NLRB v. Food & Commercial Workers Local 23*, 484 U.S. 112, 122 (1987). For a more complete description of the Board's procedures for processing unfair labor practice charges, see Sec. 102 Part B of the Board's Rules and Regulations.

are filed ever come before the Board. [22] Further, only a fraction of the cases decided by the Board involve deferral issues. Consequently, there is no reason to fear, as Member Miscimarra suggests, that the Board will "inject itself more aggressively in every suspension and discharge case that [is] subject to binding grievance arbitration (or a grievance settlement) regarding the existence or non-existence of 'cause.'"

4. The proponent of deferral has the burden to show that the standards for deferral have been met

Finally, we return to the rule enunciated in *Yourga Trucking, Inc.*, 197 NLRB at 928, and reaffirmed in *Suburban Motor Freight*, 247 NLRB at 147, that the party urging deferral has the burden to prove that the substantive requirements for deferral have been met. It is well settled that deferral is an affirmative defense. *SEIU United Healthcare Workers-West*, 350 NLRB 284, 284 fn. 1 (2007), enfd. 574 F.3d 1213 (9th Cir. 2009). Ordinarily, the proponent of an affirmative defense has the burden of establishing it. See, e.g., *Broadway Volkswagen*, 342 NLRB 1244, 1246 (2004) (finding the burden on the party raising an untimely charge defense under Section 10(b) of the Act), enfd. 483 F.3d 628 (9th Cir. 2007).[23] Moreover, as the Board observed in *Yourga Trucking*, the party urging deferral "may be presumed to have the strongest interest in establishing that the issue has been previously litigated[,]" and "in the usual case, that party will have ready access to documentary proof, or to the testimony of competent witnesses, to establish the scope of the issue submitted to the arbitrator." 197 NLRB at 928.[24] Similar considerations apply with regard to the other requirements for deferral (i.e., whether the arbitrator was explicitly authorized to decide the unfair labor practice issue; whether the arbitrator actually considered that issue; and whether Board law reasonably permits the award). In addition, as remarked by Member

Zimmerman in his dissent in *Olin,* there is "no sound procedural basis at all for imposing on the General Counsel—the one party in unfair labor practice litigation who is not in privity through a collective-bargaining agreement—the responsibility of producing evidence about arbitral proceedings under that agreement." 268 NLRB at 580.

In overruling *Yourga Trucking* and *Suburban Motor Freight* and placing the burden on the party opposing deferral to demonstrate that the standards for deferral had not been met, the Board majority in *Olin* was guided by its perception that the Board had previously been deferring too infrequently, and that this was inconsistent with the "goals of national labor policy." 268 NLRB at 574, 575.[25] We find this reasoning unpersuasive. The test of an appropriate deferral policy is not the frequency or infrequency with which the Board defers. It is, rather, whether the Board's policy gives due consideration to the vital role that arbitration plays in our national labor policy while ensuring that employees' statutory rights are given adequate protection—in the public interest—by *some* tribunal, be it the Board or an arbitrator. As we have stated above, we think that the standard we adopt today implements that test, and that the current standard does not. Moreover, we think that by providing guidance to parties and arbitrators as to the appropriate handling of unfair labor practice issues in the arbitral process, we will increase the likelihood that the decisions that result from that process will be more, not less, likely to be appropriate for deferral.[26]

D. Rejection of Arguments in Opposition to the New Standard

The Respondent, several amici, and our dissenting colleagues have raised various arguments against changing the current standard or adopting the standard we endorse today. We have carefully considered those arguments, but are not persuaded by them.

The Respondent and several amici oppose changing the current standard on the ground that it will discourage parties from settling their disputes informally through the grievance-arbitration process. Ironically, the same objection to the standard adopted in *Olin* was raised by dis-

---

[22] See the Board's Performance and Accountability Report for FY 2013 at www.nlrb.gov/reportsandguidance/reports/performance_and_accountability_reports (PAR).

[23] In general, the proponent of a rule has the burden to show that the rule applies in the circumstances presented; the proponent of an exception to the rule has the burden to show that the exception applies. See, e.g., 29 Am. Jur. 2d Evidence Sec. 174, 176. Deferral obviously is an exception to the general rule that if the Board has jurisdiction to decide an unfair labor practice issue, it will do so.

[24] See also Paul Alan Levy, *Deferral and the Dissident,* 24 U. Mich. J. Law. Ref. 479, 499 (1991) (noting under *Olin* that the "burden of showing the defects in the arbitration is placed on the General Counsel even when he seeks to enforce the statutory rights ... [while] [i]ronically, it is the parties to the CBA . . . [who] are in the best position to say what actually was litigated and decided.") Contrary to Member Johnson's suggestion, if the General Counsel is in possession of the facts concerning the arbitration, it is only because he was so informed by the parties.

[25] The *Olin* majority also stated that "[o]ur primary concern is with the failure of the Board itself to defer *in a consistent manner* thus setting an improper example for the General Counsel and administrative law judges." 268 NLRB at 575 fn. 9 (emphasis added). Although we, too, favor consistency in deferral cases (and elsewhere), it is unclear to us what consistency has to do with which party has the burden of proof.

[26] COLLE notes that in arbitral proceedings, the employer has the burden to demonstrate that an employee's discipline or discharge was for "just cause." It would seem no great chore, then, for an employer that prevailed in arbitration under that standard to show that the facts and arguments presented to the arbitrator satisfy our deferral standard, if that is the case.

senting Member Zimmerman. 268 NLRB at 581. However, the Board has never cited actual evidence of such ill effects when adopting and revising its deferral standards. In any event, the standard we adopt today simply requires that parties explicitly decide whether they want an arbitrator to decide unfair labor practice issues, and if so, that those issues be *actually* presented to the arbitrator and *actually* decided in a manner reasonably permitted by Board law. We find it difficult to believe that many employers or unions will abandon the benefits of arbitration in cases implicating Section 8(a)(3) and (1) of the Act because of the new standards, but if some parties do decide not to arbitrate these statutory issues, that is their privilege. That some may do so because they may no longer benefit from the defects of the current standard is hardly a compelling argument against the new standard.

Member Miscimarra fears that our new standard will essentially force parties either to renegotiate their contractual provisions concerning "cause" and limits on the scope of the arbitrator's authority to interpret the collective-bargaining agreement, or to submit to duplicative litigation when the Board declines to defer to arbitral awards. Again, these fears are unfounded. As we have stated, under our standard, even if a particular contract does not authorize arbitration of unfair labor practice issues, the parties can still authorize the arbitrator to decide such an issue in a given case; they do not have to renegotiate their contract to achieve that result. On the other hand, parties who wish to can draft appropriate contract language prohibiting retaliation for engaging in union activity, as the parties did in this case, or authorizing the arbitrator to decide such issues.[27] Because arbitration is a consensual matter, all that need be shown under our standard is that the parties have, in some fashion, explicitly authorized the arbitrator to decide the unfair labor practice issue. Under the new standard, the Board will not assume such grant of authority—it will be up to the parties to agree or not. It is not our province to hold them to a choice they have not made.[28]

We also disagree with Member Miscimarra's suggestion that unless parties renegotiate their contractual "just cause" provisions, the Board will not defer to arbitral decisions in cases involving discharge or discipline. Our

colleague himself asserts (as do several amici) that arbitrators know that engaging in activity protected by the Act can never constitute "just cause" for discipline or discharge, and therefore that an arbitrator who finds "just cause" for an employer's action has implicitly found that the employer did not retaliate against the employee for his protected conduct. There is reason to doubt this claim, as we have suggested. But even if it is correct, it would seem a simple matter for the arbitrator to say so, and thus make explicit what is claimed to be implicit. In short, the policy and practical concerns identified by Member Miscimarra are more illusory than real and do not outweigh the Board's statutory obligation to protect the public rights defined in the Act.

Member Johnson opposes the new standard for many of the same reasons as Member Miscimarra. We reject his position. First, Member Johnson opposes the requirement that the arbitrator must be explicitly authorized to decide the unfair labor practice issue, which he contends is inconsistent with the presumption of arbitrability established by the Supreme Court.[29] But Member Johnson is mistaken, as the Supreme Court itself has made clear. In *Wright v. Universal Maritime Service Corp.*, 525 U.S. 70 (1998), the Court held that an employee was not required, under the general language of a collective-bargaining agreement, to submit a claim alleging a violation of the Americans with Disabilities Act of 1990 (ADA), 42 U.S.C. §§12101 et seq., to the arbitration procedure. In the process, the Court explicitly rejected the employer's reliance on the presumption of arbitrability announced in the *Steelworkers Trilogy*[30] and later decisions. The Court reasoned that "[t]hat presumption . . . does not extend beyond the reach of the principal rationale that justifies it, which is that arbitrators are in a better position than courts *to interpret the terms of a CBA.*" 363 U.S. at 78 (emphasis in original). "The dispute in the present case," the Court observed, "ultimately concerns not the application or interpretation of any CBA, but the meaning of a federal statute. " Id. at 78–79. Moreover, the Court continued, "Not only is petitioner's statutory claim not subject to a presumption of arbitrability; we think any CBA requirement to arbitrate must be particularly clear," citing *Metropolitan Edison Co.* v. *NLRB*, 460 U. S. 693 (1983). Id. at 79–80.

---

[27] If parties do not wish to reopen their entire collective-bargaining agreement midterm, they have the option of drafting side agreements or agreeing on a case-by-case basis.

[28] See *Raytheon Co.*, supra, 140 NLRB at 886 (deferral inappropriate where arbitrator had been informed that he could not consider evidence that employees might have been discharged for engaging in union and other protected activity). As a general matter, the Board has no remedial authority to impose contract terms on collective-bargaining parties, including terms affecting the scope of arbitration provisions. *H.K. Porter Co., Inc. v. NLRB*, 397 U.S. 99 (1970).

[29] See *Steelworkers v. Warrior & Gulf*, supra, 363 U.S. at 582–583 ("An order to arbitrate the particular grievance should not be denied unless it may be said with positive assurance that the arbitration clause is not susceptible of an interpretation that covers the asserted dispute.").

[30] *Steelworkers v. Enterprise Wheel & Car*, supra; *Steelworkers v. American Mfg. Co.*, 363 U.S. 564 (1960); *Steelworkers v. Warrior & Gulf*, supra.

As stated, the issue in *Wright* was whether to require the employee to arbitrate his statutory discrimination claims—not whether to give effect to an arbitral decision that may or may not have addressed such claims.[31] But the Supreme Court addressed the latter issue in *14 Penn Plaza LLC v. Pyett*, 556 U.S. 247 (2009); and again, its decision supports our new standard. In *Pyett*, the Court found that , unlike in *Wright*, the employee was required to arbitrate his claim arising under the Age Discrimination in Employment Act of 1967 (ADEA), 29 U.S.C. §§621 et seq., because the arbitration provision in the collective-bargaining agreement clearly and unmistakably required employees to arbitrate ADEA claims. 556 U.S. at 258–259. However, the Court distinguished earlier decisions in which it had found that employees had not waived their right to litigate employment discrimination claims by previously submitting contractual claims to arbitration, because the arbitration provisions did not encompass the statutory claims at issue.[32] 556 U.S. at 260–264. The Court stressed that those decisions

> did not involve the issue of the enforceability of an agreement to arbitrate statutory claims [, but] instead "involved the quite different issue whether arbitration of contract-based claims precluded subsequent judicial resolution of statutory claims. *Since the employees there had not agreed to arbitrate their statutory claims, and the labor arbitrators were not authorized to resolve such claims, the arbitration in those cases understandably was held not to preclude subsequent statutory actions.*"

556 U.S. at 264, quoting *Gilmer v. Interstate/Johnson Lane Corp.*, 500 U.S. 20, 35 (1991) (emphasis added, internal citations omitted).[33] Thus, contrary to Member

Johnson's assertion, the new standard's requirement that the arbitrator be explicitly authorized by the parties to decide the statutory issue is solidly in line with Supreme Court precedent.[34]

Nor is Member Johnson persuasive when he urges the Board to give collateral-estoppel effect to arbitrators' factual findings. He objects that our "new collateral-estoppel standard" (i.e., our statement, above, that the Board will assess an arbitral award in light of the evidence presented during the arbitration) is "nowhere near[ly] specific or efficient enough to preclude relitigation of essential fact issues." This suggestion misses the point. Our statement does not address collateral-estoppel. It is well settled that the Board does *not* give collateral estoppel effect to the resolution of private claims asserted by private parties, where the Board was not a party to the prior proceedings. See, e.g., *Field Bridge Associates*, 306 NLRB 322, 322 (1992), enfd. 982 F.2d 845 (2d Cir. 1993), cert. denied 509 U.S. 904 (1993).[35] We are simply cautioning parties that if they withhold evidence relative to statutory claims in arbitration proceedings, they do so at their peril.

E. Changes to Prearbitral Deferral Standard

As noted above, when the Board solicited briefs concerning whether to change its postarbitral deferral standard, we asked the parties and amici whether, if the Board modified its postarbitral deferral standard, changes would need to be made to the Board's prearbitral deferral practices under *Collyer Insulated Wire*, 192 NLRB 837 (1971), and *United Technologies Corp.*, 268 NLRB 557 (1984). The AFL–CIO argues that the Board should not defer to the arbitral process unless the first prong of the postarbitral deferral standard is satisfied, that is, unless

---

[31] The Court in *Wright* did not address whether the Federal Arbitration Act (FAA), 9 U.S.C. §§ et seq., was applicable in that case, because the issue had not been raised. The Court did note that it had previously "discerned a presumption of arbitrability under the FAA," citing *Mitsubishi Motors Corp. v. Soler Chrysler-Plymouth, Inc.*, 473 U.S. 614 (1985). 525 U.S. at 77–78 fn. 1. In *Mitsubishi Motors*, however, the Court expressly relied in part on *Steelworkers v. Warrior & Gulf*, supra, 363 U.S. at 582–583, where the Court first announced the presumption of arbitrability under Sec. 301 of the LMRA. 473 U.S. at 626. It would seem, then, that at least where collective-bargaining agreements are concerned, that the presumption of arbitrability under the FAA would extend no farther than the Court indicated in *Wright*. That is, the presumption would extend only to disputes concerning the application or interpretation of a contract, and not to disputes over the meaning or application of a Federal statute.

[32] See *Alexander v. Gardner-Denver Co.*, 415 U.S. 36 (1974) (Title VII); *Barrentine v. Arkansas-Best Freight System, Inc.*, 450 U.S. 728 (1981) (Fair Labor Standards Act); *McDonald v. West Branch*, 466 U.S. 284 (1984) (42 U.S.C. Sec. 1983).

[33] The Court disavowed certain other aspects of the analysis in *Gardner-Denver* and its progeny. See 556 U.S. at 265–272. It did not,

however, disturb the reasoning quoted above, which it characterized as a "legal rule." Id. at 263.

[34] Citing *CompuCredit Corp. v. Greenwood*, 132 S.Ct. 665 (2012), Member Johnson contends that a "flurry of FAA [Federal Arbitration Act] cases" decided since *Wright* and *Pyett*, supra, sap those decisions of their vitality. We disagree. The issue in *CompuCredit* was whether a party was contractually bound to arbitrate claims arising under a Federal statute, not the effect (if any) that an administrative agency must give to an arbitral award. There is no mention of either *Wright* or *Pyett* in the Court's opinion, and the Court relied on cases that predate *Wright* and *Pyett*.

Member Johnson also argues that *Wright* supports, at most, only the requirement that the arbitrator be explicitly authorized to decide the statutory issue. But that is the only proposition for which *Wright* is cited. It is not otherwise relevant to the Board's standard for giving deference to an already issued arbitral decision.

[35] To say that the Board will not give collateral estoppel effect to an arbitrator's findings does not mean, as Member Johnson suggests, that they will be "discarded." Rather, the Board will give them whatever weight is appropriate. In many labor arbitration cases, of course, there is no transcript or other evidentiary record and the arbitrator makes no formal findings.

the arbitrator was explicitly authorized to decide the unfair labor practice issue. We agree. There is no apparent reason to defer to the arbitral *process* if it is plain at the outset that deferral to the arbitral *decision* would be improper. Thus, we shall no longer defer unfair labor practice allegations to the arbitral process unless the parties have explicitly authorized the arbitrator to decide the unfair labor practice issue, either in the collective-bargaining agreement or by agreement of the parties in a particular case.

COLLE and NAM suggest that if the Board adopts a more demanding postarbitral deferral standard, it should also, inter alia, require a completed investigation and merit determination before deciding whether to defer an unfair labor practice charge to the arbitral process. These suggestions are more appropriately addressed to the General Counsel. The General Counsel has unreviewable discretion as to whether or not to issue complaints in unfair labor practice cases; it follows that the General Counsel's choice of procedures for processing unfair labor practice charges, including whether and under what circumstances to defer to arbitration before issuing complaints, are matters left to the General Counsel's discretion. See *BCI Coca-Cola*, 361 NLRB No. 75, slip op. at 5 fn. 11 (2014).[36]

F. Changes to Standard for Determining Whether to Defer to Settlement Agreements Arising from the Grievance-Arbitration Process

The Board also asked the parties and amici whether, if the Board modified its postarbitral deferral standard, changes would need to be made to the Board's standards for determining whether to defer to prearbitral grievance settlements under *Alpha Beta Co.*, 273 NLRB 1546 (1985), review denied sub nom. *Mahon v. NLRB*, 808 F.2d 1342 (9th Cir. 1987); and *Postal Service*, 300 NLRB 196 (1990). In response, the General Counsel and the AFL–CIO contend that we should apply essentially the same standard to settlement agreements as to arbitral decisions. The General Counsel also argues the Board should decide whether to accept the settlement agreement under current nonBoard settlement practices, including review under the standards of *Independent Stave Co.*, 287 NLRB 740, 743 (1987). COLLE, NAM, and Member Johnson, by contrast, argue that no change should be made to the Board's standards for deferring to grievance settlements. In this regard, COLLE and Member Johnson stress that grievances often are settled by nonlawyer

representatives prior to the filing of Board charges, and therefore that parties typically do not focus on unfair labor practice issues when negotiating settlements.

We find it appropriate to apply the same deferral principles to prearbitral settlement agreements as to arbitral awards (i.e., as the Board has done under the current standard). See *Alpha Beta*, 273 NLRB at 1547. Thus, it must be shown that the parties intended to settle the unfair labor practice issue; that they addressed it in the settlement agreement; and that Board law reasonably permits the settlement agreement. As with arbitral awards, the Board will not expect the parties to have addressed the statutory issue in the same manner as administrative law judges, and the Board will not engage in de novo review of settlement agreements. Rather, we will assess such agreements in light of the factors set forth in *Independent Stave*, as the General Counsel suggests.[37] We specifically reject the argument raised by COLLE and Member Johnson that we should adopt a different standard merely because nonlawyers typically craft settlement agreements, often without being advised that an unfair labor practice charge may be waiting in the wings. We perceive no reason why settlement agreements that do not reflect the parties' consideration of statutory issues should stand on better footing than arbitral awards with similar drawbacks.[38]

II. PROSPECTIVE APPLICATION OF THE NEW STANDARD

We turn now to the question whether to apply the new standard retroactively (i.e., in all pending cases) or only prospectively (in future cases). For the reasons explained below, we find prospective application to be appropriate.

The Board's usual practice is to apply all new policies and standards in "all pending cases, in whatever stage." *Levitz Furniture Co. of the Pacific*, 333 NLRB 717, 729 (2001), quoting *John Deklewa & Sons*, 282 NLRB 1375, 1389 (1987), enfd. 843 F.2d 770 (3d Cir. 1988), cert.

---

[36] Our approach here is deliberately incremental, to permit fuller experience and deliberation over time. However, the General Counsel's suggestion that prearbitral deferral should normally be for no more than 1 year is one that the General Counsel himself may wish to consider implementing in cases that are in the investigative stage.

[37] Under *Independent Stave*, the Board considers all the circumstances surrounding a settlement agreement, including (1) whether the charging party(ies), the respondent(s), and any of the individual discriminatees have agreed to be bound, and the position taken by the General Counsel regarding the settlement; (2) whether the settlement is reasonable in light of the nature of the violations alleged, the risks inherent in litigation, and the stage of the litigation; (3) whether there has been any fraud, coercion, or duress by any of the parties in reaching the settlement; and (4) whether the respondent has engaged in a history of unlawful conduct or has breached previous settlement agreements resolving unfair labor practice disputes. 287 NLRB at 743.

[38] Obviously, then, we also reject NEBA's contention that the Board should defer to *all* settlement agreements voluntarily reached in bargaining by employers and unions.

Member Johnson suggests that the Board should craft "safe harbor" language for parties to incorporate in settlement agreements. That issue is better left for a future case, presenting the issue squarely.

denied 488 U.S. 889 (1988) (internal citation omitted). However, the effects of retroactive application must be balanced against "the mischief of producing a result which is contrary to a statutory design or to legal and equitable principles." *Levitz*, 333 NLRB at 729 (internal citations omitted).

We think that applying our new standard in pending cases would be unfair to parties that have relied on the current deferral standard in negotiating contracts and in determining whether, and in what manner, to process cases involving unfair labor practice issues through the grievance-arbitration process. Granted, retroactive application of the new standard would hasten the day when arbitral decisions more surely protect employees' statutory rights. However, a principal purpose of the Act is to promote collective bargaining, which necessarily involves giving effect to the bargains the parties have struck in concluding collective-bargaining agreements. Retroactive application would tend to frustrate that aspect of the Act's purpose. Thus, we find those concerns supporting retroactive application are outweighed by the injustice that would result from applying the new standard in pending cases. Accordingly, we will apply the new standard only prospectively.

Where parties' contracts already provide for arbitration of unfair labor practice issues, or where parties have explicitly authorized arbitrators to consider such issues in particular cases, the first prong of the new deferral standard has been met. In such cases, applying the remaining criteria of the new standard in arbitrations that have yet to take place will not result in injustice because it will not contravene the parties' settled expectations. Accordingly, where parties have already, either contractually or explicitly for a particular case or cases, authorized arbitrators to decide unfair labor practice claims, we shall apply the new standard to all future arbitrations. By contrast, where current contracts do not authorize arbitrators to decide unfair labor practice issues, we will not apply the new standards until those contracts have expired, or the parties have agreed to present particular statutory issues to the arbitrator.[39]

III. DEFERRAL IS APPROPRIATE IN THIS CASE

Having declined to apply our new deferral standard in pending cases, we must decide whether deferral is appropriate in this case under the current standard. The judge found, and we agree, that it is. As noted above, it is con-

ceded that the arbitral procedure was fair and equitable and that all parties agreed to be bound. It is also conceded that the contractual issue was factually parallel to the unfair labor practice issue and that the Subcommittee was presented generally with the facts relevant to deciding the statutory issue. The General Counsel excepts only to the judge's finding that the Subcommittee's decision was not clearly repugnant to the Act. The General Counsel asserts that Beneli was discharged primarily because of her activities as a union steward, and the Subcommittee's decision upholding her discharge therefore was "palpably wrong" and not susceptible to any interpretation consistent with the Act. The Subcommittee phrased the issue before it as whether the Respondent terminated Beneli without just cause for her use of profanity, and its decision stated only that, having reviewed the facts presented (which included the facts concerning Beneli's steward activities), it found no violation of the contract. Contrary to the General Counsel, the decision is arguably consistent with a finding that the Subcommittee considered and rejected the Union's contention that Beneli's discharge was motivated by her steward activities; at least, the General Counsel has failed to prove otherwise. See, e.g., *Airborne Express Corp.*, 343 NLRB at 581. The Subcommittee's finding that Beneli was discharged for using profanity is therefore susceptible to an interpretation consistent with the Act. Because the General Counsel has failed to demonstrate that the Subcommittee's decision was clearly repugnant to the Act, we shall defer to the decision and dismiss the complaint.

ORDER

The recommended Order of the administrative law judge is adopted and the complaint is dismissed.

Dated, Washington, D.C. December 15, 2014

Mark Gaston Pearce,	Chairman
Kent Y. Hirozawa,	Member
Nancy Schiffer,	Member

(SEAL) NATIONAL LABOR RELATIONS BOARD

MEMBER MISCIMARRA, concurring in part and dissenting in part.

The majority in this case performs surgery on two venerable institutions—final and binding grievance arbitration and the collectively bargained requirement of "cause"—that have benefited millions of employees. No

---

[39] We recognize that in some instances it will be several years before existing contracts expire and new contracts are concluded. In our view, however, the resulting delay in applying the new standard in those instances is justified by the need to avoid unfairness to contracting parties. In any event, by its very nature, this problem will become less and less serious with the passage of time.

sickness warrants the majority's treatment. Labor arbitration and the concept of "cause" have been lauded by Congress, the Supreme Court, other courts, labor relations scholars, and arbitrators.[1] The majority wields a scalpel whose bluntness will cause injury to employees, unions and employers alike, particularly those that have existing collective-bargaining agreements. Worse, the tissue cut away has existed for decades: the *Spielberg* standard has governed this area for nearly 60 years,[2] and the *Olin* standard for 30 years.[3] Most important, in my view, is the fact that the majority's changes are contradicted by our statute. Section 10(c) prohibits the Board from making the very distinction that forms the basis for the majority's reformulated deferral standards.

I concur in the outcome here only because the majority refrains from applying its changed deferral standards to the instant case.[4] However, the changed standards cut a wide swath, prospectively affecting at least three types of deferral: (i) deferral to existing arbitration awards (governed by *Olin* and *Spielberg*), (ii) deferral to prospective arbitration procedures (governed by *Collyer Insulated Wire*, supra, 192 NLRB at 839),[5] and (iii) deferral to grievance settlements reached prior to arbitration (governed by *Alpha Beta Co.*, 273 NLRB 1546 (1985), review denied sub nom. *Mahon v. NLRB*, 808 F.2d 1342 (9th Cir. 1987), and *Postal Service*, 300 NLRB 196 (1990)).

For several reasons, I dissent from the changes adopted by my colleagues in the majority.[6]

First, the majority's approach is premised on a false dichotomy—between "statutory" issues, on the one hand, and the issue of "cause," on the other—that is contradicted by the Act's language. My colleagues preclude deferral in all arbitration cases that determine whether "cause" supported an employee's suspension or discharge, unless the party seeking deferral proves that the arbitrator considered what the majority regards as different and more onerous "statutory" or "unfair labor practice" issues. Yet, Section 10(c) precludes the Board from making this distinction. In Section 10(c), Congress imposed a requirement on the Board prohibiting reinstatement or backpay *whenever "cause" exists for an employee's suspension or discharge*. In other words, the Act makes "cause" the "statutory issue" as a matter of law in *every* discharge and suspension case.

Second, the Board will not defer to grievance arbitration in most cases under the newly adopted standards unless the parties rewrite their collective bargaining agreement (CBA) provisions relating to discipline and grievance arbitration. This aspect of the majority's approach is objectionable not only because the Act prohibits the Board from imposing substantive contract terms on parties, but also because my colleagues all but compel the renegotiation of extremely important contract provisions, which will cause increased conflict among the parties for whom the Board should most strive to foster stability—i.e., employers and unions that have existing collective-bargaining relationships. Alternatively, if parties do not rewrite their collective-bargaining agreements, the majority's new standards make two track arbitration/Board litigation a near certainty, thereby eliminating the benefits previously afforded by "final and bind-

---

[1] In *USWA v. Warrior & Gulf Navigation Co.*, 363 U.S. 574, 578 (1960), the Supreme Court stated that "arbitration of labor disputes under collective bargaining agreements is part and parcel of the collective bargaining process itself." The Court continued: "[T]he grievance machinery under a collective bargaining agreement is at the very heart of the system of industrial self-government. Arbitration is the means of solving the unforeseeable by molding a system of private law for all the problems which may arise and to provide for their solution in a way which will generally accord with the variant needs and desires of the parties. The processing of disputes through the grievance machinery is actually a vehicle by which meaning and content are given to the collective bargaining agreement." Id. at 581. See also Labor Management Relations Act (LMRA) Sec. 203(d) ("Final adjustment by a method agreed upon by the parties is hereby declared to be the desirable method for settlement of grievance disputes arising over the application or interpretation of an existing collective-bargaining agreement."); *Collyer Insulated Wire*, 192 NLRB 837, 839 (1971) ("In our view, disputes such as these can better be resolved by arbitrators with special skill and experience in deciding matters arising under established bargaining relationships than by the application by this Board of a particular provision of our statute."); Archibald Cox, *Reflections Upon Labor Arbitration*, 72 HARV. L. REV. 1482, 1491 (1959) ("[J]ust cause" provisions are "an obvious illustration" of the fact that many provisions "must be expressed in general and flexible terms."). See generally *Triple Play Sports Bar & Grille*, 361 NLRB No. 31, slip op. at 9 (2014) (Member Miscimarra, dissenting in part), where I stated that "just cause" provisions have been ubiquitous in collective-bargaining agreements throughout the Act's history. Id., slip op. at 11 fn. 9, citing *Burgie Vinegar Co.*, 71 NLRB 829, 840 (1946) ("It is agreed that the right to discharge employees for just cause is a management prerogative."); *Solutia, Inc.*, 357 NLRB No. 15, slip op. at 4 fn. 8 (2011) (contract reserves to the company the right to "discipline or discharge for just cause"), enfd. 699 F.3d 50 (1st Cir. 2012).

[2] *Spielberg Mfg. Co.*, 112 NLRB 1080 (1955).

[3] *Olin Corp.*, 268 NLRB 573 (1984).

[4] The majority has announced that their changed deferral standards will only apply prospectively to cases arising after the issuance of today's decision.

[5] The Board has recognized a variation of *Collyer* prospective deferral when a pending grievance awaits arbitration. See *Dubo Mfg. Corp.*, 142 NLRB 431 (1963).

[6] In this separate opinion, I occasionally use the phrase "my colleagues" as a shorthand reference to my colleagues in the majority. However, I do not mean to suggest any disagreement with the separate opinion authored by another of my colleagues, Member Johnson, who dissents from the changes in Board deferral standards that have been adopted by the majority. I agree with the separate reasons articulated by Member Johnson in his own disagreement with the standards adopted by the majority.

ing" arbitration. In this respect, the majority deprives unions of a major benefit they could otherwise offer to unionized employers and represented employees. In the same way, because any newly negotiated arbitration and "cause" provisions will produce greater costs, burdens and delays (instead of facilitating the quick, inexpensive and final resolution of workplace disputes), nonunion employers are likely to more vigorously exercise their lawful right to oppose union representation during union organizing campaigns.

Third, I believe the changed deferral standards reflect an underlying hostility towards final and binding grievance arbitration and "cause" determinations, contrary to the federal policies favoring arbitration that Congress incorporated into the Federal Arbitration Act (in 1925) and into the Labor Management Relations Act (in 1947). The most important characteristic of "final and binding" arbitration is the notion that adjudicated outcomes will, in fact, be "final" and "binding." Yet, my colleagues now effectively guarantee that, in most cases involving existing CBAs, arbitration will *not* be final and binding. The outcome will be more work for the Board, at the expense of speed, predictability, and certainty for the parties, and the virtual elimination of finality given the long litigation treadmill that is associated with Board and court litigation of unfair labor practice claims.

In my view, there is no reason for the Board to deviate from the well-established deferral standards applicable to existing arbitration awards (governed by *Olin* and *Spielberg*), prospective arbitration procedures (governed by *Collyer*), and grievance settlements reached prior to arbitration (governed by *Alpha Beta* and *Postal Service*). These standards are understandable and have been widely applied and enforced. These standards afford appropriate deference to final and binding arbitration *and* the concept of "cause." These standards are consistent with our statute, including Section 10(c)'s requirement that makes "cause" a *statutory* issue binding on the Board in suspension and discharge cases. Finally, the existing deferral standards—instead of forcing parties to dramatically change existing labor contracts—would preserve the substantial benefits that existing arbitration and "cause" provisions confer on employees, unions and unionized employers.

A. The Majority's New Deferral Standards Are Improper Because Section 10(c) Requires the Board to Treat "Cause" as a <u>Statutory</u> Issue in All Suspension and Discharge Cases

Under the new standards established by my colleagues, the Board will never defer to a determination that "cause" existed for a discharge or suspension unless the party urging deferral proves, first, that the parties "explicitly authorized" resolution of "the unfair labor prac-

tice issue," and second, that the "the statutory issue" was presented and considered (or any failure on this score was caused by the party opposing deferral).[7] Deferral cases most often arise from employee discharges or suspensions—subject to challenge in arbitration under a contractual "cause" standard—that are also alleged in Board charges to violate Section 8(a)(3) or (1). My colleagues justify a much more narrow deferral standard by drawing a distinction between the "cause" standard, on the one hand, and what they apparently view as a more onerous and demanding "statutory" or "unfair labor practice" standard, on the other. However, the Act prohibits such reasoning and precludes the Board from making this distinction. Section 10(c) states: "*No order of the Board shall require the reinstatement of any individual as an employee . . . or the payment to him of any backpay, if such individual was suspended or discharged for cause*" (emphasis added).

In other words, the majority today finds the Board must independently redecide *every* case in which an arbitrator determines only that "cause" existed for a suspension or discharge. However, the majority presumes, incorrectly, that "cause" is inferior to a more rigorous and exacting "unfair labor practice" or "statutory" issue unique to the NLRA. Section 10(c) *makes "cause" the relevant statutory issue* in all cases involving discharges and suspensions alleged to violate the Act. Obviously, this statutory mandate is binding on the Board, and it explicitly constrains the Board's remedial authority.

Congress incorporated the "cause" requirement into the Act for good reason. The requirement of "cause"—whether referred to as "cause," "just cause," "proper cause" or similar other phrases[8]—has been called "the most important principle of labor relations in the unionized firm."[9] The meaning of "cause" in collective-bargaining agreements was explained nearly 60 years ago

---

[7] My colleagues also impose a third deferral requirement— that "Board law reasonably permits the award."

[8] Different collective-bargaining agreements articulate "cause" requirements in different ways, referring (for example) to "just cause," "proper cause" or "just and proper cause," but these different formulations are generally regarded as identical. See, e.g., *Worthington Corp.*, 24 Lab. Arb. (BNA) 1, 6–7 (McGoldrick, 1955) (regarding the right to suspend and discharge for "just cause," "proper cause," "obvious cause" or "cause," arbitrator states "[t]here is no significant difference between these various phrases"); Alan Miles Ruben, ed., Elkouri & Elkouri, *How Arbitration Works* 932 fn. 37 (6th ed. 2003) (collecting decisions "finding no significant difference between these terms"). I have previously noted that "just cause" provisions have been ubiquitous in collective-bargaining agreements throughout the Act's history. See supra fn. 1.

[9] Robert I. Abrams & Dennis R. Nolan, *Toward a Theory of "Just Cause" in Employee Discipline Cases*, Duke L.J. 594 (1985).

in *Worthington Corp.*, 24 Lab. Arb. (BNA) 1, 6–7 (McGoldrick, 1955):

> [I]t is common to include the right to suspend and discharge for "just cause," "proper cause," "obvious cause," or quite commonly simply for "cause." There is no significant difference between these various phrases. These exclude discharge for mere whim or caprice. They are, obviously, intended to include those things for which employees have traditionally been fired. They include the traditional causes of discharge in the particular trade or industry, the practices which develop in the day-to-day relations of management and labor and most recently they include the decisions of courts and arbitrators. . . . Where they are not expressed in posted rules, they may very well be implied, provided they are applied in a uniform, non-discriminatory manner.

I am at a loss to understand the majority's insistence that the Board must inject itself more aggressively in suspension and discharge arbitration regarding the existence or nonexistence of "cause."[10] Virtually everybody understands that "cause" will not exist if an arbitrator determines an employee's suspension or discharge–instead of resulting from legitimate reasons—stemmed from antiunion discrimination or other protected activities, such that the suspension or discharge, if adjudicated by the Board, would be a violation of Section 8(a)(3), (1) or both.

More importantly, the Act clearly establishes that *Congress* understood this concept, which is why Congress imposed on the Board a requirement that the issue of "cause" be deemed controlling and coextensive with any other "statutory" issues pertaining to employee discharges or suspensions alleged to violate the Act. And contrary to the majority's decision, which imposes the burden on the party seeking deferral to show that deferral is warranted, Congress prohibited the Board from impos-

ing the burden of proof on any party to establish "cause" for discharge. Rather, Congress required that the Board's General Counsel prove, by a preponderance of the evidence, that an alleged unlawful suspension or discharge was not "for cause."[11] When an existing arbitration award indicates an employee was suspended or discharged for "cause," therefore, I believe this makes deferral appropriate unless the General Counsel satisfies his or her burden to prove that deferral is unwarranted and "cause" did not exist.

The "cause" language in Section 10(c) was added as part of the Labor Management Relations Act (LMRA) amendments to the NLRA that were adopted in 1947.[12] During the Senate debates on the LMRA, Senator Taft— the legislation's principal sponsor in the Senate— commented on the "cause" language set forth in Section 10(c) and stated: "If a man is *discharged for cause*, he cannot be reinstated. If he is *discharged for union activity*, he must be reinstated."[13]

The legislative history likewise indicates that the Board was constrained to accept and apply a "cause" standard in all discharge and suspension cases. Thus, the Conference Report—commenting on House changes adopted by the Conference Committee—stated:

> [I]n section 10(c) of the amended act, as proposed in the conference agreement, it is specifically provided that no order of the Board shall require the reinstatement of any individual or the payment to him of any back pay if such individual was suspended or discharged for cause, and this, of course, applies with equal force whether or not the acts consti-

---

[10] The requirement of "cause" has nearly universal acceptance in most collective-bargaining agreements as a fundamental limitation on an employer's authority to discipline or discharge employees. Over 90 percent of all collective-bargaining agreements include an explicit "just cause" provision for discipline. See Bureau of National Affairs, *Basic Patterns in Union Contracts* (BNA, 14th ed. 1995). Just cause provisions have been called "an obvious illustration" of the fact that many provisions "must be expressed in general and flexible terms." Archibald Cox, *Reflections Upon Labor Arbitration*, 72 HARV. L. REV. 1482, 1491 (1959). To the same effect, the Supreme Court has stated, in reference to collective-bargaining agreements, that there are "a myriad of cases which the draftsmen cannot wholly anticipate," and "[t]here are too many people, too many problems, too many unforeseeable contingencies to make the words . . . the exclusive source of rights and duties." *Steelworkers v. Warrior & Gulf Navigation Co.*, 363 U.S. 574, 578–579 (1960) (internal quotation omitted).

[11] The Supreme Court has reaffirmed the settled principle, stated explicitly in Sec. 10(c), that the General Counsel has the burden of proving, "upon the preponderance of the testimony," the elements of an unfair labor practice. See, e.g., *NLRB v. Transportation Management Corp*, 462 U.S. 393, 401 (1983). In a mixed motive case, where there is evidence of both discrimination and "cause," the General Counsel bears the burden of showing by a preponderance of the evidence that a suspension or discharge was motivated by animus against the employee's union or other protected concerted activity. Although the Board allocates to the employer the burden of proving its affirmative defense, *Wright Line*, 251 NLRB 1083, 1088–1089 (1980) (subsequent history omitted), the ultimate burden of proving a violation remains with the General Counsel, id. at 1088 fn. 11. Regardless of intermediate burdens, the General Counsel must satisfy his ultimate burden to prove a violation of the Act. In such cases, it necessarily follows that the employee was not suspended or discharged for "cause." See also fn. 20 below.

[12] See, e.g., Labor Management Relations Act (Taft-Hartley Act or LMRA), 61 Stat. 136 (1947), 29 U.S.C. §§ 141 et seq.

[13] 93 Cong. Rec. 6677 (daily ed. June 6, 1947) (statement of Sen. Taft), reprinted in 2 NLRB, Legislative History of the Labor Management Relations Act, 1947 (hereinafter LMRA Hist.) at 1593.

tuting the cause for discharge were committed in connection with a concerted activity.[14]

The report accompanying the House bill—H.R. 3020, 80th Cong. (1947)—likewise indicated that the "cause" standard would be binding on the Board in all suspension and discharge cases:

A third change forbids the Board to reinstate an individual *unless the weight of the evidence shows that the individual was not suspended or discharged for cause.* In the past, the Board, admitting that an employee was guilty of gross misconduct, nevertheless frequently reinstated him, "inferring" that, because he was a member or an official of a union, this, not his misconduct, was the reason for his discharge. Matter of Wyman-Gordon Company, 62 N.L.R.B. 561 (1945), is typical of the Board's attitude in such cases. . . . The Board may not "infer" an improper motive *when the evidence shows cause for discipline or discharge.*[15]

The "cause" language in Section 10(c) was not a minor technical amendment of the Act. Rather, the Section 10(c) language was specifically referenced by President Truman when he vetoed the LMRA,[16] and by Senator Taft in opposition to President Truman's veto.[17] Senator Taft reiterated that the "cause" standard—which the Board would be constrained to accept and apply—*was to be coextensive with the "statutory" standards governing suspension and discharge cases.* Senator Taft stated:

The President says an employer can discharge a man on the pretext of a slight infraction, even though his real motive is to discriminate against the em-

ployee for union activity. This is not so. The Board decides under the new law, as under the former law, whether the man was really discharged for union activity *or for good cause.*[18]

As noted above, during its deliberations resulting in the LMRA amendments, Congress also focused on which party should bear the *burden* of establishing whether an employee's suspension or discharge violated the Act or was supported by "cause." Here, the legislation clearly placed the burden on the Board. Initially, the legislation stated that the Board could not order reinstatement or backpay "unless the *weight of the evidence* shows that the individual was not suspended or discharged for cause."[19] This "weight of the evidence" language was eventually deleted, but only because Section 10(c) independently requires (based on another amendment made in 1947) that Board determinations generally be supported by a "preponderance" of the evidence.[20]

---

[14] H.R. Rep. 80–510 at 39 (1947), reprinted in 1 LMRA Hist. 543 (emphasis added).

[15] H.R. Rep. 80–245 at 42 (1947), reprinted in 1 LMRA Hist. 333 (emphasis added).

[16] President Truman's veto message received in House argued that the "cause" language would be controlling (therefore precluding reinstatement or backpay) even if the evidence established that a suspension or discharge resulted from antiunion discrimination. Thus, President Truman's veto message stated: "The bill would make it easier for an employer to get rid of employees whom he wanted to discharge because they exercised their right of self-organization guaranteed by the act. It would permit an employer to dismiss a man on the pretext of a slight infraction of shop rules, even though his real motive was to discriminate against this employee for union activity." 93 Cong. Rec. 7501, reprinted in 1 LMRA Hist. 916 (veto message received in the House).

[17] The LMRA was enacted over President Truman's veto when two-thirds majorities in the House and Senate voted to override the President's veto. 93 Cong. Rec. 7504 (June 20, 1947), reprinted in 2 LMRA Hist. 922–923 (reflecting two-thirds majority vote in the House); 93 Cong. Rec. 7692 (June 23, 1947), reprinted in 2 LMRA Hist. 1656–1657 (reflecting two-thirds majority vote in the Senate).

[18] 93 Cong. Rec. S A3233 (daily ed. June 21, 1947) (statement of Sen. Taft).

[19] H.R. Rep. 80–245 at 42 (1947), reprinted in 1 LMRA Hist. 333.

[20] See H.R. Rep. –80510 at 55 (1947), reprinted in 1 LMRA Hist. 559 ("The conference agreement omits the 'weight of evidence' language, since the Board, under the general provisions of section 10, must act on a preponderance of evidence, and simply provides that no order of the Board shall require reinstatement or back pay for any individual who was suspended or discharged for cause.").

As noted in the text, Sec. 10(c) and its legislative history reveal that the General Counsel bears the burden of proof that disputed discipline violates the Act, which also entails establishing there was no "cause" for the discipline in question, and this makes in inappropriate for the majority, when evaluating whether to defer to a "cause" determination made by an arbitrator, to place the burden of proof on the party seeking deferral. The decision in *Transportation Management*, relied upon by the majority, does not dictate otherwise. Indeed, the Supreme Court in *Transportation Management* held that Sec. 10(c)'s "preponderance of the testimony" language meant the General Counsel has the burden "throughout the proceedings" of proving "the elements of an unfair labor practice," 462 U.S. at 401, and the Court stated that the "preponderance of the testimony" requirement was "*closely related*" to Sec. 10(c)'s provision "that no order of the Board reinstate or compensate any employee who was fired for cause," id. at 401 fn. 6 (emphasis added). Moreover, *Transportation Management* did not involve deferral to arbitration; rather, it dealt only with the employer's intermediate burden in *Wright Line* "mixed-motive" cases, where the employer asserts an "affirmative defense" by "showing what his actions would have been regardless of his forbidden motivation." Id. at 401; see also *Wright Line*, 251 NLRB at 1088 fn. 11 ("The shifting burden merely requires the employer to make out what is actually an affirmative defense."). Not only did the Supreme Court hold that the *Wright Line* mixed-motive standard "does *not* change or add to the elements of the unfair labor practice *that the General Counsel has the burden of proving* under § 10(c)," 462 U.S. at 401 (emphasis added; footnote omitted), the Court held that this mixed-motive issue was *unrelated* to the "cause" language set forth in Sec. 10(c), id. at 401 fn. 6 ("the drafters of § 10(c) were not thinking of the mixed-motive case"). Therefore, Sec. 10(c) and its legislative history indicate that Congress intended the General Counsel would bear the burden of proving any alleged viola-

In my view, the "cause" language set forth in Section 10(c), combined with the Act's legislative history as described above, warrant two important conclusions.

First, the majority's changed standards regarding deferral are premised on a misreading of the Act, and the majority impermissibly disregards the statutory "cause" standard that Section 10(c) makes binding on the Board in all suspension and discharge cases. As noted above, under the new standard the Board will not defer to any arbitration award finding that "cause" existed for an employee's discharge or suspension unless the party urging deferral proves (1) that the parties "explicitly authorized" resolution of "the unfair labor practice issue," (2) that "the statutory issue" was presented and considered (or any failure on this score was caused by the party opposing deferral), and (3) that "Board law reasonably permits the award." In suspension and discharge cases, *neither* of the first two requirements is permissible unless (i) the Board writes out of the Act the statutory "cause" standard set forth in Section 10(c), or (ii) the Board somehow goes back in time and restores the pre-1947 state of affairs that existed before Congress enacted the LMRA. In this regard, it is worth noting that Congress enacted the "cause" language in Section 10(c), as part of the LMRA amendments, at the same time final and binding arbitration received the unqualified endorsement of Congress in LMRA Section 203(d).[21]

Certainly, the Board might resolve the issue of "cause" differently than an arbitrator. However, this possibility relates to the majority's third deferral requirement (that Board law "reasonably permits" whatever award is rendered by an arbitrator). As to the majority's first two deferral requirements, Section 10(c) prohibits what the Board majority now asserts it will do—i.e., find that employee suspensions or discharges violate the Act, even if they are supported by "cause," because the Board determination will be based on a more stringent Board-created "unfair labor practice issue" or "statutory issue" separate from "cause."[22]

There is a second conclusion that, in my view, follows from Section 10(c) and the Act's legislative history: they provide ample support for the longstanding deferral standards—set forth in *Olin* and *Spielberg, Collyer, Alpha Beta* and *Postal Service*—that my colleagues now cast aside. Under *Olin*, as my colleagues note, deferral is appropriate as long as (1) the contractual issue is "factually parallel" to the unfair labor practice issue and the arbitrator was presented generally with the facts relevant to resolving that issue (268 NLRB at 573–574), and (2) the award is not "clearly repugnant" to the Act (defined as being "palpably wrong" or "not susceptible to an interpretation consistent with the Act") (id. at 574). In addition, the party opposing deferral (e.g., the Board's General Counsel) has the burden of proving that deferral is inappropriate. Id. The first requirement—evaluating whether the contractual issue is "factually parallel" to the unfair labor practice issue—recognizes the close relation between any collectively bargained "cause" standard and Section 10(c)'s prohibition against backpay or reinstatement where an employee is discharged or suspended for "cause." The second requirement recognizes the primary purpose of deferral, which is to give effect to the parties' agreement that arbitration shall constitute the final and binding means of resolving grievances regarding em-

---

tion, *including* the statutory requirement that the employee in question was *not* disciplined for "cause," and the Supreme Court regarded this as separate and distinct from whatever burdens the Board devised or applied in mixed-motive cases. Id.; see also id. at 399 fn. 4 ("[N]owhere in the legislative history is reference made to any of the mixed-motive cases decided by the Board or by the Courts.").

[21] LMRA Section 203(d) states that "[f]inal adjustment by a method agreed upon by the parties is hereby declared to be the desirable method for settlement of grievance disputes arising over the application or interpretation of an existing collective-bargaining agreement. . . ."

[22] I believe Sec. 10(c) also renders implausible the majority's stated reason for rewriting the Board's multifaceted standards regarding deferral. My colleagues maintain that the current deferral standard "creates an unacceptably high risk that the Board will defer *when an arbitrator has not adequately considered the statutory issue*, or when it is *impos-*

sible to tell whether he or she has done so" (emphasis added). Because virtually all arbitrated discipline cases turn on whether "cause" existed for an employee's suspension or discharge, and because Sec. 10(c) makes the presence or absence of "cause" controlling for the Board, the arbitrator in every case will, by definition, have "adequately considered the statutory issue" except in a rare case where the arbitrator refuses to apply the collectively bargained "cause" standard or otherwise resolves a case based on his or her "own brand of industrial justice." *Steelworkers v. Enterprise Wheel & Car Corp.*, 363 U.S. 593, 597 (1960). In the latter case, the arbitrator's award will be clearly repugnant to the Act, and thus not entitled to deferral under the existing *Spielberg* and *Olin* standards. In my view, therefore, the majority does not identify any reasons existing deferral standards are insufficient to address such exceptional cases. I also respectfully disagree with the majority's reliance on *Mobil Oil Exploration & Producing, Inc.*, 325 NLRB 176 (1997), enfd. 200 F.3d 230 (5th Cir. 1999); *Garland Coal & Mining Co.*, 276 NLRB 963 (1985); and *Cone Mills Corp.*, 298 NLRB 661 (1990). In each of these cases—decided under the *Spielberg/Olin* deferral standard—the Board *refused* to defer to an arbitrator's decision on the ground that the award was clearly repugnant to the Act. These cases, therefore, illustrate the sufficiency of the preexisting *Spielberg/Olin* deferral standard, pursuant to which the Board has decided *not* to defer in appropriate circumstances.

Sec. 10(a) of the Act provides that the Board's power to prevent unfair labor practices "shall not be affected by any other means of adjustment or prevention that has been or may be established by agreement, law, or otherwise." But this statutory language does nothing more than make clear that the Board retains authority to overturn arbitration decisions that are contrary to the Act. Nothing in Sec. 10(a) indicates or establishes that the issue of "cause" is different from and inferior to the "statutory" issue in unfair labor practice cases involving suspensions and discharges. To the contrary, Sec. 10(c) expressly *makes* "cause" the "statutory" issue in such cases.

ployee suspensions and discharges, even though an arbitrator may resolve some disputes differently than would the Board, with the caveat that the Board will not defer to awards that are plainly contrary to the Act.[23] The final requirement—favoring deferral unless the party opposing it proves that deferral is inappropriate—is consistent with Section 10(c) and its legislative history, which show that Congress intended to require *the Board's General Counsel* to prove any alleged violation. This allocation of burdens also recognizes that federal policy, reflected in LMRA Section 203(d), strongly favors "[f]inal adjustment by a method agreed upon by the parties" over other means of resolving disputes between employers, unions, and employees.[24]

The Board's traditional standards regarding deferral to arbitration awards—based on "cause" provisions in collective-bargaining agreements that have been freely negotiated by companies and unions, are easily understood by employees, and have been interpreted by thousands of arbitrators—reflect an appropriate balance between our strong federal policies favoring arbitration and the protection of statutory rights. Conversely, the majority here announces changed standards that reflect an intention to find suspensions and discharges unlawful—even if supported by "cause"—based on what the majority believes must be more stringent scrutiny of "statutory" or "unfair labor practice" issues. This is precisely what Section 10(c) prohibits because it expressly *requires* the Board to treat "cause" as the statutory standard.

I recognize that the majority characterizes deferral as a matter involving Board "discretion," but we cannot take actions that are directly prohibited by the Act. In my view, this is the problem with the majority's new deferral standards. I believe the new standards are irreconcilable with Section 10(c).

B. The Majority Dramatically Curtails Board Deferral to Arbitration or Requires a Wholesale Rewriting of CBA "Cause" and Arbitration Provisions

Collective-bargaining agreements typically span multiple years. When arbitration procedures and "cause" requirements have been agreed upon by employers and unions in existing collective-bargaining agreements, the Board should celebrate such agreements, since they are the successful culmination of good-faith bargaining required by the Act.[25] In many cases, existing collective-bargaining agreements also result from longstanding relationships between employers and unions that the Board should support and encourage.[26] And because labor arbitration procedures are mutually agreed upon between employers and unions, arbitration in this context should be afforded no less deference than the types of nonunion arbitration agreements that have received such deferential treatment by the Supreme Court. See, e.g., *Circuit City Stores v. Adams,* 532 U.S. 105 (2001) (upholding binding arbitration agreements in employment contracts subject to the Federal Arbitration Act); *Gilmer v. Interstate/Johnson Lane Corp.,* 500 U.S. 20 (1991) (same).

These considerations make it important to examine how the majority's changed deferral standards will affect existing collective-bargaining agreements—specifically, existing "cause" requirements and labor arbitration provisions. If one looks at existing *"cause"* requirements, the majority's changed deferral standards will basically

---

[23] See *Steelworkers v. American Mfg. Co.,* 363 U.S. 564, 567 (1960) (The judicial function should be "very limited when the parties have agreed to submit all questions of contract interpretation to the arbitrator. It is then confined to ascertaining whether the party seeking arbitration is making a claim which on its face is governed by the contract. Whether the moving party is right or wrong is a question of contract interpretation for the arbitrator."). I interpret the majority's changed standard as recognizing this same principle, although the majority's "Board law reasonably permits" standard will predictably permit deferral in fewer cases than the "clearly repugnant" standard.

[24] See also *Steelworkers v. Warrior & Gulf Navigation Co.,* 363 U.S. 574, 581 (1960) (Arbitration "should not be denied unless it may be said with positive assurance that the arbitration clause is not susceptible of an interpretation that covers the asserted dispute. Doubts should be resolved in favor of coverage."); *Nolde Brothers v. Bakery & Confectionary Works,* 430 U.S. 243, 254 (1977) (noting that the Supreme Court "has established a strong presumption favoring arbitrability" and describing as "noteworthy" the fact that "parties drafted their broad arbitration clause against a backdrop of well established federal labor policy favoring arbitration as the means of resolving disputes over the meaning and effect of collective bargaining agreements") (citations omitted).

[25] Sec. 8(a)(5) and 8(b)(3) of the Act impose a duty to bargain collectively on employers and unions, respectively, which Sec. 8(d) defines as "the mutual obligation of the employer and the representative of the employees to meet at reasonable times and confer in good faith with respect to wages, hours, and other terms and conditions of employment. . . ."

[26] One of the Board's primary functions is to foster stability in labor relations, to encourage good-faith negotiation, and to give effect to the parties' agreements. See, e.g., *Colgate-Palmolive-Peet Co. v. NLRB,* 338 U.S. 355, 362–363 (1949) ("To achieve stability of labor relations was the primary objective of Congress in enacting the National Labor Relations Act."); *NLRB v. Appleton Electric Co.,* 296 F.2d 202, 206 (7th Cir. 1961) ("a basic policy of the Act [is] to achieve stability of labor relations"). Arbitration plays a central role in achieving these goals. *Steelworkers v. Warrior & Gulf Navigation Co.,* 363 U.S. at 578 ("[A]rbitration is the substitute for industrial strife."). Stability is also clearly undermined when the Board adopts policies that detract from final and binding arbitration procedures that have been agreed to by employers and unions. As the Supreme Court stated in *Steelworkers v. Enterprise Wheel & Car Corp.,* 363 U.S. at 596, 599: "The federal policy of settling labor disputes by arbitration would be undermined if courts had the final say on the merits of the awards. . . . [P]lenary review by a court of the merits would make meaningless the provisions that the arbitrator's decision is final, for in reality it would almost never be final."

never permit deferral (because my colleagues believe, mistakenly, that "cause" is different from and inferior to the "statutory" and "unfair labor practice" issues uniquely examined in Board litigation). If one looks at existing *arbitration* provisions, these typically limit the arbitrator's authority to the "interpretation and application of this agreement" and typically prohibit the arbitrator from "adding to, subtracting from or modifying" the CBA.[27] Here too, therefore, the majority's changed deferral standards will basically never permit deferral (because my colleagues would require proof that different and more onerous "statutory" and "unfair labor practice" issues were presented and considered by the arbitrator). In short, therefore, the changed standards mean existing "cause" and arbitration provisions, in most existing collective-bargaining agreements, will give rise to duplicative NLRB litigation over disputed suspensions and discharges unless, first, the CBA reproduces the text of the statute or incorporates statutory provisions by reference, or second, the parties engage in a case-by-case renegotiation of the CBA "cause" provisions, abandon arbitration-clause language limiting the arbitrator's authority, and/or explicitly authorize the arbitrator to adjudicate 8(a)(3) and (1) issues in addition to whatever "cause" and other contractual issues pertain to the dispute.

In my view, this approach to deferral has several serious infirmities.

The most obvious problem is that the changed standards essentially *eliminate* Board deferral to arbitration in the overwhelming majority of cases involving current collective-bargaining agreements. As noted above, most current CBAs contain conventional "cause" requirements *and* standard restrictions on an arbitrator's authority—for example, restricting the arbitrator to the "interpretation and application of this agreement," and prohibiting the arbitrator from "adding to, subtracting from or modifying" the terms of the CBA.[28]

The second infirmity is even more significant. In my view, the majority fails to appreciate the challenges associated with forcing parties to renegotiate fundamental contract provisions governing discipline (e.g., "cause" restrictions on discipline or discharge decisions) and grievance arbitration (e.g., restrictions on an arbitrator's authority). Countless agreements contain discipline and grievance-arbitration provisions that have remained unchanged for decades. And with all due respect to the majority, many parties will be reluctant to convert their grievance-arbitration procedures into something resembling full-fledged NLRB and court litigation. Several other obvious points also warrant mention here.

1. The Board, of course, lacks authority to impose any substantive contract terms on any party. Section 8(d) explicitly states that the duty to bargain "does not compel either party to agree to a proposal or require the making of a concession." And the Supreme Court stated in *H. K. Porter Co., Inc. v. NLRB*, 397 U.S. 99 (1970):

> It is implicit in the entire structure of the Act that the Board acts to oversee and referee the process of collective bargaining, *leaving the results of the contest to the bargaining strengths of the parties....* The Board's remedial powers under § 10 of the Act are broad, but they are limited to carrying out the policies of the Act itself. *One of these fundamental policies is freedom of contract.* While the parties' freedom of contract is not absolute under the Act, allowing the Board to compel agreement when the parties themselves are unable to agree would violate *the fundamental premise on which the Act is based – private bargaining under governmental supervision of the procedure alone, without any official compulsion over the actual terms of the contract.*[29]

---

[27] For example, in *Steelworkers v. American Mfg. Co.*, supra, which dealt with what the Court called the "standard form" of arbitration agreement (363 U.S. at 565), the contract provided for arbitration only regarding "disputes, misunderstandings, differences or grievances arising between the parties as to the meaning, interpretation and application of the provisions of this agreement," and the contract also stated that "[t]he arbitrator may interpret this agreement and apply it to the particular case under consideration but shall, however, have no authority to add to, subtract from, or modify the terms of the agreement." Id. at 565 fn. 1.

[28] These types of restrictions on an arbitrator's authority exist in most CBAs. Elkouri & Elkouri, supra fn. 8, at 1235 (citing "[t]he oft-included language denying the arbitrator the power to add or subtract from or modify any of the terms of the agreement") (internal quotation omitted); Walter J. Gershenfeld & Gladys Gershenfeld, *Current Issues in Discharge Arbitration*, 55 Dispute Resolution Journal 48, 52 (May 2000) (citing "[t]he statement found in most contracts that arbitrators

may not add to, subtract from, alter, or modify the terms of an agreement"); Ann C. Hodges, *The Steelworkers Trilogy in the Public Sector*, 66 CHI-KENT L. REV. 631, 652 (1990) (citing "the common contractual restriction that arbitrators cannot add to, subtract from, or modify the contract").

[29] Id. at 107–108 (emphasis added). Although the majority may contend that their changed deferral standards do not require any party to rewrite their arbitration agreements, this is only true to the extent that the employer and union are prepared to accept concurrent arbitration and NLRB/court proceedings whenever the employee or union fears that an arbitrator will sustain a particular suspension or discharge, or choose to ignore the new standard and simply forego the possibility of deferral to arbitration. I respectfully submit that such a Hobson's choice is, by definition, no choice at all.

It is no answer to say that, instead of requiring parties to modify existing labor contract discipline provisions so they incorporate the Act (or portions of the Act), the majority's standard provides an alternative—i.e., case-by-case authorization of the arbitrator to apply the Act. As explained elsewhere in the text, the majority's new deferral standards effectively require major changes in fundamental contract terms, and this is true *regardless* of whether one focuses on discipline provi-

2. For many reasons, companies and unions predictably will have difficulty negotiating new or expanded standards—separate from a "cause" requirement—governing employee discipline, such as suspensions or discharges. Employees, unions and employers *already* have access to courts and agencies for the resolution of legal disputes that arise over discipline. For this reason, many parties will be reluctant to propose or accept expanded "contractual" discipline standards that duplicate legal rights and obligations. Unions may also be reluctant to make themselves responsible for pursuing what would otherwise be statutory claims that individual employees would pursue for themselves.

3. It is even more implausible that companies and unions will freely renegotiate existing grievance-arbitration provisions. In many cases, these have remained substantially unchanged for many years. Nobody could reasonably suggest it is routine, unimportant, or inconsequential to substantially revise a collective-bargaining agreement's labor arbitration procedures. As the Supreme Court recognized in the *Steelworkers Trilogy* cases more than 50 years ago,[30] "the grievance machinery under a collective bargaining agreement is at the very heart of the system of industrial self-government," and "arbitration is the means of solving the unforeseeable by molding a system of private law for all the problems which may arise and to provide for their solution in a way which will generally accord with the variant needs and desires of the parties." *Steelworkers v. Warrior & Gulf Navigation Co.*, 363 U.S. at 581.

4. Parties are likely to be even more reluctant to renegotiate restrictions on an arbitrator's authority or the scope of issues that are subject to grievance arbitration. It is well known that, once a dispute is submitted to arbitration, it is very difficult to obtain meaningful review on

---

sions (e.g., explicitly expanding contractual remedies to encompass violations of the Act) or the CBA's grievance-arbitration process (e.g., modifying contract language that states arbitrators may only resolve questions involving interpretation or application of the CBA, or that precludes them from "adding to, subtracting from or modifying" the CBA) (see fn. 28, supra). If anything, however, it is worse to condition deferral to arbitration on a "case-by-case" departure from the CBA's existing grievance-arbitration process, since LMRA Sec. 203(d) explicitly favors the final resolution of disputes based on the "method *agreed upon* by the parties" (emphasis added), and the entire point of a CBA's dispute resolution procedure is to *prevent* a case-by-case renegotiation of grievance-arbitration provisions that constitute the "very heart of the system of industrial self-government." *Steelworkers v. Warrior & Gulf Navigation Co.*, 363 U.S. 574, 581 (1960) (labor arbitration is desirable, in part, because it avoids "leaving each and every matter subject to a temporary resolution dependent solely upon the relative strength, at any given moment, of the contending forces").

[30] *Steelworkers v. American Mfg. Co.*, 363 U.S. 564 (1960); *Steelworkers v. Warrior & Gulf Navigation Co.*, 363 U.S. 574 (1960); *Steelworkers v. Enterprise Wheel & Car Corp.*, 363 U.S. 593 (1960).

appeal (putting aside Board review under the changed standards adopted by my colleagues).[31] The great deference afforded to arbitration frequently makes parties devote significant attention to contract provisions identifying those matters that can—and cannot—be submitted to arbitration or be considered by the arbitrator. The care exercised by parties in this area is consistent with numerous Supreme Court cases establishing that labor arbitration is a creation of the labor contract, and parties cannot be required to submit a dispute to arbitration absent an agreement to do so.[32]

The current deferral standards have provided a stable, consistent backdrop for the negotiation of collective-bargaining agreements. The concept of deferral originated nearly 60 years ago in *Spielberg* (decided in 1955), which remains the controlling case regarding Board deferral to existing arbitration awards. The more refined *Olin* standards (adopted in 1984) have governed this area for the past 30 years. Especially in this area, stability and consistency are important.

I recognize that my colleagues have a well-intentioned desire to ensure that the Board satisfies its statutory obligations. Yet, the majority gives inadequate consideration to the unintended consequences that are likely to follow

---

[31] As the Supreme Court stated in *W. R. Grace & Co. v. Local 759, Int'l Union of Rubber Workers*, 461 U.S. 757, 759 (1983): "Under well established standards for the review of labor arbitration awards, a federal court may not overrule an arbitrator's decision simply because the court believes its own interpretation of the contract would be the better one." See also *Steelworkers v. Enterprise Wheel & Car Corp.*, 363 U.S. 593, 599 (1960) ("[P]lenary review by a court of the merits would make meaningless the provisions that the arbitrator's decision is final, for, in reality, it would almost never be final. . . . It is the arbitrator's construction which was bargained for; and so far as the arbitrator's decision concerns construction of the contract, the courts have no business overruling him because their interpretation of the contract is different from his."); *Paperworkers v. Misco, Inc.*, 484 U.S. 29, 39 (1987) ("grievous error" and "improvident, even silly fact-finding" is "hardly a sufficient basis" for overturning an arbitration award).

[32] *AT&T Technologies Inc. v. CWA*, 475 U.S. 643, 648 (1986); *Steelworkers v. Warrior & Gulf Navigation Co.*, 363 U.S. at 582; *Steelworkers v. American Mfg. Co.*, 363 U.S. at 570–571; *Gateway Coal Co. v. UMW*, 414 U.S. 368, 374 (1974). The considerations described in the text render implausible the majority's suggestion that, whenever a particular contract does not authorize the arbitration of unfair labor practice issues, on a case-by-case basis parties can simply "authorize" the arbitrator to decide such issues. Given the central role played by grievance arbitration in most collective-bargaining agreements, and given the care and importance that parties, the Board and courts understandably attach to contractual restrictions on an arbitrator's authority, it is unreasonable to suggest that parties can or should deviate from the labor contract provisions that govern and limit the arbitrator's authority, particularly since the Board is without authority to compel parties to do so, Sec. 8(d); *H. K. Porter*, 397 U.S. at 108–109, and the Board has the statutory responsibility to foster stability rather than instability in bargaining relationships. See also fn. 26, supra.

from these changed deferral standards. In my view, they will impose higher costs and delays on parties in mature bargaining relationships that are covered by collective-bargaining agreements by effectively eliminating the finality associated with grievance arbitration. The changed standards will cause substantially greater conflict as parties attempt to renegotiate CBA provisions that, as noted above, involve the most fundamental aspects of their relationship. Again, I believe there is also likely to be greater conflict in union organizing campaigns based on employer resistance to the costs and burdens associated with two-track litigation that, in turn, would be considered part and parcel of a new union's demands for grievance-arbitration procedures and disciplinary "cause" restrictions.

C. The Majority's Changed Deferral Standards Are Ill-Advised as a Matter of Labor Relations Policy

As a final matter, I believe the majority's changed deferral standards are ill-advised as a matter of public policy because they reflect a deep-seated hostility towards arbitration that Congress rejected when it adopted the Federal Arbitration Act (in 1925) and again when it articulated a strong presumption favoring arbitration when adopting (in 1947) Section 203(d) of the LMRA.

The Federal Arbitration Act (FAA) was enacted to "reverse longstanding judicial hostility towards arbitration agreements and to place arbitration agreements upon the same footing as other contracts." *Seawright v. American General Financial Services, Inc.*, 507 F.3d 967, 979 (6th Cir. 2007) (citing *Gilmer v. Interstate/Johnson Lane Corp.*, 500 U.S. 20, 24 (1991)). Consistent with the FAA, the Supreme Court has "rejected generalized attacks on arbitration that rest on suspicion of arbitration as a method of weakening the protection afforded in the substantive law to would-be complainants." *Green Tree Financial Corp. v. Randolph,* 531 U.S. 79, 89–90 (2000). And the Court stated that "arbitral tribunals are readily capable of handling ... factual and legal complexities" and that "there is no reason to assume at the outset that arbitrators will not follow the law." *14 Penn Plaza LLC v. Pyett*, 556 U.S. 247, 268 (2009) (citations omitted).

Congress reaffirmed the importance of arbitration in the Section 203(d) of the LMRA, which states: "Final adjustment by a method agreed upon by the parties is declared to be the desirable method for settlement of grievance disputes arising over the application or interpretation of an existing collective-bargaining agreement." The unique importance of labor arbitration was underscored by the Supreme Court in the *Steelworkers Trilogy* cases.[33] Among other things, the Court stated:

In the commercial case, arbitration is the substitute for litigation. Here, arbitration is the substitute for industrial strife. Since arbitration of labor disputes has quite different functions from arbitration under an ordinary commercial agreement, *the hostility evinced by courts toward arbitration of commercial agreements has no place here. For arbitration of labor disputes under collective bargaining agreements is part and parcel of the collective bargaining process itself.*[34]

The majority's adoption of a much more narrow standard governing deferral to arbitration reveals the same hostility and suspicion towards arbitration that Congress repudiated and the FAA was enacted to reverse almost a century ago. In the 30 years since the Board has applied the *Olin* standard, no evidence suggests that arbitrators have declined to follow the law or have failed to protect employees' statutory rights.[35]

The Board's traditional deferral policies also typically involve potential Board review at many points in the grievance-arbitration process. Thus, even with broad deferral (and without mandating duplicative Board litigation of cases already subject to grievance-arbitration procedures), the Board has been afforded multiple opportunities to review and reconsider the appropriateness of deferral in particular cases. Disputes not yet the subject of grievances pending arbitration are reviewed to determine whether deferral is appropriate under *Collyer*.[36] Disputes where there are pending grievances subject to arbitration are reviewed for possible deferral under *Dubo*.[37] Settlements can be reviewed by the Board under *Alpha Beta*[38] and *Postal Services*.[39] Cases previously deferred under *Collyer* or *Dubo* can be (and frequently are) subject to further postarbitration review under *Spielberg* and *Olin*. Finally, the practice of the Regions regarding *Dubo* and *Collyer* deferral is to require parties to provide timely reports regarding whether deferred cases

---

[33] Supra fn. 69.

[34] *Steelworkers v. Warrior & Gulf Navigation Co.,* 363 U.S. at 579 (emphasis added).

[35] My colleagues find that the prior deferral standard created an "unacceptably high risk" that the Board would defer when an arbitrator had not adequately considered the statutory issue. However, to illustrate this risk, the majority cited to only *two* cases from the last 30 years: *Airborne Freight Corp.*, 343 NLRB 580 (2004), and *Andersen Sand & Gravel Co.*, 277 NLRB 1204 (1985). Further, in the cited cases, as in the underlying case here, there is no evidence that the arbitrator *failed to consider* the charging parties' discrimination or retaliation claims, but only the absence of any explicit statement by the tribunal proving and explaining its consideration of those claims. The majority's evidence thus reveals no risk at all to employees' rights.

[36] *Collyer Insulated Wire*, 192 NLRB 837 (1971).

[37] *Dubo Mfg. Corp.*, 142 NLRB 431 (1963).

[38] 273 NLRB 1546 (1985).

[39] 300 NLRB 196 (1990).

have proceeded to arbitration, which can (and does) re-sult in the resumption of Board proceedings if arbitration is not occurring in a timely manner. These safeguards provide further assurances that employee rights are pro-tected throughout the grievance-arbitration process, which reinforces the absence of any reasonable need to change existing deferral policies.

D. Conclusion

Today's decision disregards nearly a century of sup-port by Congress and the courts for arbitration. It is es-pecially surprising that the Board discredits "cause" re-quirements and labor arbitration, when both have result-ed from good-faith collective bargaining that the Act requires and the Board should encourage.[40] Finally, as noted previously, the majority's changed deferral stand-ards are based on the false premise that a difference ex-ists, in cases involving suspensions or discharges, be-tween "cause" determinations, on the one hand, and more onerous "statutory" and "unfair labor practice" issues, on the other. In Section 10(c), Congress prohibits the Board from making this distinction in employee suspension or discharge cases. In such cases, the Act *makes* "cause" the controlling "statutory" issue.

More generally, I believe the majority fails to ade-quately consider the damage their changed deferral standards are likely to inflict on "final and binding" arbi-tration. As the Supreme Court cautioned more than 60 years ago when discussing judicial review, our "federal policy of settling labor disputes by arbitration would be undermined if courts had the final say on the merits of the awards. . . . [P]lenary review . . . of the merits would make meaningless the provisions that the arbitrator's decision is final, for in reality it would almost never be final." *Steelworkers v. Enterprise Wheel & Car Corp.*, 363 U.S. at 596, 599.

The Board's traditional deferral standards, for good reasons, have existed without substantial change over the past three decades. I do not believe any reasonable justi-fication warrants the new standards adopted by the ma-jority. For these reasons, as to the above issues, I re-spectfully dissent.

Dated, Washington, D.C. December 15, 2014

Philip A. Miscimarra,   Member

---

[40] Sec. 1 of the Act relevantly provides that "[i]t is declared to be the policy of the United States to eliminate the causes of certain sub-stantial obstructions to the free flow of commerce and to mitigate and eliminate these obstructions when they have occurred by encouraging the practice and procedure of collective bargaining . . . ."

NATIONAL LABOR RELATIONS BOARD

MEMBER JOHNSON, concurring in part and dissenting in part.

The decision to overrule [extant precedent on Board deferral to arbitration awards] represents yet another step in the ill-considered retreat from a fair, balanced, comprehensive, and efficacious accom-modation between public and private mechanisms for the resolution of disputes. Once again, a Board majority has rendered a decision which will promote the proliferation of litigation and impede the matura-tion of peaceable labor-management relations. Once again, my colleagues have endorsed a policy which tightens the bureaucratic fetters on employees, un-ions, and employers alike, and so contravenes the very purposes of the Act which that policy is meant to serve. Once again, I must dissent.[1]

Dissenting Member Penello wrote the foregoing in 1980, protesting what he correctly regarded as an arbi-trary and inappropriate retreat by the majority in *Subur-ban Motor Freight* from Board precedent implementing a national labor policy, entrenched in statutory language and decades of judicial precedent, favoring the resolution of disputes in collective-bargaining relationships through mutually agreed private grievance and arbitration proce-dures. Thankfully, the regressive approach taken in *Sub-urban Motor Freight* was overruled only 4 years later in *Olin Corp.*, 268 NLRB 573 (1984). Regretfully, after 30 years of collective-bargaining relations conducted under that standard, the majority returns in substantial part to a significantly more restrictive and inimical deferral policy towards both arbitration awards and prearbitral proceed-ings, including settlements. They do so based largely on the speculative supposition that the policy they overrule has not adequately protected employees' statutory rights in an unknown number of grievance and arbitration pro-ceedings that have never been brought to our attention. Like Member Penello before me, and for many of the same reasons as he and my dissenting colleague Member Miscimarra articulate, I must dissent.[2]

---

[1] *Suburban Motor Freight, Inc.*, 247 NLRB 146, 147 (1980) (cita-tions and footnotes omitted).

[2] I note that I am dissenting from the change in law announced in this decision. Technically, I concur in the result reached by the majori-ty because it applies the change prospectively while dismissing the complaint here under extant deferral policy. My colleagues state that the immediate imposition of their new deferral policy would disrupt practices under current collectively-bargained agreements and thereby frustrate the Act's purpose of promoting collective bargaining. A cynic might say that this is a convenient way to prevent immediate judicial review of the change in law, but I will take them at their word. To that point, not only do I agree that concern about the disruptive

I. THE CHANGE IN DEFERRAL STANDARDS

For the past 30 years, the standard for Board deferral to the results of arbitration awards made under collective-bargaining agreements has been that:

> The Board will defer to an arbitration award when the proceedings appear to have been fair and regular, all parties have agreed to be bound, and the decision of the arbitrator is not clearly repugnant to the purposes and policies of the Act. See *Spielberg Mfg. Co.*, 112 NLRB 1080 (1955). Additionally, the arbitrator must have considered the unfair labor practice issue which is before the Board. In *Olin Corp.*, 268 NLRB 573 (1984), the Board clarified that an arbitrator has adequately considered the unfair labor practice issue if (1) the contractual issue is factually parallel to the unfair labor practice issue, (2) the arbitrator was presented generally with the facts relevant to resolving the unfair labor practice, and (3) the decision is susceptible to an interpretation consistent with the Act. Id. at 574. The party seeking to have the Board reject deferral bears the burden of proof. Id.[3]

This *Spielberg/Olin* standard has been uniformly applied by the Board in all unfair labor practice cases where a party has urged deferral to an arbitration award. The Board has also applied this standard in determining whether to defer to prearbitral grievance settlements.[4]

Today that longstanding uniform deferral standard is substantially changed. Under the majority's new standard, the Board will defer to an arbitral decision in unfair labor cases addressing alleged violations of Section 8(a)(3) and (1) of the Act only "[i]f the arbitration procedures appear to have been fair and regular, and if the parties agreed to be bound [traditional *Spielberg* requirements] . . . [*and*] the party urging deferral shows that: (1) the arbitrator was explicitly authorized, either in the collective-bargaining agreement or by agreement of the parties in the particular case, to decide the unfair labor practice issue; (2) the arbitrator was presented with and considered the statutory issue, or was prevented from doing so by the party opposing deferral; and (3) Board law reasonably permits the award." It is the addition of this three-pronged requirement, and the imposition of the burden of proof on the party urging deferral, that so substantially departs from the existing deferral standard.

Corollary to the new standard for deferral to arbitration awards, the majority modifies the *Collyer*[5] standard for deferral to the grievance and arbitration process. Deferral will no longer be appropriate unless the General Counsel has sufficient evidence from the party urging deferral that prong (1) above of the new standard has been met. Implicitly then, the Board's deferral policy under *Dubo Manufacturing*[6] will also be modified to the same extent, so that even when the parties are already voluntarily engaged in grievance and arbitration proceedings relevant to conduct alleged as Section 8(a)(3) or (1) discrimination in an unfair labor practice charge, the General Counsel will not defer proceeding on that charge unless he has evidence that the arbitrator has the parties' express authority to resolve it. Finally, the Board will not itself defer to prearbitral grievance settlements unless the party urging deferral can meet its burden of proof with respect to all three prongs of the new test. Thus, the majority today overrules in significant part the entire body of precedent that has governed the Board's deferral practices for decades under *Spielberg/Olin*, *Collyer*, *Dubo*, and *Alpha Beta*.

II. THE DEPARTURE FROM CURRENT DEFERRAL POLICY IS UNWARRANTED.

The problems with the majority's standard are manifold. Among those problems, three are paramount. First, as with their prohibition of individual class action waiver agreements,[7] the majority's new deferral standard fails to make the required accommodation of the national policy strongly favoring arbitration. Indeed, as Member Miscimarra states in his dissent, the new standard reflects an implicit hostility towards arbitration on matters where the Board claims jurisdiction. Second, the majority offers no rational basis in law or fact for departing from longstanding precedent that has been followed regardless of partisan shifts in Board membership. In particular, they can point to no nationwide wave of rogue arbitral decisions that threatens to undermine rights protected by Section 7 of the Act for workers in the United States. As such, their complete rewriting of existing deferral standards rests on nothing more than speculation about the possibility that these standards offer inadequate protection of employees' statutory rights to be free from retaliation for engaging in Section 7 activity. Speculation is an inadequate basis for such a wide-ranging revision of legal standards. Finally, I believe that my colleagues greatly understate the adverse impact of their new standard on the ability of parties in a collective-bargaining

---

nature of the majority's change in law is a valid reason for not applying the new policy retroactively, I find that it is an extremely sound reason against making the change at all.

[3] *Smurfit-Stone Container Corp.*, 344 NLRB 658, 659 (2005).

[4] *Alpha Beta Co.*, 273 NLRB 1546 (1985), rev. denied sub nom. *Mahon v. NLRB*, 808 F.2d 1342 (9th Cir. 1987).

---

[5] *Collyer Insulated Wire*, 192 NLRB 837 (1971).

[6] *Dubo Mfg. Corp.*, 142 NLRB 431 (1963).

[7] See *Murphy Oil*, 361 NLRB No. 72 (2014).

relationship to achieve final adjustment of employee grievances through their mutually agreed grievance and arbitration procedures. In lieu of a single, more expeditious and less formal procedure for resolution of most cases addressing adverse employment actions, the majority's new standard practically guarantees a process in which almost any employee or his union representative dissatisfied with the result of grievance and arbitration can pursue an unfair labor practice claim at public expense with little or no regard for that prior result. Further, as in *Murphy Oil*, the majority's action here poses a significant risk that the Board's caseload will swell substantially, with a corresponding delay in our own ability to reach final decision in cases before us.

A. The New Standard Disfavors Arbitration in Contravention of Clear National Policy

"It hardly needs repeating that national policy strongly favors the voluntary arbitration of disputes. The importance of arbitration in the overall scheme of Federal labor law has been stressed in innumerable contexts and forums." *Olin*, 268 NLRB at 574 and fn. 5 (citations omitted). Apparently, the *Olin* majority was mistaken about the need for repetition. In spite of the fact that their decision put an end to several years of back and forth debate fully addressing the pros and cons of an expansive deferral policy that accords with national policy favoring arbitration, in spite of a host of Supreme Court opinions since 1984 that repeatedly endorse and expand that national policy,[8] in spite of the majority's own lukewarm acknowledgment of the importance of arbitration in our Act and in the overall scheme of Federal laws, the majority today finds it appropriate to mount a full retreat to a past where arbitration is accorded far less importance and finality in Board proceedings. There is no reason to disregard this historical record that points only one way—in favor of recognizing arbitration as the primary, favored resolution system for labor disputes.

Congressional preference that parties to collective-bargaining agreements resolve their disputes through mutually agreed procedures was made plain in Section 203(d) of the Labor Management Relations Act: "Final adjustment by a method agreed upon by the parties is declared to be the desirable method for settlement of grievance disputes arising over the application or inter-

pretation of an existing collective-bargaining agreement." 29 U.S.C. § 173(d). The addition of this provision to the Act in 1947 was consistent with prior expressions of Federal policy dating back to the enactment of the Federal Arbitration Act (FAA) in 1925. The central purpose of the FAA was to force courts to enforce agreements to arbitrate, just as they would enforce any other contract provision, and reflects a national policy favoring arbitration and the enforcement of agreements to arbitrate disputes. See *Southland Corp. v. Keating*, 465 U.S. 1, 28 (1984) ("In enacting [the FAA], Congress declared a national policy favoring arbitration...."); *Mitsubishi Motors Corp. v. Soler Chrysler-Plymouth, Inc*, above, 473 U.S. at 625 (1985); *Gilmer v. Interstate/Johnson Lane Corp.*, above, 500 U.S. at 25 (1991). The language of Section 203(d) is also fully compatible with the statement of general policy and purpose in Section 1 of the National Labor Relations Act, which states in relevant part:

> Experience has proved that protection by law of the right of employees to organize and bargain collectively safeguards commerce from injury, impairment, or interruption, and promotes the flow of commerce by removing certain recognized sources of industrial strife and unrest, *by encouraging practices fundamental to the friendly adjustment of industrial disputes arising out of differences as to wages, hours, or other working conditions*, and by restoring equality of bargaining power between employers and employees. (Emphasis added).

29 U.S.C. § 151.

The central role of arbitration as the means for parties to collective-bargaining agreements to provide for final adjustment of their disputes was emphatically confirmed in 1960 by the Supreme Court in the *Steelworkers Trilogy* cases. *United Steelworkers v. Enterprise Wheel & Car Corp.*, 363 U.S. 593 (1960); *United Steelworkers v. Warrior & Gulf Navigation Co.*, 363 U.S. 574 (1960); *United Steelworkers v. American Mfg. Co.*, 363 U.S. 564 (1960). The Supreme Court made clear that arbitration was seen as the preferred mechanism for resolving all disputes between the parties. Thus, in *Warrior & Gulf Navigation Co.*, the Court described the grievance procedure and arbitration in a collective-bargaining agreement as being "at the very heart of the system of industrial self-government":

> *Arbitration is the means of solving* the unforeseeable by molding a system of private law for *all the problems which may arise and to provide for their solution* in a way which will generally accord with

---

[8] See, e.g., *American Express Co. v. Italian Colors Restaurant*, 133 S.Ct. 2304 (2013). *Oxford Health Plans LLC v. Sutter*, 133 S.Ct. 2064 (2013), *CompuCredit Corp. v. Greenwood*, 132 S.Ct. 665 (2012), *AT&T Mobility, LLC v. Concepcion*, 131 S.Ct. 1740 (2011), *Stolt-Nielsen S.A v. AnimalFeeds International Corp.*, 559 U.S. 662 (2010), *14 Penn Plaza LLC v. Pyett*, 129 S.Ct. 1456 (2009), *Gilmer v. Interstate/Johnson-Lane Corp.*, 500 U.S. 20 (1991), and *Mitsubishi Motors Corp. v. Soler Chrysler-Plymouth, Inc.*, 473 U.S. 614 (1985).

the variant needs and desires of the parties. (Emphasis added).

Warrior & Gulf Navigation Co., 363 U.S. at 580.

The Court further acknowledged the centrality of "[t]he grievance procedure [a]s…a part of the continuous collective bargaining process." Id. at 581–582.

In *American Mfg.*, the Court similarly stated, "Arbitration is a stabilizing influence only as it serves as a vehicle for handling *any and all* disputes that arise under the agreement." 363 U.S. at 567 (emphasis added). The Court also stressed the importance of finality of arbitration decisions in *Enterprise Wheel & Car* holding, "The refusal of courts to review the merits of an arbitration award is the proper approach to arbitration under collective bargaining agreements." 363 U.S. at 596.

Soon after the *Steelworkers Trilogy,* the Board acknowledged that "the Board, which is entrusted with the administration of one of the many facets of national labor policy, should give hospitable acceptance to the arbitral process . . . ." *International Harvester Co.,* 138 NLRB 923, 927 (1962) (quoted with approval in *Carey v. Westinghouse Elec. Corp.*, 375 U.S. 261, 271 (1964). See id. at 925–926 (recognizing "[e]xperience has demonstrated that collective-bargaining agreements that provide for final and binding arbitration of grievance and disputes arising thereunder, 'as a substitute for industrial strife,' contribute significantly to the attainment of th[e] statutory objective" of "promot[ing] industrial peace and stability by encouraging the practice and procedure of collective-bargaining"); *Olin Corp.*, 268 NLRB at 574 (stressing "[t]he importance of arbitration in the overall scheme of Federal labor law"); see also *Boys Markets, Inc. v. Retail Clerks Union, Local 770,* 398 U.S. 235, 252 (1970) (recognizing the importance of "voluntary settlement of labor disputes without resort to self-help and more particularly to arbitration as a means to this end" and suggesting that arbitration is the "central institution in the administration of collective bargaining contracts").

Though giving a nominal nod to arbitration's role, the majority's return to a more restrictive deferral standard rests on a suspicion that private arbitration's assurance of the Act's antidiscrimination protections is so inadequate that the Board may be "abdicating" its enforcement obligations under Section 10(a) by deferring too readily. But long ago the Court of Appeals for the District of Columbia Circuit "recognized that the Board 'does not abdicate its responsibilities to implement the National Labor Relations Act by respecting peaceful resolution of disputes through voluntarily agreed upon administrative techniques.'" *Plumbers & Pipefitters Local Union No. 520 v. NLRB*, 955 F.2d 744, 752 (D.C. Cir. 1992) (quoting

Associated Press v. NLRB, 492 F.2d 662, 667 (D.C. Cir. 1974)).

To be sure, the Board's deferral to arbitration awards must balance two policies in the Act. On one hand, Section 10(a) of the Act gives the Board authority to prevent and remedy unfair labor practices, unaffected by other means of dispute resolution including procedures provided for in collective-bargaining agreements. On the other hand, Section 203(d) expresses the Congressional preference that parties to collective-bargaining agreements resolve their disputes through their own grievance and arbitration procedures.

The majority's standard fails to strike the appropriate balance between these two policies by imposing significant legalistic impediments to the prospect of achieving final adjustment of grievances through arbitration. Even assuming that the parties have authorized an arbitrator to decide an unfair labor practice issue, and that evidence relating to the issue has been presented and considered by the arbitrator, the majority's new policy provides for Board review of the reasonableness of the arbitrator's award. This is tantamount to requiring de novo review of the award by an administrative law judge in the unfair labor practice case and, upon exceptions, by the Board itself. There may be instances in which an award will survive this review even if the judge or Board might interpret the facts differently, but it seems far more likely that the current Board majority will defer only in circumstances where it would reach the same result under the facts as they would find them and under the law as they presently construe it.

This is not true deferral in any meaningful sense. The Board review required under the new deferral standard will predictably lead again to the "overzealous dissection of [arbitrators'] opinions by the NLRB" that was criticized in *Douglas Aircraft Co. v. NLRB*, 609 F.2d 352, 355 (9th Cir. 1979). Other courts of appeals voiced this same criticism, which in significant part prompted the Board to adopt the broader deferral policy in *Olin.* See *Olin Corp.*, 268 NLRB at 575 fn. 11 (collecting cases), *NLRB v. Pincus Bros.*, 620 F.2d 367, 367 (3d Cir. 1980), *Liquor Salesmen's Local 2 v. NLRB (Charmer Industries)*, 664 F.2d 318, 327, *NLRB v. Motor Convoy, Inc.*, 673 F.2d 734 (4th Cir.1982), and *American Freight Systems v. NLRB*, 722 F.2d 828 (D.C. Cir. 1983); see also *Richmond Tank Car Co. v. NLRB*, 721 F.2d 499 (5th Cir. 1983).

Notably, there is a sharp contrast between the majority's deferral standard and the standard for judicial review of arbitration awards. As summarized by the Supreme Court, "we have indicated that there is no reason to assume at the outset that arbitrators will not follow the law;

although judicial scrutiny of arbitration awards necessarily is limited, such review is sufficient to ensure that arbitrators comply with the requirements of the statute."[9] What is the limited judicial review standard that the Supreme Court deemed to be sufficient?: "[u]nder the FAA, courts may vacate an arbitrator's decision 'only in very unusual circumstances.'"[10] Thus, while courts have essentially the same obligation as the Board to ensure that statutory requirements are met in arbitration proceedings, that obligation is deemed satisfied by a very limited review. So, too, should it be with the Board.

The Board's deferral standard under *Spielberg/Olin* effectively accommodates the arbitral process, which stands as "the central institution in the administration of collective bargaining contracts,"[11] without jeopardizing, much less abdicating, the Board's statutory enforcement obligation. In contrast, the majority's new standard falls far short of striking the appropriate balance, effectively subordinating private party dispute resolution systems to final Board de novo review in most cases involving 8(a)(3) and (1) allegations.

B. There Is No Experiential or Legal Justification for Changing the Deferral Standard.

Certainly, there are circumstances in which the Board's expertise and experience under a particular legal regime may lead it to reconsider and overrule precedent for sound practical reasons, although I maintain that the more venerable the precedent, the more cautiously we ought to approach its revision. In other instances, a change in law may be viewed as a required response to intervening Supreme Court precedent or as a rational response to judicial criticism of extant precedent. However, the majority here has failed to justify overruling *Spielberg/Olin* and related deferral standards on either basis.

---

[9] *Shearson/American Express Inc. v. McMahon*, 482 U.S. 220, 232 (1987).

[10] *Oxford Health Plans LLC v. Sutter*, 569 U.S. ——, 133 S.Ct. 2064, 2068 (2013) (quoting *First Options of Chicago, Inc. v. Kaplan*, 514 U.S. 938, 942 (1995)).

Sec. 10(a) of the FAA permits an award to be vacated only:

(1) where the award was procured by corruption, fraud, or undue means;

(2) where there was evident partiality or corruption in the arbitrators, or either of them;

(3) where the arbitrators were guilty of misconduct in refusing to postpone the hearing, upon sufficient cause shown, or in refusing to hear evidence pertinent and material to the controversy; or of any other misbehavior by which the rights of any party have been prejudiced; or

(4) where the arbitrators exceeded their powers, or so imperfectly executed them that a mutual, final, and definite award upon the subject matter submitted was not made.

[11] *Boys Markets, Inc*, supra, 398 U.S. at 252 (1970).

1. *Experience with the Spielberg/Olin Deferral Standard.* The majority claims that employees may be left without any forum for the vindication of their statutory rights because the *Spielberg/Olin* standard permits deferral when there is no evidence the arbitrator actually considered the unfair labor practice issue. As an abstract concept, it is difficult to reconcile this claim with the Supreme Court's statement that "there is no reason to assume at the outset that arbitrators will not follow the law."[12] Consistent with this statement, it was reasonable for the Board in *Olin* to place the burden on the party opposing deferral to prove that which should not be assumed.[13] Still, a litany of instances in which arbitration decisions were in fact shown not to have considered the statutory issue when resolving a grievance on a factually parallel contractual issue might support a change in law. Certainly, if there were an epidemic of labor arbitrators handing down decisions that let stand obvious employer 8(a)(3) and (1) violations, it would be the Board's duty to adjust its deferral standards to put a stop to that. But, despite over 30 years of experience applying the *Spielberg/Olin* deferral standard, the majority can cite only the present case and two past cases—*Andersen Sand & Gravel Co.*, 277 NLRB 1204 (1985), and *Airborne Freight Corp.*, 343 NLRB 580 (2004)—as alleged proof that a grievant was unable to secure arbitral consideration of the unfair labor practice issue. This hardly suffices to justify a wholesale change in deferral law, even if the cases stood for the proposition asserted. One case every 10 or 20 years does not an epidemic make.

Moreover, in *Andersen Sand & Gravel Co.*, the Board had a reasonable basis for deferring to the arbitration award upholding the termination of employees for violating a contractual no-strike clause. In light of the General Counsel's concession that the contractual and statutory issues were "coextensive," the Board found deferral was "particularly appropriate." 277 NLRB at 1204. While the arbitration panel did not expressly indicate that it considered and resolved the unfair labor practice issue, the Board reasonably assumed from the evidence presented to the panel and the panel's resolution of

---

[12] *Shearson/American Express Inc.*, above, 482 U.S. at 232.

[13] The majority now shifts the burden to the party urging deferral. It is true that deferral must be raised as an affirmative defense, but I would find the initial burden met by proof of an arbitration decision adverse to the unfair labor practice claimant. Beyond that, the General Counsel should have the burden of proving why the Board should not defer. This is no disadvantage. The General Counsel brings complaint on behalf of the charging party grievant or union that has participated in the arbitration proceeding, is in possession of the facts and evidence in support of the statutory claim, and, as advocate of that claim, is in a stronger position to pursue it.

the coextensive contractual issue that the statutory issue was adequately considered. Id. at 1205.

Airborne Freight, the other case cited by the majority, involved several deferral questions. The majority points only to the one where the Board panel unanimously deferred to a joint committee's resolution even though the hearing record before the administrative law judge did not show what arguments and evidence had been presented by the parties to the joint committee in that proceeding. 343 NLRB at 581. As I will shortly explain, the panel's disposition of other deferral issues in that case contradicts the majority's contention that the *Spielberg/Olin* standard fails adequately to protect statutory rights. In any event, the fact that the Board in this one case unanimously deferred to an arbitral award when the record did not show what evidence was presented and considered in arbitration is hardly an excuse to ignore a 30-year history in myriad cases where the same perceived shortcoming is not apparent.

To fill a considerable void in actual precedent, the majority relies on makeweight speculation that more cases challenging deferral to arbitration may have never been brought to the Board's attention because challengers and/or the General Counsel assumed that they could not meet *Olin*'s allegedly impossible burden of proof. Thus, the majority pronounces that "[they] are no longer willing to countenance such results," albeit those results have not been shown to exist. Indeed, the Board invited "the parties and amici . . . to submit empirical and other evidence" in "answering" whether the deferral standard should be changed in this matter. *Notice and Invitation to File Briefs,* February 7, 2014. Given this, where is the empirical evidence before we undertake this nationwide reform? Where is the lengthy discussion of how such evidence points to the need for resetting decades of time-honored rules and policies? Neither is to be found in the majority's rationale. The most recent "evidence" they present, besides the facts themselves of this case, is one case, *Airborne Freight Corp.,* from 10 years ago. This is no way to make public policy, especially one that will fundamentally affect every collective-bargaining relationship in the United States.

Contrary to the majority's speculative concern, the Board's actual experience shows that the *Spielberg/Olin* limited review deferral standard has been more than adequate to protect employees' Section 7 rights. It is not, as the majority states, "virtually impossible" for the party opposing deferral to meet the evidentiary burden imposed under that standard. Far from conveying the impression that it would rubber stamp every arbitration award, the Board has not hesitated to refuse to defer where the current standards are not met. For instance, as

to the other deferral issues presented in *Airborne Freight,* the transcript was introduced into the record and showed that the union had been precluded from arguing or introducing evidence of antiunion motivation. The Board unanimously agreed that deferral was inappropriate because the grievance committee had not been not generally presented the relevant facts and thus it could not "adequately consider" the statutory issue. 343 NLRB at 582. See also, *ABF Freight System, Inc.,* 304 NLRB 585, 587 fn.5 (1991) (affirming judge's refusal to defer to an arbitration award because the record showed there was inadequate consideration of the unfair labor practice issues), and *Dick Gidron Cadillac,* 287 NLRB 1107, 1111 (1988) (affirming without comment judge's refusal to defer because the record showed evidence on the statutory issue was not presented to the arbitrator), enfd. mem. 862 F.2d 304 (2d Cir. 1988).

The Board has also declined to defer where it has been shown that an arbitration award is so clearly contrary to policy or precedent as to be "repugnant to the Act." See, e.g., *U.S. Postal Service,* 332 NLRB 340, 343–344 (2000) (finding arbitrator's decision upholding terminations for "insubordination" of employees engaging in concerted protected activity by attempting to enforce collective-bargaining agreement provisions was "repugnant to the Act"); *Mobil Oil Exploration & Producing,* 325 NLRB 176, 177–178, 179 (1997) (reversing judge and finding inappropriate deferral to arbitration award upholding employee's discipline based on his protected concerted activities); *110 Greenwich Street Corp.,* 319 NLRB 331 (1995) (agreeing with judge's failure to defer to arbitrator upholding discharge of employees for displaying "controversial placards" that were insufficient to constitute "gross disloyalty" warranting discipline under the Act); *Cirker's Moving & Storage Co.,* 313 NLRB 1318, 1318 fn. 2 (1994) (agreeing with judge that deferral inappropriate where contractual issue and statutory issue are not factually parallel); *United Cable Television Corporation,* 299 NLRB 138 (1990) (finding arbitrator's denial of backpay to employee disciplined for protected concerted activity because it was only "partially protected" was repugnant); *Barton Brands,* 298 NLRB 976, 979–980 (1990) (finding inappropriate deferral to arbitration award because issue not factually parallel with unfair labor practice issue and also repugnant); *Key Food Stores,* 286 NLRB 1056, 1056–1057, 1071–1072 (1987) (finding deferral inappropriate where arbitrator sustained discharge based on protected activities, including activities as shop steward), *Garland Coal & Mining Co.,* 276 NLRB 963 (1985) (finding deferral inappropriate to award upholding discipline for "insubordination" issued to employee "for actions he took in his capacity as union representative" was not susceptible to any interpretation consistent with the Act).

In short, there is no sound basis in the Board's 30-year experience operating under the *Spielberg/Olin* standard for substantial revision of that standard.

2. *Judicial Precedent Weighs in Favor of a Broad Deferral Policy Rather than Against It.* As previously discussed, there has been a steady, unrelenting tide of Supreme Court cases favoring private party arbitration as a preferred means of dispute resolution over which the judiciary should exercise limited review. The majority dismisses this precedent out of hand, branding it irrelevant to the question whether an administrative agency should exercise discretion to defer to arbitral resolution of statutory employment claims. Obviously, I could not disagree more, particularly when considering the administration of an Act that affirmatively endorses "*final* adjustment by a method agreed upon by the parties" as "the desirable method for settlement of grievance disputes."

Of course, I could be wrong in my view that the deference accorded arbitration awards under the *Spielberg/Olin* standard is impermissibly overbroad. If so, one would expect that 30 years of judicial review of this standard would produce a cacophony of judicial criticism, especially where this standard gave rise to results that "one could not countenance," in the majority's words. That cacophony has not sounded. In fact, reviewing federal courts of appeals have routinely approved or applied without adverse comment the *Spielberg/Olin* standards. See *Bakery, Confectionery and Tobacco Workers v. NLRB,* 730 F.2d 812, 815–816 (D.C. Cir. 1984); *NLRB v. Aces Mechanical Corp.,* 837 F.2d 570, 574 (2nd Cir. 1988); *NLRB v. Yellow Freight Systems,* 930 F.2d 316, 321 (3rd Cir. 1991); *Equitable Gas Co. v. NLRB,* 966 F.2d 861, 864–865 (4th Cir. 1992); *NLRB v. Ryder/P.I.E. Nationwide,* 810 F.2d 502, 506 (5th Cir.1987); *Grand Rapids Die Casting v. NLRB,* 831 F.2d 112, 115–116 (6th Cir. 1987); *Doerfer Engineering v. NLRB,* 79 F.3d 101, 103 (8th Cir. 1996); *Garcia v. NLRB,* 785 F.2d 807, 809–810 (9th Cir. 1986); *Harberson v. NLRB,* 810 F.2d 977, 984 (10th Cir.1987). See also *Goodwin v. NLRB,* 979 F.2d 854 (Table) 1992 WL 337118 at *7 (9th Cir. 1992) (collecting cases approving *Olin* standards).

Against this legion of precedent, the majority stands two court of appeals decisions: *Stephenson v. NLRB,* 550 F.2d 535 (9th Cir. 1977), and *Taylor v. NLRB,* 786 F.2d 1516 (11th Cir. 1986). *Stephenson,* a pre-*Olin* case, focused on application of a requirement in an earlier Board deferral standard that "no more than an 'opportunity' to present the unfair labor practice issue to the arbitrator" was needed to warrant deferral. *Electronic Reproduction*

Services Corp., 213 NLRB 758 (1974). The Board in *Olin* explicitly did not adopt that part of *Electronic Reproduction* standard. 268 NLRB at 575 fn. 10. In decisions subsequent to *Stephenson,* the Ninth Circuit has acknowledged that Board deferral need not be contingent on proof that an arbitrator has explicitly decided the unfair labor practice issue. See *Servair, Inc. v. NLRB,* 726 F.2d 1435, 1440–1441 (9th Cir. 1984) (deference warranted when resolution of statutory issue depends on resolution of contractual issue even if arbitrator does not purport to resolve statutory issue); *NLRB v. Max Factor & Co.,* 640 F.2d 197, 203 fn. 6 (9th Cir. 1980) ("We see no useful purpose served, in cases where the arbitral award is not clearly repugnant to the Act, by precluding deferral because of uncertainty about whether the arbitrator intended to decide the statutory unfair labor practice issues."). *Goodwin v. NLRB,* 1992 WL 337118 at *5 ("[The Ninth] Circuit has held that deferral may be appropriate even where the arbitrator did not clearly decide the statutory issue if the statutory issue is primarily factual or contractual and its resolution is dependent on the resolution of the contractual issue the arbitrator decided.") (citing *Servair, supra,* 726 F.2d at 1440–1441). Thus, the law of this circuit is not contrary to the *Spielberg/Olin* deferral standard.

It is true that Eleventh Circuit was sharply critical of the *Olin* deferral standard in *Taylor,* finding that it "does not protect sufficiently an employee's [statutory] rights." 786 F.2d at 1521. However, the court's finding that the Board had improperly deferred seems also to have been much influenced by its view that the Board had simply failed to follow its own *Spielberg/Olin* standard in the circumstances of that case. 786 F.2d at 1522. Indeed, the decision to defer there seems questionable. Employee Taylor first presented evidence in support of his discharge grievance to a multistate joint union-management committee, which was unable to resolve the matter. The hearing transcript and issue were then presented to an area wide joint committee. Only the employer presented evidence at the hearing before this committee. Taylor was not permitted to attend, and his union representative made no statement. The area wide committee summarily denied his grievance in a terse nine word statement. Reviewing these record facts, the court noted that "the ALJ found that the statutory issue clearly was considered at the Multi-State Committee hearing. If that hearing had produced a dispositive result, *then deferral to that result would have been proper under any of the many variations of the Spielberg standard.* It is the Area Committee's decision, however, that is relevant for deferral purposes and the ALJ had no indication from the transcript of that proceeding whether the Area Committee considered any unfair labor practice claim." Id. (emphasis added).[14]

Even accepting the Eleventh Circuit's broad criticism of the *Spielberg/Olin* standard on its face, without reference to the unfavorable facts of the case, this single decision hardly seems sufficient to warrant the majority's revisions of the Board's current deferral practices. On this point, it is impossible to ignore the contrast between my colleagues' willingness to follow the guidance of two dated court of appeals decisions in this case with their refusal to "acquiesce" to dozens of federal court decisions that either expressly or implicitly contradict the position they hold with respect to the legality of individual class action arbitration waivers in their recent *Murphy Oil* decision. 361 NLRB No. 72 (2014). It would seem that adverse judicial precedent matters only when it favors Board adjudication over private arbitration.

C. The Majority's New Deferral Standard Will Adversely Impact Both Private Collectively Bargained Dispute Resolution Systems and Board Unfair Labor Practice Proceedings.

Let us suppose that the majority had presented a rational basis in Board experience and/or judicial criticism for changing the *Spielberg/Olin* deferral standard. I would then be willing to join in defining a revised standard. But that process would still have to be consistent with the Supreme Court's and other federal courts' endorsement of arbitration as a favored mechanism in dispute resolution. What is presented here would still not be the way to do that. The majority's test has a number of major flaws. I will discuss each of these in turn.

1. The majority's new test is inconsistent with the Federal Arbitration Act because of its cramped view of contract construction

Begin with the majority's threshold requirement that the party opposing deferral must show that the arbitrator was "explicitly authorized," either in the collective-bargaining agreement or by agreement of the parties in the particular case, to decide the unfair labor practice issue. The majority unfortunately does not define "explicit authorization" here. But it is most likely that the majority would require this authorization to be "clear and unmistakable," as a waiver of the statutory right to exclusive Board consideration of a statutory discrimination claim.[15] I assume as well that they reserve to the Board

final determination of whether an arbitrator has such authority. If this is the majority's approach, it flies in the face of the Supreme Court's long-settled, liberal standard for construing the coverage of arbitration clauses in collective-bargaining agreements. *E.g., AT & T Technologies, Inc. v. Communications Workers*, 475 U.S. 643, 650 (1986) ("there is a presumption of arbitrability in the sense that '[a]n order to arbitrate the particular grievance should not be denied unless it may be said with positive assurance that the arbitration clause is not susceptible of an interpretation that covers the asserted dispute. Doubts should be resolved in favor of coverage.'") (quoting *Warrior & Gulf Nav. Co.*, 363 U.S., at 582–583); see also *John Wiley & Sons, Inc. v. Livingston*, 376 U.S. 543, 550 fn. 4 (1964) ("[W]hen a contract is scrutinized for evidence of an intention to arbitrate a particular kind of dispute, national labor policy requires, within reason, that an interpretation that covers the asserted dispute ... be favored" (emphasis deleted; internal quotation marks omitted)).

The majority's approach is also directly contrary to the general arbitration clause construction standard under the Federal Arbitration Act, which is identically liberal to the "presumption of arbitrability" of labor contracts. Under the FAA, the Supreme Court has held "that questions of arbitrability must be addressed with a healthy regard for the federal policy favoring arbitration. . . . The Arbitration Act establishes that, as a matter of federal law, any doubts concerning the scope of arbitrable issues should be resolved in favor of arbitration, whether the problem at hand is the construction of the contract language itself or an allegation of waiver, delay, or a like defense to arbitrability." *Moses H. Cone Memorial Hospital v. Mercury Construction Corp.*, 460 U.S. 1, 24 (1983). See also *Shearson/American Express, Inc. v. McMahon*, 482 U.S. 220, 226 (1987) (FAA "mandates enforcement of agreements to arbitrate statutory claims"); *Mitsubishi Motors Corp. v. Soler Chrysler-Plymouth, Inc.*, 473 U.S. 614, 625 (1985) ("no warrant in [FAA] for implying ... presumption against arbitration of statutory claims"); *Dean Witter Reynolds Inc. v. Byrd*, 470 U.S. 213, 221 (1985) (FAA "requires that [the Court] rigorously enforce agreements to arbitrate"). In the end, "the parties' intentions control, but those intentions are *generously*

---

[14] The court also expressed skepticism that a bipartite committee lacking any neutral member can provide the requisite fair and regular proceeding for resolution of a grievance. Id.

[15] See generally *Provena St. Joseph Medical Center*, 350 NLRB 808 (2007) (reaffirming clear and unmistakable standard for waiver of statutory rights). By citing *14 Penn Plaza LLC v. Pyett*, 556 U.S. 247

(2009), infra, the majority presumably would allow a comparable arbitration agreement to serve as a clear and unmistakable waiver. Also, as discussed below, the majority casts doubt on whether an arbitrator's "just cause" determination will suffice to meet the requirement that the unfair labor practice issue was considered. They do not speak directly to the fundamental issue of whether an otherwise vanilla "just cause" contractual provision would suffice as proof that an arbitrator is even authorized to consider the unfair labor practice issue.

construed as to issues of arbitrability." *Mitsubishi Motors Corp.*, 473 U.S. at 626 (italics for emphasis).

The majority cites *Wright v. Universal Maritime Service Corp.*, 525 U.S. 70 (1998), and its arguable reaffirmation in *Penn Plaza* in claiming that the new deferral standard is entirely consistent with Supreme Court precedent on arbitration. The majority's position would be ironclad if the only issue posed by the new standard was the "explicit contractual authorization" question, and if development of the law had stopped in 2009. But neither of those things is true.

Let's start with the latter problem with the majority's analysis. The Supreme Court has made it increasingly clear in a flurry of FAA cases, decided after *Wright* in 1998 and *14 Penn Plaza* in 2009, that the burden lies with the party resisting arbitration to demonstrate, even for federal statutory claims, either that: a plain-text reading of the arbitration contract's terms does not require that contract's enforcement, or the federal statute at issue contains an express command disavowing arbitration. See, e.g., *CompuCredit Corp. v. Greenwood*, 132 S.Ct. 665, 669 (2012) ("[The FAA] requires courts to enforce agreements to arbitrate *according to their terms*. That is the case *even when the claims at issue are federal statutory claims*, unless the FAA's mandate has been overridden by a *contrary congressional command*." (internal quotations and citations omitted; emphasis added)). As one can read in this precedent, there is no requirement of showing "explicit contract authorization" before federal statutory claims go to arbitration. Moreover, as detailed in my dissent in *Murphy Oil*, supra, the text of the Act obviously does not contain a command to override the FAA—especially in relation to *already-completed* arbitrations. Indeed, the force of the FAA should be far greater here, given that we are not dealing with any provision of the Act, but only, as the majority concedes, with a completely discretionary policy of deferral.

Second, and more importantly, even if the *Wright* principle still endures today (independently or as construed in *Penn Plaza*), it cannot sustain the great weight that the majority places upon it. *Wright* stands only for the proposition that, before a statutory right will be sent to arbitration, the arbitration contract's language must constitute a "clear and unmistakable waiver" of the judicial forum. In other words, *Wright* conceivably supports only the first prong of the majority's test, i.e. a standalone requirement of "explicit authorization" in the labor contract. By the same token, *Wright* actually undercuts the majority's total deferral standard, because that standard is "explicit authorization plus two more prongs." To wit, *Wright* looks solely to contract language, and does not require more before effectuating an

arbitration process. Nowhere in *Wright* or any related cases does there appear a notion that, *in addition*, a claim must still be technically "presented" to an arbitrator and the arbitrator's award must be "reasonably permissible." These extra conditions go far beyond recognized boundaries. Thus, the majority's new standard is a sizeable divergence from the standards mandated by the Supreme Court for construction of both (1) labor agreements specifically and (2) contracts in general under the FAA. This guarantees the new rule will be disfavored on court review.

2. The majority's new test will impede labor peace, not enhance it, in the long run

Moreover, as more fully explored in Member Miscimarra's dissent and accurately predicted by Member Penello 34 years ago, the new standards are guaranteed to produce less labor peace, not more. Why, exactly, would any exclusive collective-bargaining representative be willing to make an agreement that expressly waives its right to unlimited Board review of a statutory claim in favor of arbitration with an employer? Absent such agreement, a represented grievant is guaranteed two bites of the litigation apple, and the second bite in unfair labor practice litigation is "on the house," because the government will pay for it. The majority's new standard simply introduces a new stumbling block to productive negotiations over a grievance and arbitration procedure.

3. The majority's new test will still encourage strategic claim splitting

The same "two bites" problem may apply even in instances where the parties have agreed that an arbitrator has the authority to consider the statutory claim. The majority states that deferral remains possible if the arbitrator was presented with and considered the statutory issue, *or was "affirmatively" prevented from doing so by the party opposing deferral*. This suggests a prohibition against claim splitting, albeit a very limited one. However, the majority then belies this suggestion by stating that an employer can easily raise the issue by simply informing the arbitrator of the unfair labor practice "allegation." What if the employer is unaware of any such allegation, because the grievant has not made it yet, i.e. has effectively decided to reserve it? That is, what if the grievant and union representative, with a 6-month grace period in which to file an unfair labor charge under Section 10(b) of the Act, simply keep silent as to the statutory claim while taking the expeditious grievance and arbitration route in pursuit of the contractual claim? Would this be considered acting "affirmatively" to prevent consideration of the unfair labor practice claim? What if the employer asks the claimant/grievant—in prearbitral discovery or during the course of the arbitration case or hearing—if the grievant intends to initiate any unfair labor practice claims against the employer as a result of the same events, and the grievant answers "no"? By keeping silent or answering "no" at the time of the arbitration, a grievant or claimant could effectively preserve the second litigation option independent of any adverse outcome from the first. This is another fault with the majority's test.

4. The majority's new test is an impermissible standard of de novo review

There is also the adverse impact of the Board's review standard to be considered. As previously stated, the Board will now engage in what is essentially de novo review of an arbitrator's award to determine whether Board law reasonably permits the award. Not only does the availability of this standard encourage a losing grievant to pursue this second chance litigation, but it reduces the arbitration decision to the stature of an administrative law judge's decision, or even less so if any credibility resolutions and factual findings made in arbitration may be ignored or rebutted, as I note below. The limited extent to which actual deference will be given to the legal reasoning of the arbitrator is best measured by the majority's summary rejection of "just cause" as textual protection for statutory rights.[16] The majority's supposition that an arbitrator who is forthrightly applying a "just cause" provision will somehow likely trample Section 7 rights is unexplained and unwarranted. As more fully discussed in Member Miscimarra's dissent, Section 10(c) of the Act and its legislative history show that Congress was aware that "just cause" provisions in collective-bargaining agreements were interpreted by arbitrators to protect employees' statutory rights. Thus, even though an arbitrator is applying a contractual "just cause" standard, and not Board principles per se, history shows us that an arbitrator will not uphold discipline issued in response to union or concerted activities.[17] The "reason-

ably permissible" standard needs flesh on its bones ensuring that the Board is not simply substituting its after-the-fact judgment for the arbitrator's.[18] The majority supplies none.

5. The majority inexplicably fails to assign significant or specific collateral-estoppel value to any prior arbitration findings

Further, either when considering whether to defer *or* in those cases where deferral is held improper, the majority has severely cut back the collateral-estoppel impact of any fact findings by the arbitrator, which are, of course, made after taking testimony under oath. This unfortunately ensures that the arbitrator's decision will have little effect, evidentiary or analytical, on subsequent litigation before the Board. Although the majority seems to allow a limited form of collateral estoppel, it is nowhere near specific or efficient enough to preclude relitigation of essential fact issues, or even seemingly factual representations made 180 degrees different than before the arbitrator. The majority's new collateral-estoppel standard merely states that "the Board will assess the arbitrator's decision in light of the evidence that was presented." This will apparently preclude a party from withholding evidence in arbitration and then seeking to introduce it in a subsequent unfair labor practice proceeding.[19]

The majority, however, assigns no inherent deference to the fact finding or even the credibility determinations of the arbitrator whom the *parties themselves* voluntarily selected, and who will presumably have great experience

---

[V]irtually every arbitrator who found union activity or concerted activities to be the motivation behind discipline would sustain a challenging grievance. Indeed, arbitrators are prone to find just cause violations for any reason that appears to be arbitrary and without a foundation in fundamental fairness. That would include any discharge or discipline that had no satisfactory explanation. That is so much a part of the fabric of grievance arbitration that an arbitrator who had never heard of the NLRA or read an NLRB decision would undoubtedly find discipline action based on union or concerted activities to be without just cause.

[18] The majority says that their standard means that the "arbitrator's decision must constitute a reasonable application of the statutory principles that would govern the Board's decision, if the case were presented to it, to the facts of the case." But determining whether the arbitrator reasonably applied the statutory principles to the "facts" of the case—particularly since, as noted below, the majority seems unwilling to consider any deference to the arbitrator's fact finding—seems a ripe opportunity to engage in de novo review, despite the majority's claims to the contrary.

[19] Presumably, this limited preclusion rule applies as well to the General Counsel, even though he was not a party to the arbitration. Otherwise, the rule is essentially meaningless. But this is far from certain given the majority's pointed assertion that it is "well settled" that the Board does *not* give collateral estoppel effect to the resolution of private litigation, where the Board was not a party to the prior proceedings.

---

[16] A related problem with the new deferral standard is the assumption that in all instances the statutory issue can be easily separated from the contractual issue. That is not always the case, as for example, when the union has waived employees' statutory rights. *American Freight System, Inc. v. NLRB*, 722 F.2d 828, 831–833 (D.C. Cir. 1983) (finding that the "obvious fallacy in the Board's analysis is its contention that there is a statutory issue apart from the contractual issue," where union had waived employees' statutory rights in labor contract); *Fournelle v. NLRB*, 670 F.2d 331, 341–345 (D.C. Cir. 1982) (finding Board should have given precedential effect by deferring to prior arbitration decision permitting selective discipline of union officials under contract).

[17] See Reginald Alleyne, *Courts, Arbitrators, and the NLRB The Nature of the Deferral Beast, in 33 Proceedings of the National Academy of Arbitrators* 249 (1980):

in fact finding in adversarial proceedings. The majority merely points to the traditional rule that—for the Board's determination of deferral under the traditional standard—no collateral estoppel attaches. However, the majority misses that the traditional deferral standard would automatically "weed out" weak arbitrator decisions for collateral-estoppel purposes; decisions that are evaluated under and fail under the traditional deferral standard would be unworthy of any collateral-estoppel effect on any type of issue.

But, that same parallelism does not hold true for the new deferral standard. For example, an unfair labor practice issue may not have been technically "presented" to an arbitrator (in the sense that would satisfy the majority's new rule and trigger deferral to the arbitrator's ultimate decision), but that arbitrator may have made very detailed factual findings and credibility determinations that bear on the commission of the alleged unfair labor practice. The majority presents no reason or standards why, and how, those findings and determinations should be discarded, under the new rule.[20] If the arbitrator firmly considered and decided the issue of whether the stoplight was "red" or "green" and decided that it was "red," how does it advance the enforcement of the Act to undermine that determination by allowing it to be relitigated de novo? In other words, in order to serve fairness, a wholesale reformulation of one set of legal standards often requires modification of other, related legal standards. But, the majority apparently will still woodenly apply the no-estoppel rule, even though it has obliterated the underlying deferral precedent that would supply any logical support for the rule's premise.

Simply stated, arbitrators deserve far more deference than this. Indeed, the majority does not even supply a rule for parties or administrative law judges to determine how much deference to give the express or implicit fact finding made by an arbitrator. Nor does the majority discuss to what extent admissions or representations made in an arbitral transcript continue to bind a party before the Board. The majority's standard guarantees duplicative, wasteful proceedings and leaves parties in the dark about how much the workings of the arbitral process will count before the Board, if they count for anything at all. The majority's test needs improvement, which will probably be supplied by a court, unfortunately, on remand.

6. The majority's application of its highly technical new standards to prearbitral settlements confounds and undermines the settlement process, but the majority inexplicably provides no "safe harbor" for parties to utilize in settlement agreements whatsoever

The majority's overreach in reform of our postarbitral deferral policy becomes even more egregious by its application of the new restrictive standards to prearbitral grievance settlements, overruling *Alpha Beta Co.*, 273 NLRB 1546. Grievance settlements, including settlement of discipline or discharge disputes, are often reached at the work site, at the lower informal steps of the grievance process, and before any unfair labor practice charge is filed. They are agreements between the employer's operating managers, supervisors, or human resources officials, and the local union business representatives, stewards, or grievance committee members, as well as the employee involved. At this stage, the parties are seeking a compromise that, from the employer's perspective, assesses a suitable disciplinary penalty and, from the union's perspective, returns the employee to work with limited or no financial loss. Their concern is a prompt and final resolution of the matter and not a hypothetical unfair labor practice charge. The settlement itself may be extremely informal, memorialized by little more than a hand-written statement on a grievance form, an entry or authorization made in the employer's payroll system, and a notation in the employee's personnel record. Bear in mind that many of the individuals involved in creating such settlements are laypersons, not lawyers, and more still are unaware of every specific nuance in the Board's Section 7 jurisprudence. They are not well-served by imposing high standards before any settlement is given binding weight by the Board.

It is important to remember that "[b]y recognizing the validity and finality of [grievance] settlements, the Board promotes the integrity of the collective bargaining process, thereby effectuating a primary goal of the national labor policy." *Plumbers & Pipefitters Local Union No. 520*, 955 F.2d at 752. The majority's imposition of a stricter review standard makes little sense in this context. It simply adds to the heightened degree of uncertainty about the actual finality of the voluntary adjustment of disputes, even at the earliest stage of a collectively bargained grievance and arbitration procedure. This is anathema to our statutory policy of assuring labor relations stability through collective bargaining.

The majority identifies a problem here that does not exist, and I would not change the *Alpha Beta* standard. But, even accepting the ostensible problem on the majority's terms, one would think the majority could simply provide a safe harbor by stating that their test would be

---

[20] Any contention by the majority that the arbitrator's findings will not be automatically discarded but will be accorded "whatever weight is appropriate," besides reinforcing the notion that the review will likely be de novo, provides no guidance to the parties, the presiding administrative law judge, or the arbitrator about what is needed to satisfy the new standard.

automatically satisfied if the grievance settlement had particular language in it. At least for some group of employers, this might provide a method to avoid duplicative litigation. Although I disagree the *Alpha Beta* standard should be altered at all, if the majority is going to upend a 30-year old standard for settlements entered into mostly by laypeople, it should provide a workable drafting solution rather than leave the details for another day. The majority's approach abandons parties to twist in the wind as they attempt to figure out how to write a settlement agreement that actually and finally settles their dispute—which, of course, is supposed to be the core function of settlement agreements.

Contrary to the majority, giving parties safe harbor guidance is the rational administrative law approach. The Board has taken this approach where the ultimate issue was the Board's future interpretation of contracts, just as in this case. See *Keystone Coat, Apron & Towel Supply Co.*, 121 NLRB 880, 885 (1958) (construction of maintenance of membership clauses). There, the Board set forth safe harbor language so that unions could conform their legitimate union security needs to the law, and have their contracts serve as a valid basis for an election bar. The Board did not consign these unions to the "mercy" of a case-by-case Board adjudication process until the unions eventually stumbled upon language that would pass Board muster. Surely, we can do the same for parties who want to settle labor contract disputes with finality.

Finally, this task is not that hard. I can perform it in 39 words: "The parties realize that this dispute may include what could be alleged as unfair labor practice violations of the National Labor Relations Act. Notwithstanding, the parties intend to fully and finally resolve all such potential allegations in this settlement."[21] State legislatures have addressed analogous problems using a few lines of text as well. See, e.g., Cal. Civ. Code § 1542 (language to be used within a general release to effectively release unknown claims). I disagree strongly with the

majority's approach here, and its lack of a valid excuse to take the same path.

7. The majority's test is very likely to further delay the parties and reduce agency efficiency in these and other matters

The institution of the majority's new standards also portends that more and more cases that could and should be resolved through collective bargaining will now be dropped on our doorstep. The Board already struggles with the processing of its current unfair labor practice caseload, without the extra increment of cases posed here. For fiscal years 2011 through the last completed fiscal year 2014, the Board's production has been at the following level of contested cases per year: 248 (2014); 213 (2013); 342 (2012); and 368 (2011). Adding a hundred—or even a few dozen—arbitration cases each year to the Board's overall case load out of the many arbitration proceedings that are initiated nationwide each year will seriously detract from the Board's enforcement of the Act in other milieus. That is a simple mathematical fact.

Parties also do not need the extra delay posed by the prospect of a new, highly technical Board review before they know that an arbitrator's decision is final. This is not an abstract concern; the danger of delay is manifest in this very case, in the contrast between how quickly an arbitral process handles a disputed termination and how fast the Board does. As noted in the amicus brief provided by the Council on Labor Law Equality (COLLE):

> The procedural history of the underlying case here, Babcock & Wilcox Construction Co., JD(SF)-15-12, exemplifies [the concern about delay]. Pursuant to the contractual procedure, the union in this case filed a grievance on behalf of the Charging Party approximately one week after her termination, on March 19, 2009. The case quickly progressed to Step 4 of the contractual grievance procedure, in which the parties participated in a hearing before the subcommittee panel and submitted position statements and documentary evidence. The subcommittee rendered a decision on October 8 of that same year. The contractual grievance procedure, from start to finish, thus provided the parties with a resolution less than seven months after the challenged disciplinary action took place.
>
> By contrast, the Board proceedings in this case have prolonged this dispute for almost five years. The Region issued a complaint in this case on August 29, 2011, almost two years after the subcommittee's decision. ALJ's decision issued on April 9, 2012, over three years after the employee's dis-

---

[21] The Board in *Keystone Coat* managed to craft a 136-word clause for its safe harbor: "It shall be a condition of employment that all employees of the Employer covered by this agreement who are members of the Union in good standing on the effective date of this agreement shall remain members in good standing and those who are not members on the effective date of this agreement shall, on the thirtieth day [or such longer period as the parties may specify] following the effective date of this agreement, become and remain members in good standing in the Union. It shall also be a condition of employment that all employees covered by this agreement and hired on or after its effective date shall, on the thirtieth day following the beginning of such employment [or such longer period as the parties may specify] become and remain members in good standing in the Union." [note omitted]. 121 NLRB at 885.

charge, and upheld the subcommittee's decision. The case has now been pending at the Board for nearly two additional years. As of today [March 25, 2014], the parties have spent five years waiting for this matter to be finally resolved.

COLLE amicus brief at 19–20 (emphasis added). It makes no sense for us to impose a system that will only encourage delays of this nature.

There may be occasions when it is nevertheless necessary to take on an increased caseload in order to assure the prevention of unfair labor practices. This is not such an occasion, not when we have for 30 years followed a deferral practice that fulfills our obligation to accommodate arbitration without any proven derogation of our statutory enforcement obligation. We should not effectively become "the nation's just cause arbitrator," when our own cases take too long to issue, and adding more will only delay this process and frustrate finality in the nation's workplaces whenever a grievance arises.

In conclusion, I note that my colleagues downplay the possibility that their new deferral standard will have significant ramifications for arbitration, the incidence of deferral, and Board litigation. I disagree. The new policy virtually guarantees the proliferation of bifurcated, prolonged litigation in many more cases. Grievants and/or their union representatives will be encouraged to split their litigation claims, proceeding first solely on the contractual issue in arbitration, then, should they lose in that forum, turning to the General Counsel to proceed with litigation of the unfair labor practice claim at public expense. For that matter, even if they do zealously litigate the statutory claim in arbitration, but lose, they will be encouraged to pursue litigation before the Board with the prospect that the arbitration decision will be accorded little deference.

CONCLUSION

Although I dissent from my colleagues' broadscale revision of Board deferral policy, I do not mean to suggest that certain refinements of the current policy would be out of order. If the majority had proposed a rational, less radical test, the lack of necessity for overall change would not weigh as heavily from my perspective. Despite the absence of any showing that a drastic departure was necessary, not only do my colleagues radically revamp the deferral policy, they do so by substantially returning to the regressive approach taken in *Suburban Motor Freight*, which the Board wisely overruled 30 years ago in *Olin Corp.*

I certainly endorse the majority's general observation that "[a]n important and attractive feature of the grievance/ arbitration system is that it is less formal, less

structured, and less costly than litigation." Unfortunately, however, the fundamental problem here, as well as in the recent *Murphy Oil* decision, is that the majority's decision blights that attractive feature. By subordinating the arbitral process to Board litigation, rather than accommodating that process, they impose an overall system that is more formal, more structured, and potentially much more costly.

I yield to no one in faithfully assuring that the Board meets its statutory obligation to prevent unfair labor practices. Thirty years of experience under the *Spielberg/Olin* deferral standard fail to show that our statutory obligation has not been met. I also strongly adhere to the view that the Act and Supreme Court precedent mandate that the Board encourage final adjustment of work disputes through collectively bargained grievance and arbitration procedures. A broad discretionary deferral policy serves that mandate. The majority's new restrictive deferral policy does not. Even if there was a basis for changing all the deferral standards the majority uproots here, there are too many flaws in the majority's new test that will manifest themselves in too many scenarios. I therefore respectfully dissent.

Dated, Washington, D.C. December 15, 2014

Harry I. Johnson, III,   Member

NATIONAL LABOR RELATIONS BOARD

William Mabry III, for the General Counsel.
Dean E. Westman (Kastner, Westman & Wilkins), of Akron, Ohio, for the Respondent.

DECISION

STATEMENT OF THE CASE

JAY R. POLLACK, Administrative Law Judge. I heard this case in trial at Show Low, Arizona, on January 17–18, 2012. On July 30, 2009, Coletta Kim Beneli (Beneli) filed a charge alleging that Babcock & Wilcox Construction Co., Inc. (Respondent or the Employer) committed certain violations of Section 8(a)(3) and (1) of the National Labor Relations Act (the Act). On September 29, 2009, Beneli filed an amended charge against Respondent. On August 29, 2011, the Regional Director for Region 28, issued a complaint and notice of hearing alleging that Respondent violated Section 8(a) (3) and (1) of the Act. Respondent filed a timely answer to the complaint, denying all wrongdoing.

All parties have been afforded full opportunity to appear, to introduce relevant evidence, to examine and cross-examine witnesses, and to file briefs. Upon the entire record, from my observation of the demeanor of the witnesses,[1] and having considered the post-hearing briefs of the parties, I make the following

FINDINGS OF FACT

I. JURISDICTION

Respondent, a Delaware corporation, at times material here, was engaged as a construction contractor providing field construction and maintenance service for Arizona Public Service at Joseph City, Arizona. During the 12 months prior to the filing of the charge, Respondent received gross revenues in excess of $50,000 from services provided outside Arizona. Accordingly, Respondent admits and I find that Respondent is an employer engaged in commerce within the meaning of Section 2(2), (6), and (7) of the Act.

Respondent admits and I find, the International Union of Operating Engineers Local 428 has been a labor organization within the meaning of Section 2(5) of the Act.

II. THE ALLEGED UNFAIR LABOR PRACTICES

A. Factual Summary

Since 1996, Respondent and the International Union of Operating Engineers (the International) and its Local 428 (the Union) have been parties to the National Maintenance Agreement, which is currently in effect. Respondent has also been signatory to a multiemployer association agreement between the Union and the Arizona Chapter of the Associated General Contractors of America, Inc. At all times material here, Respondent was performing construction and maintenance work for Arizona Public Service (APS) at a coal plant in Joseph City, Arizona.

On January 12, 2009, Beneli began working for Respondent at the Joseph City jobsite as a utility operator, operating a forklift and a crane. Shortly after beginning work for Respondent, Beneli became the union job steward for the worksite. On February 2, Respondent brought in a new operator, Ian Christianson, to work at the jobsite. Beneli called the Union and found out that Christianson had not been dispatched through the Union's hiring hall. Beneli spoke to Christianson and told the employee that he needed a dispatch from the Union's hiring hall. Christianson told Beneli that he would speak with management and take care of it. Later that day Christianson told Beneli that he had spoken to Respondent's timekeeper.

On February 16, Robert Alsop, a foreman and union member, told Beneli that he had not been paid properly for a full 40-hour week. Beneli spoke with Christopher Goff, Respondent's project superintendent. Beneli told Goff that Alsop was short 10 hours on his paycheck. Goff asked why and Beneli responded that the collective-bargaining agreement guaranteed

[1] The credibility resolutions here have been derived from a review of the entire testimonial record and exhibits, with due regard for the logic of probability, the demeanor of the witnesses, and the teachings of *NLRB v. Walton Mfg. Co.*, 369 U.S. 404, 408 (1962). As to those witnesses testifying in contradiction to the findings here, their testimony has been discredited, either as having been in conflict with credited documentary or testimonial evidence or because it was in and of itself incredible and unworthy of belief.

foremen 40 hours a week. Goff then asked Beneli to tell the timekeeper, Rhonda Roberson, to cut Alsop a check for the full 40 hours.

On March 10, Beneli saw another new operator on the job. Beneli asked the new operator, Heath Riley, whether he was referred from the Union's hiring hall. Riley answered that he had been called directly by Goff. Beneli called the Union and then had Riley speak with the union dispatcher. Beneli told Riley that the Union and Respondent would work it out.

On March 11, Alsop told Beneli that Bill Roberson, APS representative, wanted to speak with her. After a short discussion, Beneli stated that she had spoken to the Union about Alsop's guaranteed pay. Beneli told Roberson that it would be a lot better if Goff did not bring operators from outside the State without using the Union's hiring hall. Goff walked in at the end of the conversation.

On March 11, after meeting with Roberson, Beneli was late for the morning's job safety analysis (jsa) meeting. Goff told Beneli that he wanted to speak with her. When Beneli asked if he wanted to speak at that moment, Goff angrily responded, "I will take care of you later missy." After the meeting, Goff asked Beneli what she had discussed with Roberson. Beneli said she had told Roberson that Riley had not been dispatched from the Union's hiring hall and about Alsop's pay issue. Goff asked why Beneli had not discussed the matter with him. Beneli explained that Roberson had asked her to talk with him. Goff said that the contract was with Respondent and not with APS. Beneli said that she had made a mistake and that it would not happen again. Goff said that he did not say Alsop should be paid for 40 hours. Beneli disagreed telling Goff where and when he had told her to tell Rhonda Roberson to pay Alsop the full amount. Goff said that it was none of Beneli's business. Goff told Beneli that she had no business talking to APS. Beneli stated that she had made a mistake but that Bill Roberson had asked to talk to her. Goff told Beneli that she was sticking her nose where it does not belong and asking questions that were none of her business. Goff told Beneli that she was not supposed to take care of union business on company time. After this meeting, Beneli called Shawn Williams, union assistant business manager.

Williams testified that at about 8 a.m. on March 11, he received a call from Goff. Ralph McDesmond, safety representative was also on the call. Goff told Williams that he wanted to terminate Beneli because she had overstepped her boundaries as the Union's steward and was crossing the line into management. Williams testified that Goff said Beneli was raising contractual issues and trying to tell Respondent what they are supposed to pay employees. Williams stated that in his view Beneli was acting as a steward should. Goff stated that Beneli should not be getting APS, Respondent's customer, involved by raising contractual issues with APS. Williams said that in the future Beneli would raise contractual issues solely with Respondent. Williams stated that if Goff discharged Beneli, the Union would fight the discharge and file a grievance.

On March 11, sometime after 2 p.m., Alsop told Beneli that Goff had called him and wanted them both to go to Respondent's office. Beneli and Alsop went to Goff's office, where they found McDesmond and Matt Winklestine, safety representative, waiting. Winklestine told Beneli that she was being suspended for violating two safety policies earlier that day. Specifically Winkelstine said Beneli had been observed eating a pastry during the jsa meeting, and that she had failed to fill out a separate jsa form. Beneli laughed and asked Winklestine where it stated she could not eat a pastry during the jsa meeting. Winklestine said he would look for it. Beneli again asked to see it in writing. Winklestine said he did not have to show Beneli anything. Winklestine then stated that Beneli was being suspended for 3 days without pay for the two safety violations.

Beneli turned to McDesmond and said, "So this is the f—g game you guys are going to play?" Almost immediately Winklestine and McDesmond pointed their fingers at Beneli and stated that she was terminated. McDesmond said that Beneli had threatened them. Beneli said that she did not threaten anyone but said, "is this the f—g game you are going to play?" McDesmond stated there you go again and once more accused Beneli of threatening them. McDesmond then told Rhonda Roberson to prepare termination papers and to cut Beneli's final check. Beneli refused to sign the termination papers which stated that she was being terminated for "inappropriate conduct."

Respondent's Defense

Respondent presented evidence that Beneli was not a safety conscious employee. She used her cell phone while operating equipment, moved a crane without a spotter and drove a forklift through a prohibited area. She was given a written warning on February 2 for driving through the prohibited area.

Beneli was also late for several joint safety analysis meetings. On March 11, Beneli was late for the jsa meeting. She also admits to eating a pastry at the meeting. In addition she failed to fill out a second jsa form that day. Both Goff and McDesmond deny having a conversation with Williams on March 11.

On that day, Goff and McDesmond consulted over the telephone with Dave Crichton, Respondent's corporate manager of labor relations. They agreed to give Beneli a 3-day suspension for safety violations. Winklestine filled out the disciplinary suspension form. When Winklestine began to explain the suspension, Beneli became angry. She said in an angry tone, "if you guys want to play this f—g game, we'll see." McDesmond asked what she had said and Beneli repeated it. McDesmond immediately responded that Beneli was discharged. Respondent contends that Beneli was discharged for her angry outburst and use of profanity at this disciplinary interview. Respondent denied that Beneli was discharged because of her activities as union steward.

The Grievance

On March 19, the Union filed a grievance over Beneli's suspension and discharge. The grievance moved through the contractual grievance procedure to step 4, which calls for a hearing before the grievance review subcommittee (subcommittee). A quorum of five representatives consisting of at least two management representatives, two labor representatives, and one NAMPC staff representative considers and decides a grievance at step 4. All subcommittee determinations are based upon the facts presented, both written and oral, and any decision rendered is final, binding and not subject to any appeal.

On their step 4 grievance fact form, the Union asserted that "Beneli's termination was in violation of the National Maintenance Agreement, NLRA Section 7 . . . and decisions made by the NLRB." Additionally, the Union contended that "While engaged in a representational capacity as a Union steward [Grievant] made the following statement '. . . so this is the f—g game you guys are going to play.' She was immediately terminated without further discussion in the process."

On October 8, the step 4 hearing was conducted before the subcommittee panel. Both the Respondent and the International Union provided the subcommittee with position statements and documentary evidence. The International Union submitted a statement position and provided various documents in support of the grievance, including a 3-page report setting out a detailed timeline of Beneli's extensive union and concerted activities in the month and a half before her suspension and discharge. Respondent's position statement stated in part, that Beneli "was terminated due to the inappropriate conduct which she engaged in when the Company Supervisor informed her of their intent to administer a . . . three day disciplinary suspension for safety violations." Respondent also asserted that a supervisor had complained that "the Steward was disruptive in terms of the amount of time being spent on Union duties, and had frequently evidenced a poor attitude toward safety on the job." Additionally, attached to Respondent's position statement were statements prepared by Respondent's witnesses who were present at the March 11 meeting.

By letter dated October 8, the subcommittee denied the grievance and upheld Beneli's discharge. The subcommittee noted the "issue was the Union's contention the [Respondent] violated Article XXIII Management Clause of the National Maintenance Agreement by terminating the grievant, without just cause, for the grievant's use of profanity" and that the subcommittee "reviewed all the information submitted both written and oral" and determined that "no violation of the National Maintenance Agreement occurred and therefore, the grievance was denied."

On September 30, 2009, Region 28 issued a letter which deferred the charge to the parties grievance/arbitration procedure pursuant to *Dubo Mfg. Corp.,* 142 NLRB 431 (1963). A portion of the charge was resolved by a non-Board settlement whereby Respondent agreed to post a notice for 60 days. The parties provided the Region with a letter which stated:

> At issue was the Union's contention that Respondent violated Article XXIII Management Clause of the National Maintenance Agreement by terminating the grievant, without just cause for the grievant's use of profanity.

> Respondent contends that grievant was terminated for just cause due to the grievant's use of profanity and insubordinate conduct upon receipt of disciplinary action.

> After reviewing all the information submitted, both written and oral, the subcommittee determined that no violation of the National Maintenance Agreement occurred and therefore, the grievance was denied. This determination is based on the facts presented and reviewed in the instant case and only applies to this specific grievance.

BABCOCK & WILCOX CONSTRUCTION CO.

Thereafter Beneli informed the Region that she was not satisfied with the grievance decision and asked that the Region not defer to it. The Region considered Respondent's position but determined that the grievance decision was repugnant to the Act and reversed the deferral. On August 29, 2011, the Region issued the complaint in this matter.

Should the Board Defer to the Subcommittee's Decision?

Under the current *Spielberg/Olin* standards, the Board defers to arbitral awards and final disposition of joint employer-union committees when: (1) all parties agreed to be bound by the decision of the arbitrator; (2) the proceedings appear to be fair and regular; (3) the arbitrator adequately considered the unfair labor practice issue; and (4) the award is clearly not repugnant to the policies of the Act. *Spielberg Mfg. Co.*, 112 NLRB 1080 at 1082 (1955); *Olin Corp.*, 268 NLRB 573 at 574 (1984). See also, *K-Mechanical Services, Inc.*, 299 NLRB 114,117 (1990) (applying *Spielberg/ Olin* deferral standards to determinations by joint employer-union committees that are final dispositions of a grievance).

Here General Counsel concedes that the proceedings were fair and regular and that all parties had agreed to be bound by the decision. In addition, the contractual issue presented was factually parallel to the unfair labor practice issue and the subcommittee was generally presented with the facts relevant to resolving the unfair labor practice. General Counsel contends that the subcommittee's decision was repugnant to the Act. Here, the subcommittee found that Beleni was discharged for the use of profanity and insubordination upon receipt of her discipline. Although not stated in its decision, the subcommittee rejected the assertion that Beneli was discharged because of her duties as steward. While I credited Beneli and Williams, the subcommittee could have credited Respondent's witnesses. While I would reach a different conclusion, I do not find this factual decision by the subcommittee to be repugnant to the Act. Accordingly, I recommend that the Board defer to the arbitration and grievance procedure.

CONCLUSIONS OF LAW

1. Respondent is an employer engaged in commerce within the meaning of Section 2(2), (6), and (7) of the Act.

2. The Board should defer to the decision of the NAMPC subcommittee.

3. Respondent did not violate the Act as alleged in the complaint.

On these findings of fact and conclusions of law and on the entire record, I issue the following recommended.[2]

ORDER

The complaint should be dismissed.
Dated, Washington, D.C. April 9, 2012

---

[2] If no exceptions are filed as provided by Sec. 102.46 of the Board's Rules and Regulations, the findings, conclusions, and recommended Order shall, as provided in Sec. 102.48 of the Rules, be adopted by the Board and all objections to them shall be deemed waived for all purposes.

MEMORANDUM GC 15-02   February 10, 2015

TO: All Regional Directors, Officers-in-Charge,
                And Resident Officers

FROM: Richard F. Griffin, Jr., General Counsel /s/

SUBJECT: Guideline Memorandum Concerning Deferral to Arbitral Awards,
                the Arbitral Process, and Grievance Settlements in Section 8(a)(1)
                and (3) cases

I.   Introduction

In its seminal decision in *Spielberg Manufacturing Co.*,[1] the Board decided that it would defer, as a matter of discretion, to an arbitrator's decision in cases where the arbitral proceedings appear to have been fair and regular, all parties agreed to be bound, and the arbitrator's decision was not clearly repugnant to the purposes and policies of the Act. After some years of experience applying *Spielberg*, the Board expanded on that test by requiring an arbitrator to have considered the unfair labor practice issue (i.e., the "statutory issue").[2] In *Olin Corp.*,[3] the Board relaxed the consideration requirement, holding that it was satisfied if the contractual and statutory issues were factually parallel and the arbitrator was presented generally with the facts relevant to resolving the unfair labor practice. In addition, *Olin* placed the burden on the party opposing deferral to demonstrate that the deferral criteria were not met.[4]

In *Babcock & Wilcox Construction Co.*,[5] the Board revisited *Olin* and held that the existing postarbitral deferral standard did not adequately balance the protection of employee rights under the Act and the national policy of encouraging arbitration of disputes over the application or interpretation of collective-bargaining agreements. The Board reasoned that the existing standard created excessive risk

---

[1] 112 NLRB 1080, 1082 (1955).

[2] *See Raytheon Co.*, 140 NLRB 883, 884-85 (1963), *enforcement denied*, 326 F.2d 471 (1st Cir. 1964).

[3] 268 NLRB 573, 574 (1984).

[4] *Id.*

[5] 361 NLRB No. 132 (Dec. 15, 2014).

that the Board would defer when an arbitrator had not adequately considered the unfair labor practice issue, or when it was impossible to tell whether that issue had been considered.

In order to adequately ensure that employees' Section 7 rights are protected in the course of the arbitral process, *Babcock* announced a new standard for deferring to arbitral decisions in Section 8(a)(1) and (3) cases.[6] In so doing, the Board also modified the standards for prearbitral deferral and deferral to grievance settlements in these types of cases. This memorandum explains these new standards, describes the circumstances in which they apply to pending and future cases, and provides guidance on handling cases that implicate these issues.

II.   Postarbitral Deferral

A.   Overview of the *Babcock* Standard and Burden Allocation

Under *Babcock*, deferral to an arbitral decision is appropriate in Section 8(a)(1) and (3) cases where the arbitration procedures appear to have been fair and regular, the parties agreed to be bound,[7] and the party urging deferral demonstrates that: (1) the arbitrator was explicitly authorized to decide the unfair labor practice issue; (2) the arbitrator was presented with and considered the statutory issue, or was prevented from doing so by the party opposing deferral; and (3) Board law "reasonably permits" the arbitral award.[8] The meaning of each of these three new prongs in the postarbitral deferral test is discussed in more detail below. It is important to underscore that *Babcock* places the burden of proving that the deferral standard is satisfied on the party urging deferral, typically the employer, which is another significant change from the *Olin* standard.[9]

---

[6] We interpret *Babcock* as applying not only to cases involving Section 8(a)(1) and (3) discipline and discharge, but also to other Section 8(a)(1) and (3) conduct cognizable under a contractual grievance provision. Such conduct likewise implicates employees' Section 7 rights, and therefore falls within the scope of the Board's policy rationale for adopting new deferral standards. By contrast, the processing of Section 8(a)(5) allegations will be unchanged, except where they are entwined with related Section 8(a)(1) and/or (3) allegations. *See, infra*, fn. 50.

[7] These traditional requirements under *Spielberg* and *Olin* were not affected by the *Babcock* decision.

[8] Since the Board has now adopted a new postarbitral deferral standard, Regions should no longer follow Memorandum GC 11-05 (Jan. 20, 2011), which outlined a different proposed framework.

[9] 361 NLRB No. 132, slip op. at 10.

B. Explanation of the *Babcock* Requirements

1. Explicit Authorization

Under *Babcock*, an arbitrator must be explicitly authorized to decide the statutory issue in order to defer to the arbitral award. This requirement can be met by showing either that: (1) the specific statutory right at issue was incorporated in the collective-bargaining agreement, or (2) the parties agreed to authorize arbitration of the statutory issue in the particular case.[10]

Significantly, the *Babcock* standard treats explicit authorization as a threshold requirement, that is, deferral is never warranted if this requirement is not met. The Board reasoned that arbitration is a consensual matter and it will not assume that the parties have agreed to submit statutory claims to the grievance process. Consequently, each party to a collective-bargaining agreement has the prerogative to decide not to arbitrate statutory claims by refusing to agree to a contract incorporating the statutory right or to otherwise agree to arbitrate the statutory issue.[11] That is, a party will retain the option of adjudicating a statutory claim before the Board in the event the arbitrator denies the grievance where the collective-bargaining agreement is silent as to the statutory right and the party refused to authorize arbitration of the claim in the particular case.

CASEHANDLING INSTRUCTIONS: The Region should submit to the Division of Advice any questions about whether a specific statutory right was incorporated into the collective-bargaining agreement or whether the parties agreed to arbitrate the statutory issue in the particular case.

2. Statutory Issue was Presented and Considered

The *Babcock* standard requires that the arbitrator was "actually presented" with and "actually considered" the statutory issue in order to defer to an arbitral award.[12] It therefore abandons *Olin*'s *de facto* presumption that "if an arbitrator is presented in some fashion with facts relevant to both an alleged contract violation

---

[10] *Id.*, slip op. at 2, 5. The Board noted that contract language prohibiting retaliation for engaging in union activity would be sufficient to show that the statutory right was incorporated in the collective-bargaining agreement in a case, like *Babcock*, where the union argued during the grievance process that the employee was discharged for engaging in steward activities. *Id.*, slip op. at 6, 11.

[11] *Id.*, slip op. at 11.

[12] *Id.*, slip op. at 6, 7, 10, 11 (emphasis omitted).

and an alleged unfair labor practice, the arbitrator necessarily was presented with, and decided, the latter allegation in the course of deciding the former."[13]

The *Babcock* Board observed that either party can raise the statutory issue before the arbitrator.[14] Merely informing the arbitrator of the unfair labor practice allegation in a pending charge will usually be sufficient to show that the issue had been presented.[15]

In order to show that the arbitrator actually considered the statutory issue, the Board will require that the arbitrator "identified that issue and at least generally explained why . . . the facts presented either do or do not support the unfair labor practice allegation."[16] The Board will not require that an arbitrator conduct a "detailed exegesis" of Board law, since many arbitrators, as well as union and employer representatives in arbitral proceedings, are not trained in labor law.[17] But the Board will not assume that an arbitrator implicitly ruled on the statutory issue if the award merely upholds disciplinary action under a "just cause" analysis; rather, the arbitrator must make explicit that the action was not in retaliation for an employee's protected activities.[18]

Although the Board did not explicitly return to the deferral principles set forth in *Suburban Motor Freight, Inc.*,[19] which predated *Olin*, certain cases decided under that earlier standard illustrate *Babcock*'s "actual consideration" principle. For example, in *Inland Steel Co.*,[20] the Board found that deferral to an arbitral

[13] *Id.*, slip op. at 5.

[14] *Id.*, slip op. at 7.

[15] *Id.*, slip op. at 7 n.14.

[16] *Id.*, slip op. at 7.

[17] *Id.* Thus, the Board declined to adopt a requirement that the arbitrator correctly enunciated the applicable statutory principles and applied them in deciding the statutory issue. *Id.*

[18] *Id.*, slip op. at 8, 11.

[19] 247 NLRB 146, 146-47 (1980) (deferral unwarranted unless the statutory issue was both presented to and considered by the arbitrator; no deference will be given where arbitral award does not indicate whether arbitrator "ruled on" the unfair labor practice issue), *overruled as recognized in Altoona Hospital*, 270 NLRB 1179, 1179 (1984).

[20] 263 NLRB 1091, 1091, 1097 (1982).

award finding "just and proper cause" for an employee's discharge was appropriate where the arbitrator expressly found that the employee was discharged for providing false information on her employment application rather than for her union activities. Specifically, the arbitrator reasoned that the employer harbored no anti-union animus in light of its longstanding knowledge and tolerance of the employee's union activities and that it merely followed its uniform policy and practice of terminating employees for such falsifications.[21] In these circumstances, the Board observed that the "parties clearly litigated the statutory issue of discrimination before the arbitrator and he clearly considered that issue in deciding [the] grievance."[22] In contrast, deferral was rejected in cases where the arbitral award did not discuss the facts relevant to the statutory issue, did not draw any conclusions based on the unfair labor practice evidence presented, or made no determination as to the real reason for the employer's actions.[23] Notably, the Board also refused to defer in cases where the arbitral award disavowed any intention of

[21] *Id.* at 1096-97.

[22] *Id.* at 1091.

[23] *See, e.g., Joyce Brothers Storage*, 263 NLRB 544, 548-49 (1982) (deferral unwarranted where arbitral panel denied grievance without any rationale; no proof panel considered whether union activity motivated discharge where hearing minutes disclosed no discussion of "factors germane to the statutory issue" and no analysis of evidence presented); *Phil Smidt & Son, Inc.*, 260 NLRB 668, 668 n.1, 670-71 (1982) (deferral unwarranted where arbitral decision merely assessed whether reasons given for discharge were supported by the evidence and amounted to "just cause"; arbitrator did not consider whether employer's proffered justifications were pretextual or whether employee's arguably protected attempt to document favoritism motivated the discharge); *Magnetics International, Inc.*, 254 NLRB 520, 520 n.2, 523 (1981) (deferral unwarranted where arbitration decision merely recited parties' contentions and announced that insubordination amounted to "just contractual cause," but did not draw conclusions as to the evidence of unlawful motive and did not decide if the legitimate basis for discharge was mixed with unlawful considerations), *enforced*, 699 F.2d 806 (6th Cir. 1983); *General Warehouse Corp.*, 247 NLRB 1073, 1074, 1076 (1980) (deferral unwarranted where arbitral decision framed the issue in terms of "just cause," only discussed absenteeism evidence, and did not make findings concerning discriminatee's protected activity of opposing waiver of cost-of-living increase), *enforced*, 643 F.2d 965 (3d Cir. 1981); *Koppel, Inc.*, 251 NLRB 567, 569-72 (1980) (deferral unwarranted where arbitral decision did not address argument that employer's decision to return employee to the dispatch hall was in retaliation for protected complaints about safety and manning; arbitrator's statement at the hearing that he would consider all the evidence and arguments insufficient).

deciding the unfair labor practice, but where the arbitrator nonetheless made gratuitous comments or findings as to the merits of the statutory claim.[24]

The *Babcock* Board articulated an exception to the above requirements, which permits deferral absent presentation and consideration if the statutory right is incorporated in the collective-bargaining agreement and one party affirmatively prevented the other party from raising the unfair labor practice issue before the arbitrator.[25] The Board anticipates that this exception will rarely apply.[26] Typically, both parties will be motivated to litigate the unfair labor practice in the arbitral proceeding, and the employer will be able to raise the statutory issue if the union does not.[27] In order to address the concern that unions might withhold evidence relevant to the statutory issue during the arbitral proceeding for the purpose of defeating deferral, *Babcock* provides that in the event the issue is placed before an arbitrator but a party fails to introduce such evidence, the Board will assess whether the arbitral award is reasonably permitted in light of the evidence that was before the arbitrator.[28] This creates a disincentive against withholding evidence in an attempt to avoid an arbitral ruling on the statutory issue if a party initially authorized arbitration of the issue and the other party at least raised it in the arbitral proceeding.

CASEHANDLING INSTRUCTIONS: The Region should submit any questions concerning whether the statutory issue was presented to and considered by the arbitrator to the Division of Advice. Likewise, any case where a party argues that it was prevented from placing the statutory issue before the arbitrator, including

---

[24] *See B & W Construction Co.*, 263 NLRB 405, 405 n.3 (1982), *enforced sub nom. NLRB v. Babcock & Wilcox Co.*, 736 F.2d 1410 (10th Cir. 1984); *Professional Porter & Window Cleaning Co.*, 263 NLRB 136, 136-37 (1982), *enforced*, 742 F.2d 1438 (2d Cir. 1983) (table decision).

[25] 361 NLRB No. 132, slip op. at 6-7.

[26] *Id.*, slip op. at 6-7 & n.12.

[27] *Id.*, slip op. at 7 & n.12. The Board also emphasized that its adoption of this narrow exception did not signal a return to *Electronic Reproduction Service Corp.*, 213 NLRB 758, 762, 764 (1974), *overruled by Suburban Motor Freight*, 247 NLRB at 146, which held that deferral would normally be appropriate so long as there was a mere opportunity to present the statutory issue, even if the record did not disclose whether it was raised by the parties or considered by the arbitrator. 361 NLRB No. 132, slip op. at 7 & n.13.

[28] *Id.*, slip op. at 7.

situations where a union waited to file an unfair labor practice charge until after the arbitration,[29] should be submitted to Advice.

3. Arbitral Award is Reasonably Permitted Under Board Law

Under *Spielberg* and *Olin*, deferral was improper if the arbitral award was "clearly repugnant" to the Act, that is, the award was "palpably wrong" or "not susceptible to an interpretation consistent with the Act."[30] In applying this standard, the Board would defer unless there was "no conceivable reading of the facts in a given case that would support the arbitrator's decision."[31] Thus, the Board routinely deferred to arbitral awards that were adverse to disciplined or discharged employees even if there was "considerable evidence" of an unlawful motive.[32]

The *Babcock* Board found that the "clearly repugnant" standard failed to adequately protect employees' statutory rights and adopted a new inquiry for assessing arbitral awards: whether Board law reasonably permits the arbitrator's decision. Under this new standard, the award must represent a "reasonable application of the statutory principles that would govern the Board's decision."[33] The arbitrator need not rule exactly as the Board would have ruled; in other words, the Board will not engage in the equivalent of *de novo* review of the arbitrator's decision. Rather, the award need only reach a result a "decision maker reasonably applying the Act could reach."[34] We interpret the Board's rejection of *de novo* review to mean that it will give some deference to the arbitrator's factual findings, including credibility resolutions, in determining whether the result is reasonably permitted under Board law.

With regard to remedial questions, the arbitrator's remedy need not exactly match the remedy the Board would have imposed, although the absence of any

---

[29] *See id.*, slip op. at 32 (Member Johnson, dissenting) (questioning whether waiting to file an unfair labor practice charge would be considered acting "affirmatively" to prevent consideration of the statutory issue in the arbitral forum).

[30] *Spielberg*, 112 NLRB at 1082; *Olin*, 268 NLRB at 574.

[31] 361 NLRB No. 132, slip op. at 8.

[32] *Id.*

[33] *Id.*, slip op. at 7.

[34] *Id.*

effective remedy would preclude deferral.[35] For example, the Board noted that deferral might be proper even if the award allowed the employer to deduct unemployment compensation from backpay, which is contrary to Board policy concerning backpay offsets.[36] We would extend this rationale to cases where an arbitrator failed to order the respondent to post a notice, compensate the discriminatee for excess Federal and State income taxes paid as a result of receiving a lump-sum backpay award covering more than one year,[37] or report the discriminatee's backpay allocation to the Social Security Administration,[38] or where there were other similar remedial deficiencies.

CASEHANDLING INSTRUCTIONS: The Region should submit to the Division of Advice any case where the arbitral ruling on the statutory issue arguably fails to satisfy the "reasonably permitted" requirement, such as where an arbitrator places no weight on facts critical to the unfair labor practice or misconstrues Board law. As to cases presenting remedial deficiencies, the Region may, at its discretion, defer whenever the relief granted by the arbitral award is such that the Region would have the authority to unilaterally accept it as settlement of the unfair labor practice charge.[39] The Region should submit to the Division of Advice any case where it seeks to issue complaint on the basis that an arbitral remedy is insufficient, including cases where the Region wishes to challenge an arbitral award on the basis that it failed to provide a notice posting in light of the circumstances of that particular case.

C.   Application of the *Babcock* Postarbitral Deferral Standard to Pending and Future Cases

The Board indicated that it would apply the new postarbitral deferral standard prospectively ("in future cases") and not retroactively ("i.e., in all pending

---

[35] *Id.*, slip op. at 7 n.16.

[36] *Id.*

[37] *See Latino Express, Inc.*, 359 NLRB No. 44 (Dec. 18, 2012), *reaffirmed in Tortillas Don Chavas*, 361 NLRB No. 10, slip op. at 2 (Aug. 8, 2014).

[38] *See id.*

[39] *See* Casehandling Manual, Compliance Proceedings § 10592.1 (defining authority of Regional Directors to accept backpay settlements agreed to by all parties and discriminatees); *see also* Casehandling Manual, Unfair Labor Practice Proceedings §§ 10150-10150.2 (outlining the procedure for regional approval of unilateral informal settlements).

cases").[40] In actuality, the Board has taken a more nuanced, hybrid approach under which the new standard will apply to some pending charges (i.e., some charges presently on administrative deferral) and the old standard will continue to apply to some charges filed after *Babcock*. The date the unfair labor practice charge was filed is, thus, irrelevant in deciding which standard applies. Rather, Regions should apply the following rules to determine whether to evaluate an arbitral award under *Olin* or *Babcock* in pending and future cases raising allegations under Section 8(a)(1) and (3):

- *Olin* applies if the arbitration hearing occurred on or before December 15, 2014, the date the *Babcock* decision issued;

- *Babcock* applies if the collective-bargaining agreement under which the grievance arose was executed after December 15, 2014.[41]

- If the collective-bargaining agreement under which the grievance arose was executed on or before December 15, 2014, and the arbitration hearing occurred after December 15, 2014, which standard applies depends on whether the arbitrator was explicitly authorized to decide the statutory question (either in the collective-bargaining agreement or by agreement of the parties in a particular case). If the arbitrator was so authorized, then *Babcock* applies, even if the Region initially placed the case on administrative deferral pursuant to the preexisting standard for prearbitral deferral.[42] If the arbitrator was not authorized to decide the statutory issue, then *Olin* applies.

Notwithstanding the Board's statement that, absent explicit authorization to arbitrate the statutory issue, it "will not apply the new standards until [contracts

---

[40] 361 NLRB No. 132, slip op. at 13-14.

[41] We would likewise apply *Babcock* if the grievance arose under a collective-bargaining agreement that automatically renewed after December 15, 2014 because neither party took action to reopen negotiations pursuant to a contractual renewal clause. Similarly, we would apply *Babcock* if the grievance arose under a post-*Babcock* agreement to extend an expired contract for a set term, unless it was a temporary extension to allow the parties to continue bargaining over a successor collective-bargaining agreement. In that case, which standard applies depends on whether the arbitrator was explicitly authorized to decide the unfair labor practice.

[42] Such cases will necessarily meet the first prong of *Babcock*, and the Board decided that it is therefore appropriate to apply the remaining criteria of the new standard because it will not contravene the parties' settled expectations. 361 NLRB No. 132, slip op. at 14.

executed prior to *Babcock*] *have expired*,"[43] we would not treat contract expiration as a strict cutoff date for applying *Olin*. Specifically, we would apply *Olin* to any grievance arising under a pre-*Babcock* contract, even if the arbitral hearing occurred after the contract's expiration, assuming there is no explicit authorization to decide the statutory issue. Such an approach best accommodates the Board's rationale surrounding retroactivity. The Board decided to delay application of the new deferral standard in cases where explicit authorization is absent because parties relied on the preexisting deferral scheme in negotiating their contracts and processing grievances. In particular, parties had no expectation that deferral would be withheld if they did not incorporate the statutory right in their agreement or otherwise agree to arbitrate the unfair labor practice. And they likewise assumed that an arbitration award resolving a grievance arising under their contract would be assessed under *Olin*, regardless of whether the arbitration took place before or after the contract expired. Thus, by applying *Olin* to all grievances that occurred during the life of a pre-*Babcock* contract in cases where the parties did not authorize arbitration of the unfair labor practice, our approach gives parties the full benefit of the bargain they struck and comports with their settled expectations as to whether the resolution of grievances arising under their contract would warrant deferral.[44]

III. **Prearbitral Deferral**

The *Babcock* Board determined that the above modifications to the standard for reviewing arbitral awards necessitated a change in the criteria for administratively placing a Section 8(a)(1) or (3) charge on deferral pending the outcome of the arbitral process, as set forth in *Collyer Insulated Wire*[45] and *United Technologies Corp.*[46] Accordingly, the Board will no longer defer cases to the arbitral process unless the arbitrator is explicitly authorized to decide the statutory issue (either in the collective-bargaining agreement or by agreement of the parties

---

[43] *Id.* (emphasis added). The Board elsewhere references the time period before "new contracts are concluded," *id.*, slip op. at 14 n.39, and appears to conflate the expiration of pre-*Babcock* agreements and the negotiation of post-*Babcock* agreements.

[44] In cases where the Region issued complaint prior to the *Babcock* decision pursuant to the theory that the arbitral award is clearly repugnant under *Olin* and that the Board should adopt a different deferral standard, the Region should continue to litigate the case and argue only that the award is repugnant.

[45] 192 NLRB 837, 841-42 (1971).

[46] 268 NLRB 557, 558 (1984).

in a particular case).[47] This is because it would be futile to place a case on hold pending arbitration if it is clear from the outset that deferral to that ultimate award would be improper.

Although the Board did not indicate whether this new standard would apply prospectively or retroactively, we infer that the new prearbitral deferral standard will apply only if the new postarbitral deferral standard would apply to the ultimate arbitration.

CASEHANDLING INSTRUCTIONS: With respect to cases currently on *Collyer* deferral, the Region should send letters (template attached) to parties notifying them of the *Babcock* decision, attaching this memorandum, and instructing them as to the circumstances under which the new deferral standards may apply. With respect to future charges in which a party raises prearbitral deferral as a defense to allegations under Section 8(a)(1) and (3), the Region must take into account which standard will apply to the ultimate arbitration in deciding whether to place the case on administrative deferral. In processing such cases, the Region should proceed as follows.[48]

First, the Region should assess whether the statutory right at issue is incorporated in the applicable collective-bargaining agreement. As with postarbitral deferral, any questions about whether a specific statutory right has been incorporated into the agreement should be submitted to the Division of Advice. If it is so incorporated, the Region should place the case on administrative deferral, provided all of the other *Collyer* requirements are met and there is arguable

---

[47] 361 NLRB No. 132, slip op. at 12-13. Although the *Babcock* decision only discussed this new requirement in the context of *Collyer* deferral, we assume that it would also apply to cases where *Dubo* deferral is raised, i.e., where the unfair labor practice issue is being processed through the grievance-arbitration machinery and there is a reasonable chance that use of that machinery will resolve the dispute or put it to rest. *See Dubo Manufacturing Corp.*, 142 NLRB 431 (1963); Memorandum GC 79-36, *Procedures for Application of the* Dubo *Policy to Pending Charges*, dated May 14, 1979, at 1.

[48] In any case where administrative deferral is appropriate, the Region should use the attached *Collyer* or *Dubo* deferral letters (instead of the *Collyer* letter appearing in the Casehandling Manual, Unfair Labor Practice Proceedings Section 10118.6) and select the appropriate pattern language relevant to the circumstances of the case. The *Collyer* and *Dubo* deferral letter templates in NxGen have been updated accordingly.

merit.[49] Once an arbitration award issues, the Region should assess it under *Babcock*.

Next, if the statutory right is not incorporated in the contract, the Region should ask both parties if they will authorize the arbitrator to decide the unfair labor practice. If the parties so authorize, the Region should obtain such commitments in writing and place the case on administrative deferral, provided all of the other *Collyer* requirements are met and there is arguable merit. Once an arbitration award issues, the Region should assess it under *Babcock*.

Finally, if the statutory right is not incorporated in the contract and one or both parties refuse to authorize arbitration of the unfair labor practice, how the case should be processed will depend on whether the applicable contract was executed before or after December 15, 2014, the date the *Babcock* decision issued. If the contract was executed on or before that date, the Region should place the case on administrative deferral, provided that *Collyer* requirements are met and there is arguable merit. Once an arbitration award issues, the Region should assess it under *Olin*. After placing the case on deferral, if the Region learns that the parties have subsequently agreed to authorize arbitration of the unfair labor practice, the Region should keep the case on administrative deferral, but apply *Babcock* once an award issues. If the contract was executed after December 15, 2014, the Region should conduct a full investigation of the merits and issue complaint or dismiss the charge accordingly. If, after issuing complaint, the Region learns that the parties have subsequently agreed to authorize arbitration of the unfair labor practice, the Region should place the case on administrative deferral and apply *Babcock* once an award issues.[50]

[49] Arguable merit should be determined based on affidavits from the charging party and witnesses within that party's control. At the Region's discretion, it may wish to undertake a more complete investigation before deciding whether to defer.

[50] *Babcock* did not change Board law finding *Collyer* deferral inappropriate where an allegation is "inextricably related" to or "closely intertwined" with "'other complaint allegations that are either inappropriate for deferral or for which deferral is not sought.'" *Arvinmeritor, Inc.*, 340 NLRB 1035, 1035 n.1 (2003) (quoting *American Commercial Lines*, 291 NLRB 1066, 1069 (1988), *overruled on other grounds by J. E. Brown Electric*, 315 NLRB 620 (1994)). *See also Clarkson Industries*, 312 NLRB 349, 351-52 (1993) (declining deferral as to "closely related" allegations where arbitrator lacked authority to fashion an appropriate remedy as to one). Thus, the Region should decline to place a Section 8(a)(5) allegation on *Collyer* deferral if it is closely related to a meritorious Section 8(a)(1) or (3) allegation that is non-deferrable (e.g., because *Babcock* applies and the parties have not authorized arbitration of the Section 8(a)(1) or (3) issue). Where a charge concerns allegations of Section 8(a)(1), (3), and (5), the *Babcock* standard applies to the 8(a)(1) and (3) allegations and the parties have authorized the arbitrator to

IV. Deferral to Grievance Settlements

A. The *Babcock* Standard

Under *Babcock*, the Board will apply essentially the same deferral standard to grievance settlements as it does to arbitral decisions in Section 8(a)(1) and (3) cases. In such cases, it must be shown that: (1) the parties intended to settle the unfair labor practice issue; (2) they addressed that issue in the settlement agreement; and (3) Board law reasonably permits the settlement agreement.[51] In assessing whether the negotiated settlement is reasonably permitted, the Board will assess the agreement in light of the factors applicable to other non-Board settlement agreements, as set forth in *Independent Stave Co.*[52]

CASEHANDLING INSTRUCTIONS: So long as a grievance settlement is satisfactory under *Independent Stave*, the Region may accept a charging party's request for withdrawal of a charge in cases with arguable merit, since such a request suggests an intent to settle the unfair labor practice and prosecution would not effectuate the purposes of the Act. Any merit cases where the charging party does not withdraw the charge following settlement of the grievance, or where a discriminatee objects to the withdrawal, should be submitted to the Division of Advice with recommendations regarding whether the parties intended that the settlement would resolve the unfair labor practice issue, whether the settlement agreement addresses that issue, and whether the agreement meets the requirements of *Independent Stave*.

B. Application of the *Babcock* Grievance Settlement Deferral Standard to Pending and Future Cases

address the statutory issue, Regions should contact the Division of Advice for instructions on how to proceed.

[51] 361 NLRB No. 132, slip op. at 13.

[52] 287 NLRB 740, 743 (1987). The Board in *Independent Stave* identified the following non-exclusive list of factors to consider in evaluating settlements: (1) whether all parties involved agreed to be bound by the non-Board settlement; (2) whether the proposed settlement is reasonable in light of the alleged violation, the risks of litigation, and the stage of litigation; (3) whether there is any indication of fraud, coercion or duress regarding the parties' settlement; and (4) whether the respondent has a history of violations or of breaching previous settlement agreements resolving unfair labor practices.

Although the Board did not articulate whether the new grievance settlement deferral standard would apply retroactively or prospectively, we assume that the policy considerations informing the Board's nuanced approach toward postarbitral deferral apply equally to the grievance settlement context. Thus, we infer that the new standard for evaluating grievance settlements should apply in parallel fashion as the new standard for reviewing arbitral awards, and should apply in all cases where *Babcock* would have applied had the parties proceeded to arbitration. The Region should apply the following rules to determine whether to evaluate a grievance settlement under *Babcock* or the pre-*Babcock* deferral standard set forth in *Alpha Beta Co.*[53] in pending and future cases raising allegations under Section 8(a)(1) and (3):

- *Alpha Beta* applies if the settlement agreement was executed on or before December 15, 2014, the date the *Babcock* decision issued;

- *Babcock* applies if the collective-bargaining agreement under which the grievance arose was executed after December 15, 2014.[54]

- If the collective-bargaining agreement under which the grievance arose was executed on or before December 15, 2014, and the grievance settlement was executed after December 15, 2014, which standard applies depends on whether the parties intended to resolve the unfair labor practice issue via arbitration or settlement. If the arbitrator was explicitly authorized to decide the unfair labor practice issue (either in the collective-bargaining agreement or by agreement of the parties in a particular case), or the parties intended to settle that issue, then *Babcock* applies.[55] As with postarbitral deferral, any questions about whether a

[53] 273 NLRB 1546, 1547 (1985), *enforced sub nom. Mahon v. NLRB*, 808 F.2d 1342 (9th Cir. 1987). *See also Postal* Service, 300 NLRB 196, 197 (1990).

[54] As with postarbitral deferral, we would likewise apply *Babcock* if the grievance arose under a collective-bargaining agreement that automatically renewed after December 15, 2014 because neither party took action to reopen negotiations pursuant to a contractual renewal clause. Similarly, we would apply *Babcock* if the grievance arose under a post-*Babcock* agreement to extend an expired contract for a set term, unless the extension was a temporary one for the purpose of allowing the parties to continue bargaining over a successor collective-bargaining agreement. In that case, which standard applies depends on whether the arbitrator was explicitly authorized to decide the unfair labor practice.

[55] *Babcock* applies in this scenario even if the Region initially placed the case on administrative deferral pursuant to the preexisting standard for prearbitral deferral.

specific statutory right has been incorporated into the agreement should be submitted to the Division of Advice. If the arbitrator was not authorized to resolve the statutory issue, and the parties did not intend to settle it, then *Alpha Beta* applies.

Any questions regarding the implementation of this memorandum should be directed to the Division of Advice.

Attachments:
1. Letter – to be sent in all currently deferred cases
2. a. *Collyer* deferral letter – *Spielberg/Olin* and *Alpha Beta* apply
   b. *Collyer* deferral letter – *Babcock* applies
   c. *Dubo* deferral letter – *Spielberg/Olin* and *Alpha Beta* apply
   d. *Dubo* deferral letter – *Babcock* applies

cc: NLRBU
Release to the Public

MEMORANDUM GC 15

Attachment 1 to Memorandum GC 15-02

[address to all parties]

Greetings:

On [insert date] the subject charge was deferred to the parties' grievance/arbitration procedures. On December 15, 2014, the Board issued its decision in *Babcock & Wilcox Construction Co.*, 361 NLRB No. 132 (2014), which altered the standards the Board will use going forward in assessing whether to defer to grievance settlements, arbitration awards, and the grievance-arbitration procedure. In this case, if the parties have explicitly agreed that the statutory issue will be considered by the arbitrator or the parties have a clause in their collective bargaining agreement to that effect, the new deferral standards enunciated in *Babcock & Wilcox* will apply. Absent that exception, the Board will use the existing standards described by *Spielberg Manufacturing Company*, 112 NLRB 1080 (1955) and *Olin Corp.*, 268 NLRB 573 (1984) (arbitration awards) and *Alpha Beta*, 273 NLRB 1546 (1985) (grievance settlements),

On February 10, 2015, the Agency's General Counsel issued a guideline memorandum instructing Regions on how to apply these new standards going forward. That guideline memorandum is available online from our Agency's web-site at www.nlrb.gov, or may be accessed from a mobile device with a QR code scanning app, by scanning the following code:

If you wish to have a hard copy of the guideline memorandum mailed to you, please contact this office.

The subject charge remains in deferred status and no action is required from you at this time. The purpose of this letter is keep you informed regarding these developments, which may impact this office's processing of your case at a later time. Please contact [insert name, contact number, and e-mail address of agent assigned to the case *or* Region's designated point person for such inquiries] if you have questions.

Very truly yours,

/s/ Regional Director

Memorandum GC 15-02, Attachment 2.a

The Region has carefully considered the charge alleging that [name of Charged Party] violated the National Labor Relations Act. As explained below, I have decided that further proceedings on the charge should be handled in accordance with the deferral policy of the National Labor Relations Board as set forth in *Collyer Insulated Wire*, 192 NLRB 837 (1971), and *United Technologies Corp.*, 268 NLRB 557 (1984). This letter explains that deferral policy, the reasons for my decision to defer further processing of the charge, and the Charging Party's right to appeal my decision.

Deferral Policy: The Board's deferral policy provides that the Board will postpone making a final determination on a charge when a grievance involving the same issue can be processed under the grievance/arbitration provision of the applicable contract. This policy is partially based on the preference that the parties use their contractual grievance procedure to achieve a prompt, fair, and effective settlement of their disputes. Therefore, if an employer agrees to waive contractual time limits and process the related grievance through arbitration if necessary, the Board's Regional Office will defer the charge.

Decision to Defer: Based on our investigation, I am deferring further proceedings on the charge in this matter to the grievance/arbitration process for the following reasons:

1. The Employer and the Union have a collective-bargaining agreement currently in effect that provides for final and binding arbitration.

2. The **[insert description of each issue being deferred]** as alleged in the charge **[is/are]** encompassed by the terms of the collective-bargaining agreement.

3. The Employer is willing to process a grievance concerning the issues in the charge, and will arbitrate the grievance if necessary. The Employer has also agreed to waive any time limitations in order to ensure that the arbitrator addresses the merits of the dispute.

4. Since the issues in the charge appear to be covered by provisions of the collective-bargaining agreement, it is likely that the issues may be resolved through the grievance/arbitration procedure.

Further Processing of the Charge: As explained below, while the charge is deferred, the Regional office will monitor the processing of the grievance and, under certain circumstances, will resume processing of the charge.

Charging Party's Obligation: Under the Board's *Collyer* deferral policy, the Charging Party has an affirmative obligation to file a grievance, if a grievance has not already been filed. If the Charging Party fails either to promptly submit the grievance to the grievance/arbitration process or declines to have the grievance arbitrated if it is not resolved, I may dismiss the charge.

Union/Employer Conduct: If the Union or Employer fails to promptly process the grievance under the grievance/arbitration process; declines to arbitrate the grievance if it is not resolved; or if a conflict develops between the interests of the Union and the Charging Party, I may revoke deferral and resume processing of the charge.

Charged Party's Conduct: If the Charged Party prevents or impedes resolution of the grievance, raises a defense that the grievance is untimely filed, or refuses to arbitrate the grievance, I will revoke deferral and resume processing of the charge.

Monitoring the Dispute: Approximately every 90 days, the Regional Office will ask the parties about the status of this dispute to determine if the dispute has been resolved and if continued deferral is appropriate. However, at any time, a party may present evidence and request dismissal of the charge, continued deferral of the charge, or issuance of a complaint.

Notice to Arbitrator Form: If the grievance is submitted to an arbitrator, please sign and submit to the arbitrator the enclosed "Notice to Arbitrator" form to ensure that the Region receives a copy of an arbitration award when the arbitrator sends the award to the parties.

Review of Arbitrator's Award or Settlement: If the grievance is arbitrated or settled, the Charging Party may ask the Board to review the arbitrator's award or settlement. The request must be in writing and addressed to me. If the request concerns an arbitrator's award, the request should analyze whether the arbitration process was fair and regular, whether the unfair labor practice allegations in the charge were considered by the arbitrator, and whether the award is consistent with the Act. Further guidance on this review is provided in *Spielberg Manufacturing Company*, 112 NLRB 1080 (1955) and *Olin Corp.*, 268 NLRB 573 (1984). If the request concerns a grievance settlement, see *Alpha Beta*, 273 NLRB 1546 (1985). These Board decisions are available on our website, www.nlrb.gov.

Change in Standards if Parties Agree to Submit Statutory Issue to Arbitrator: If during the processing of the grievance the parties agree to authorize the arbitrator to decide the statutory issue, please advise me in writing.

Charging Party's Right to Appeal: The Charging Party may appeal my decision to defer this charge by filing an appeal with the General Counsel of the National Labor Relations Board, through the Office of Appeals. An appeal may be filed by submitting the enclosed Appeal Form (form NLRB-4767), which is also available at www.nlrb.gov. However, we encourage the Charging Party to submit a complete statement setting forth the facts and reasons why the decision to defer the charge is incorrect.

Means of Filing: An appeal may be filed electronically, by mail, by delivery service, or hand-delivered. Filing an appeal electronically is preferred but not required. The appeal MAY NOT be filed by fax or email. To file an appeal electronically, go to the Agency's website at www.nlrb.gov, click on **E-File Documents,** enter the **NLRB Case Number**, and follow the detailed instructions. To file an appeal by mail or delivery service, address the appeal to the **General Counsel** at the **National Labor Relations Board, Attn: Office of Appeals, 1099 14th Street, N.W., Washington,**

D.C. 20570-0001. Unless filed electronically, a copy of the appeal should also be sent to me.

     Appeal Due Date and Time: The appeal is due on [date populates]. If the appeal is filed electronically, the transmission of the entire document through the Agency's website must be completed **no later than 11:59 p.m. Eastern Time** on the due date. If filing by mail or by delivery service an appeal will be found to be timely filed if it is postmarked or given to a delivery service no later than . **If an appeal is postmarked or given to a delivery service on the due date, it will be rejected as untimely**. If hand delivered, an appeal must be received by the General Counsel in Washington D.C. by 5:00 p.m. Eastern Time on the appeal due date. If an appeal is not submitted in accordance with this paragraph, it will be rejected.

     Extension of Time to File Appeal: The General Counsel may allow additional time to file the appeal if the Charging Party provides a good reason for doing so and the request for an extension of time is **received on or before** [date populates]. The request may be filed electronically through the **E-File Documents** link on our website www.nlrb.gov, by fax to (202)273-4283, by mail, or by delivery service. The General Counsel will not consider any request for an extension of time to file an appeal received after , **even if it is postmarked or given to the delivery service before the due date**. Unless filed electronically, a copy of the extension of time should also be sent to me.

     Confidentiality: We will not honor any claim of confidentiality or privilege or any limitations on our use of appeal statements or supporting evidence beyond those prescribed by the Federal Records Act and the Freedom of Information Act (FOIA). Thus, we may disclose an appeal statement to a party upon request during the processing of the appeal. If the appeal is successful, any statement or material submitted with the appeal may be introduced as evidence at a hearing before an administrative law judge. Because the Federal Records Act requires us to keep copies of case handling documents for some years after a case closes, we may be required by the FOIA to disclose those documents absent an applicable exemption such as those that protect confidential sources, commercial/financial information, or personal privacy interests.

The Region has carefully considered the charge alleging that [name of Charged Party] violated the National Labor Relations Act. As explained below, I have decided that further proceedings on the charge should be handled in accordance with the deferral policy of the National Labor Relations Board as set forth in *Collyer Insulated Wire*, 192 NLRB 837 (1971), and *United Technologies Corp.*, 268 NLRB 557 (1984). This letter explains that deferral policy, the reasons for my decision to defer further processing of the charge, and the Charging Party's right to appeal my decision.

Deferral Policy: The Board's deferral policy provides that the Board will postpone making a final determination on a charge when a grievance involving the same issue can be processed under the grievance/arbitration provision of the applicable contract. This policy is partially based on the preference that the parties use their contractual grievance procedure to achieve a prompt, fair, and effective settlement of their disputes. Therefore, if an employer agrees to waive contractual time limits and process the related grievance through arbitration if necessary, the Board's Regional Office will defer the charge.

Decision to Defer: Based on our investigation, I am deferring further proceedings on the charge in this matter to the grievance/arbitration process for the following reasons:

1.   The Employer and the Union have a collective-bargaining agreement currently in effect that provides for final and binding arbitration.

2.   The **[insert description of each issue being deferred]** as alleged in the charge **[is/are]** encompassed by the terms of the collective-bargaining agreement.

3.   The Employer is willing to process a grievance concerning the issues in the charge, and will arbitrate the grievance if necessary. The Employer has also agreed to waive any time limitations in order to ensure that the arbitrator addresses the merits of the dispute.

4.   Since the issues in the charge appear to be covered by provisions of the collective-bargaining agreement, it is likely that the issues may be resolved through the grievance/arbitration procedure.

Further Processing of the Charge: As explained below, while the charge is deferred, the Regional office will monitor the processing of the grievance and, under certain circumstances, will resume processing of the charge.

      Charging Party's Obligation: Under the Board's *Collyer* deferral policy, the Charging Party has an affirmative obligation to file a grievance, if a grievance has not already been filed. If the Charging Party fails either to promptly submit the grievance to the grievance/arbitration process or declines to have the grievance arbitrated if it is not resolved, I may dismiss the charge.

      Union/Employer Conduct: If the Union or Employer fails to promptly process the grievance under the grievance/arbitration process; declines to arbitrate the grievance if it is not resolved; or if a conflict develops between the interests of the Union and the Charging Party, I may revoke deferral and resume processing of the charge.

Charged Party's Conduct: If the Charged Party prevents or impedes resolution of the grievance, raises a defense that the grievance is untimely filed, or refuses to arbitrate the grievance, I will revoke deferral and resume processing of the charge.

Monitoring the Dispute: Approximately every 90 days, the Regional Office will ask the parties about the status of this dispute to determine if the dispute has been resolved and if continued deferral is appropriate. However, at any time, a party may present evidence and request dismissal of the charge, continued deferral of the charge, or issuance of a complaint.

Notice to Arbitrator Form: If the grievance is submitted to an arbitrator, please sign and submit to the arbitrator the enclosed "Notice to Arbitrator" form to ensure that the Region receives a copy of an arbitration award when the arbitrator sends the award to the parties.

Review of Arbitrator's Award: If the grievance is arbitrated, the Charging Party may ask the Board to review the arbitrator's award. The request must be in writing and addressed to me. Because the parties have explicitly authorized the arbitrator to decide the statutory issue in this case, the Board's deferral standards applicable in this case are those set forth in *Babcock & Wilcox Construction Co.*, 361 NLRB No. 132 (2014), which is available on our website, www.nlrb.gov. Any request for review of an arbitrator's award should analyze (1) whether the parties explicitly authorized the arbitrator to decide the statutory issue; (2) whether the arbitrator was presented with and considered the statutory issue, or was prevented from doing so by the party opposing deferral; and (3) whether Board law reasonably permits the award. The party urging deferral has the burden to prove these standards are met.

Review of Grievance Settlement: If the grievance is settled, the Charging Party may ask the Board to review the grievance settlement. The Board's deferral standards applicable to any grievance settlement in this case are also set forth in *Babcock & Wilcox Construction Co.*, 361 NLRB No. 132 (2014). Any request for review of a grievance settlement should analyze (1) whether the parties intended to settle the unfair labor practice issue; (2) whether the parties addressed the statutory issue in the settlement; and (3) whether Board law reasonably permits the grievance settlement agreement. The party urging deferral has the burden to prove these standards are met. In assessing whether to defer to the settlement, I will also consider the factors identified by the Board in *Independent Stave Co.*, 287 NLRB 740, 743 (1987).

Charging Party's Right to Appeal: The Charging Party may appeal my decision to defer this charge by filing an appeal with the General Counsel of the National Labor Relations Board, through the Office of Appeals. An appeal may be filed by submitting the enclosed Appeal Form (form NLRB-4767), which is also available at www.nlrb.gov. However, we encourage the Charging Party to submit a complete statement setting forth the facts and reasons why the decision to defer the charge is incorrect.

Means of Filing: An appeal may be filed electronically, by mail, by delivery service, or hand-delivered. Filing an appeal electronically is preferred but not required. The appeal <u>MAY NOT</u> be filed by fax or email. To file an appeal electronically, go to the Agency's website at www.nlrb.gov, click on **E-File Documents,** enter the **NLRB Case Number**, and follow the detailed instructions. To file an appeal by mail or delivery service, address the appeal to the **General Counsel** at the **National Labor Relations Board, Attn: Office of Appeals, 1099 14th Street, N.W., Washington, D.C. 20570-0001**. Unless filed electronically, a copy of the appeal should also be sent to me.

Appeal Due Date and Time: The appeal is due on [date populates]. If the appeal is filed electronically, the transmission of the entire document through the Agency's website must be completed **no later than 11:59 p.m. Eastern Time** on the due date. If filing by mail or by delivery service an appeal will be found to be timely filed if it is postmarked or given to a delivery service no later than . **If an appeal is postmarked or given to a delivery service on the due date, it will be rejected as untimely**. If hand delivered, an appeal must be received by the General Counsel in Washington D.C. by 5:00 p.m. Eastern Time on the appeal due date. If an appeal is not submitted in accordance with this paragraph, it will be rejected.

Extension of Time to File Appeal: The General Counsel may allow additional time to file the appeal if the Charging Party provides a good reason for doing so and the request for an extension of time is **received on or before** [date populates]. The request may be filed electronically through the *E-File Documents* link on our website www.nlrb.gov, by fax to (202)273-4283, by mail, or by delivery service. The General Counsel will not consider any request for an extension of time to file an appeal received after , **even if it is postmarked or given to the delivery service before the due date**. Unless filed electronically, a copy of the extension of time should also be sent to me.

Confidentiality: We will not honor any claim of confidentiality or privilege or any limitations on our use of appeal statements or supporting evidence beyond those prescribed by the Federal Records Act and the Freedom of Information Act (FOIA). Thus, we may disclose an appeal statement to a party upon request during the processing of the appeal. If the appeal is successful, any statement or material submitted with the appeal may be introduced as evidence at a hearing before an administrative law judge. Because the Federal Records Act requires us to keep copies of case handling documents for some years after a case closes, we may be required by the FOIA to disclose those documents absent an applicable exemption such as those that protect confidential sources, commercial/financial information, or personal privacy interests.

The Region has investigated the charge filed against [name of Charged Party] alleging it violated the National Labor Relations Act. As explained below, I have decided to defer further processing of the charge.

Decision to Defer: The investigation disclosed that the principal issues in this case are the subject of a grievance filed pursuant to the grievance/arbitration procedures established by the collective-bargaining agreement between the Employer and . Accordingly, I have concluded that deferral of those issues to the grievance/arbitration process is warranted since it appears there is a substantial likelihood that this process will resolve the issues raised by the charge. See *Dubo Manufacturing Corporation*, 142 NLRB 431 (1963).

Monitoring the Dispute: Approximately every 90 days, the Regional Office will ask the parties about the status of this dispute to determine if the dispute has been resolved and if continued deferral is appropriate. However, at any time a party may present evidence and request resumed processing of the charge.

Notice to Arbitrator Form: If the grievance is submitted to an arbitrator, please sign and submit to the arbitrator the enclosed "Notice to Arbitrator" form to ensure that the Region receives a copy of an arbitration award when the arbitrator sends the award to the parties.

Review of Arbitrator's Award or Settlement: If the grievance is arbitrated or settled, the Charging Party may ask the Board to review the arbitrator's award or settlement. The request must be in writing and addressed to me. If the request concerns an arbitrator's award, the request should analyze whether the arbitration process was fair and regular, whether the unfair labor practice allegations in the charge were considered by the arbitrator, and whether the award is consistent with the Act. Further guidance on this review is provided in *Spielberg Manufacturing Company*, 112 NLRB 1080 (1955) and *Olin Corp.*, 268 NLRB 573 (1984). If the request concerns a grievance settlement, see *Alpha Beta*, 273 NLRB 1546 (1985). These Board decisions are available on our website, www.nlrb.gov.

Change in Standards if Parties Agree to Submit Statutory Issue to Arbitrator: If during the processing of the grievance the parties agree to authorize the arbitrator to decide the statutory issue, please advise me in writing.

The Region has investigated the charge filed against [name of Charged Party] alleging it violated the National Labor Relations Act. As explained below, I have decided to defer further processing of the charge.

Decision to Defer: The investigation disclosed that the principal issues in this case are the subject of a grievance filed pursuant to the grievance/arbitration procedures established by the collective-bargaining agreement between the Employer and . Accordingly, I have concluded that deferral of those issues to the grievance/arbitration process is warranted since it appears there is a substantial likelihood that this process will resolve the issues raised by the charge. See *Dubo Manufacturing Corporation*, 142 NLRB 431 (1963).

Monitoring the Dispute: Approximately every 90 days, the Regional Office will ask the parties about the status of this dispute to determine if the dispute has been resolved and if continued deferral is appropriate. However, at any time a party may present evidence and request resumed processing of the charge.

Notice to Arbitrator Form: If the grievance is submitted to an arbitrator, please sign and submit to the arbitrator the enclosed "Notice to Arbitrator" form to ensure that the Region receives a copy of an arbitration award when the arbitrator sends the award to the parties.

Review of Arbitrator's Award: If the grievance is arbitrated, the Charging Party may ask the Board to review the arbitrator's award. The request must be in writing and addressed to me. Because the parties have explicitly authorized the arbitrator to decide the statutory issue in this case, the Board's deferral standards applicable in this case are those set forth in *Babcock & Wilcox Construction Co.*, 361 NLRB No. 132 (2014), which is available on our website, www.nlrb.gov. Any request for review of an arbitrator's award should analyze (1) whether the parties explicitly authorized the arbitrator to decide the statutory issue; (2) whether the arbitrator was presented with and considered the statutory issue, or was prevented from doing so by the party opposing deferral; and (3) whether Board law reasonably permits the award. The party urging deferral has the burden to prove these standards are met.

Review of Grievance Settlement: If the grievance is settled, the Charging Party may ask the Board to review the grievance settlement. The Board's deferral standards applicable to any grievance settlement in this case are also set forth in *Babcock & Wilcox Construction Co.*, 361 NLRB No. 132 (2014). Any request for review of a grievance settlement should analyze (1) whether the parties intended to settle the unfair labor practice issue; (2) whether the parties addressed the statutory issue in the settlement; and (3) whether Board law reasonably permits the grievance settlement agreement. The party urging deferral has the burden to prove these standards are met. In assessing whether to defer to the settlement, I will also consider the factors identified by the Board in *Independent Stave Co.*, 287 NLRB 740, 743 (1987).

WHICH DEFERRAL STANDARD TO APPLY

Babcock & Wilcox Construction Co. OR *Spielberg/Olin & Alpha Beta*

What Section of the Act is alleged to have been violated?

- 8(a)(5)
- 8(a)(1) or (3)

Did/will arbitration hearing or grievance settlement occur after 12/15/14*?

- No
- Yes

Was applicable CBA executed after 12/15/14*?

- No
- Yes

Is specific statutory right at issue incorporated into CBA?

- No
- Yes

Have parties specially agreed in writing that arbitrator is authorized to decide statutory issue or that settlement will resolve issue?

- No
- Yes

Use *Spielberg/Olin* and *Alpha Beta* letter and standards

Use *Babcock* letter and standards

*Issuance date of *Babcock & Wilcox Construction Co.*, 361 NLRB No. 132

Flowchart: Whether to apply *Babcock & Wilcox Construction Co.* or *Spielberg/Olin* and *Alpha Beta*

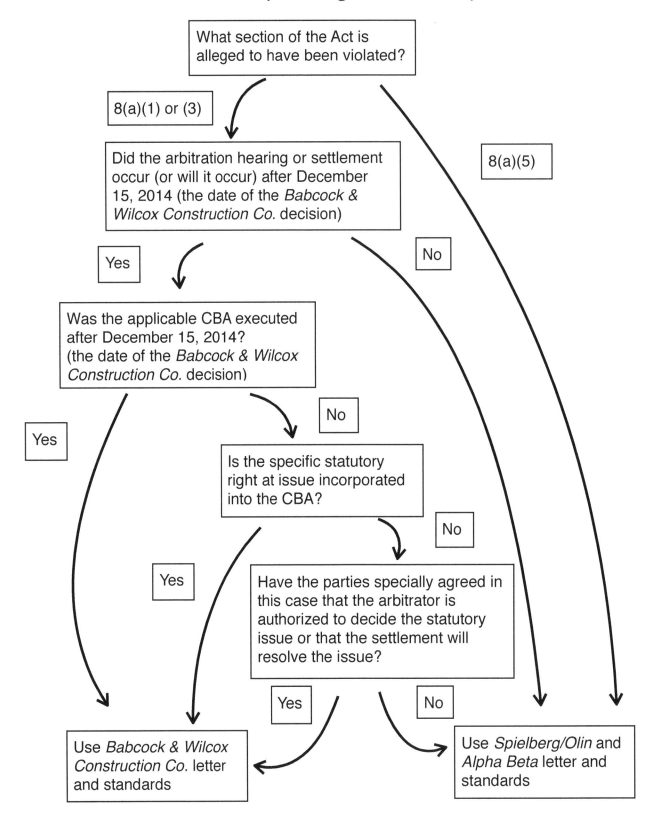

OFFICE OF THE GENERAL COUNSEL

MEMORANDUM GC 15- 04   March 18, 2015

TO: All Regional Directors, Officers-in-Charge,
              and Resident Officers

FROM: Richard F. Griffin, Jr., General Counsel

SUBJECT: Report of the General Counsel
               Concerning Employer Rules

      Attached is a report from the General Counsel concerning recent employer rule cases.

Attachment

cc: NLRBU
Release to the Public

MEMORANDUM GC 15-04

Report of the General Counsel

During my term as General Counsel, I have endeavored to keep the labor-management bar fully aware of the activities of my Office. As part of this goal, I continue the practice of issuing periodic reports of cases raising significant legal or policy issues. This report presents recent case developments arising in the context of employee handbook rules. Although I believe that most employers do not draft their employee handbooks with the object of prohibiting or restricting conduct protected by the National Labor Relations Act, the law does not allow even well-intentioned rules that would inhibit employees from engaging in activities protected by the Act. Moreover, the Office of the General Counsel continues to receive meritorious charges alleging unlawful handbook rules. I am publishing this report to offer guidance on my views of this evolving area of labor law, with the hope that it will help employers to review their handbooks and other rules, and conform them, if necessary, to ensure that they are lawful.

Under the Board's decision in *Lutheran Heritage Village-Livonia,* 343 NLRB 646 (2004), the mere maintenance of a work rule may violate Section 8(a)(1) of the Act if the rule has a chilling effect on employees' Section 7 activity. The most obvious way a rule would violate Section 8(a)(1) is by explicitly restricting protected concerted activity; by banning union activity, for example. Even if a rule does not explicitly prohibit Section 7 activity, however, it will still be found unlawful if 1) employees would reasonably construe the rule's language to prohibit Section 7 activity; 2) the rule was promulgated in response to union or other Section 7 activity; or 3) the rule was actually applied to restrict the exercise of Section 7 rights.

In our experience, the vast majority of violations are found under the first prong of the *Lutheran Heritage* test. The Board has issued a number of decisions interpreting whether "employees would reasonably construe" employer rules to prohibit Section 7 activity, finding various rules to be unlawful under that standard. I have had conversations with both labor- and management-side practitioners, who have asked for guidance regarding handbook rules that are deemed acceptable under this prong of the Board's test. Thus, I am issuing this report.

This report is divided into two parts. First, the report will compare rules we found unlawful with rules we found lawful and explain our reasoning. This section will focus on the types of rules that are frequently at issue before us, such as confidentiality rules, professionalism rules, anti-harassment rules, trademark rules, photography/recording rules, and media contact rules. Second, the report will discuss handbook rules from a recently settled unfair labor practice charge against Wendy's International LLC. The settlement was negotiated following our initial determination that several of Wendy's handbook rules were facially unlawful. The report sets forth Wendy's rules that we initially found unlawful with an explanation, along with Wendy's modified rules, adopted pursuant to a informal, bilateral Board settlement agreement, which the Office of the General Counsel does not believe violate the Act.

I hope that this report, with its specific examples of lawful and unlawful handbook policies and rules, will be of assistance to labor law practitioners and human resource professionals.

Richard F. Griffin, Jr.
General Counsel

Part 1: Examples of Lawful and Unlawful Handbook Rules

A.   Employer Handbook Rules Regarding Confidentiality

Employees have a Section 7 right to discuss wages, hours, and other terms and conditions of employment with fellow employees, as well as with nonemployees, such as union representatives. Thus, an employer's confidentiality policy that either specifically prohibits employee discussions of terms and conditions of employment—such as wages, hours, or workplace complaints—or that employees would reasonably understand to prohibit such discussions, violates the Act. Similarly, a confidentiality rule that broadly encompasses "employee" or "personnel" information, without further clarification, will reasonably be construed by employees to restrict Section 7-protected communications. *See Flamingo-Hilton Laughlin*, 330 NLRB 287, 288 n.3, 291–92 (1999).

In contrast, broad prohibitions on disclosing "confidential" information are lawful so long as they do not reference information regarding employees or anything that would reasonably be considered a term or condition of employment, because employers have a substantial and legitimate interest in maintaining the privacy of certain business information. *See Lafayette Park Hotel*, 326 NLRB 824, 826 (1998), *enforced*, 203 F.3d 52 (D.C. Cir. 1999); *Super K-Mart*, 330 NLRB 263, 263 (1999). Furthermore, an otherwise unlawful confidentiality rule will be found lawful if, when viewed in context, employees would not reasonably understand the rule to prohibit Section 7 protected activity.

Unlawful Confidentiality Rules

We found the following rules to be unlawful because they restrict disclosure of employee information and therefore are unlawfully overbroad:

- **Do not discuss "customer or employee information" outside of work, including "phone numbers [and] addresses."**

In the above rule, in addition to the overbroad reference to "employee information," the blanket ban on discussing employee contact information, without regard for how employees obtain that information, is also facially unlawful.

- **"You must not disclose proprietary or confidential information about [the Employer, or] other associates (if the proprietary or confidential** information relating to [the Employer's] associates was obtained in violation of law or lawful Company policy)."

Although this rule's restriction on disclosing information about "other associates" is not a blanket ban, it is nonetheless unlawfully overbroad because a reasonable employee would not understand how the employer determines what constitutes a "lawful Company policy."

- **"Never publish or disclose [the Employer's] or another's confidential or other proprietary information. Never publish or report on conversations that are meant to be private or internal to [the Employer]."**

While an employer may clearly ban disclosure of its own confidential information, a broad reference to "another's" information, without further clarification, as in the above rule, would reasonably be interpreted to include other *employees'* wages and other terms and conditions of employment.

We determined that the following confidentiality rules were facially unlawful, even though they did not explicitly reference terms and conditions of employment or employee information, because the rules contained broad restrictions and did not clarify, in express language or contextually, that they did not restrict Section 7 communications:

- **Prohibiting employees from "[d]isclosing . . . details about the [Employer]."**

- **"Sharing of [overheard conversations at the work site] with your co-workers, the public, or anyone outside of your immediate work group is strictly prohibited."**

- **"Discuss work matters only with other [Employer] employees who have a specific business reason to know or have access to such information. . . . Do not discuss work matters in public places."**

- **"[I]f something is not public information, you must not share it."**

Because the rule directly above bans discussion of all non-public information, we concluded that employees would reasonably understand it to encompass such non-public information as employee wages, benefits, and other terms and conditions of employment.

- **Confidential Information is: "All information in which its [sic] loss, undue use or unauthorized disclosure could adversely affect the [Employer's] interests, image and reputation or compromise personal and private information of its members."**

Employees not only have a Section 7 right to protest their wages and working conditions, but also have a right to share information in support of those complaints. This rule would reasonably lead employees to believe that they cannot disclose that kind of information because it might adversely affect the employer's interest, image, or reputation.

<u>Lawful Confidentiality Rules</u>

We concluded that the following rules that prohibit disclosure of confidential information were facially lawful because: 1) they do not reference information regarding employees or employee terms and conditions of employment, 2) although they use the general term "confidential," they do not define it in an overbroad manner, and 3) they do not otherwise contain language that would reasonably be construed to prohibit Section 7 communications:

- **No unauthorized disclosure of "business 'secrets' or other confidential information."**

- **"Misuse or unauthorized disclosure of confidential information not otherwise available to persons or firms outside [Employer] is cause for disciplinary action, including termination."**

- **"Do not disclose confidential financial data, or other non-public proprietary company information. Do not share confidential information regarding business partners, vendors or customers."**

Finally, even when a confidentiality policy contains overly broad language, the rule will be found lawful if, when viewed in context, employees would not reasonably understand the rule to prohibit Section 7-protected activity. The following confidentiality rule, which we found lawful based on a contextual analysis, well illustrates this principle:

- **Prohibition on disclosure of all "information acquired in the course of one's work."**

This rule uses expansive language that, when read in isolation, would reasonably be read to define employee wages and benefits as confidential information. However, in that case, the rule was nested among rules relating to conflicts of interest and compliance with SEC regulations and state and federal laws. Thus, we determined that employees would reasonably understand the information described as encompassing customer credit cards, contracts, and trade secrets, and not Section 7-protected activity.

B.   Employer Handbook Rules Regarding Employee Conduct toward the Company and Supervisors

Employees also have the Section 7 right to criticize or protest their employer's labor policies or treatment of employees. Thus, rules that can reasonably be read to prohibit protected concerted criticism of the employer will be found unlawfully overbroad. For instance, a rule that prohibits employees from engaging in "disrespectful," "negative," "inappropriate," or "rude" conduct towards the employer or management, absent sufficient clarification or context, will usually be found unlawful. *See Casino San Pablo*, 361 NLRB No. 148, slip op. at 3 (Dec. 16, 2014). Moreover, employee criticism of an employer will not lose the Act's protection simply because the criticism is false or defamatory, so a rule that bans false statements will be found unlawfully overbroad unless it specifies that only maliciously false statements are prohibited. *Id.* at 4. On the other hand, a rule that requires employees to be respectful and professional to coworkers, clients, or competitors, but not the employer or management, will generally be found lawful, because employers have a legitimate business interest in having employees act professionally and courteously in their dealings with coworkers, customers, employer business partners, and other third parties. In addition, rules prohibiting conduct that amounts to insubordination would also not be construed as limiting protected activities. *See Copper River of Boiling Springs, LLC*, 360 NLRB No. 60 (Feb. 28, 2014). Also, rules that employees would reasonably understand to prohibit insubordinate conduct have been found lawful.

Unlawful Rules Regulating Employee Conduct towards the Employer

We found the following rules unlawfully overbroad since employees reasonably would construe them to ban protected criticism or protests regarding their supervisors, management, or the employer in general.

- **"[B]e respectful to the company, other employees, customers, partners, and competitors."**

- **Do "not make fun of, denigrate, or defame your co-workers, customers, franchisees, suppliers, the Company, or our competitors."**

- **"Be respectful of others and the Company."**

- **No "[d]efamatory, libelous, slanderous or discriminatory comments about [the Company], its customers and/or competitors, its employees or management.**

While the following two rules ban "insubordination," they also ban conduct that does not rise to the level of insubordination, which reasonably would be understood as including protected concerted activity. Accordingly, we found these rules to be unlawful.

- **"Disrespectful conduct or insubordination, including, but not limited to, refusing to follow orders from a supervisor or a designated representative."**

- **"Chronic resistance to proper work-related orders or discipline, even though not overt insubordination" will result in discipline.**

In addition, employees' right to criticize an employer's labor policies and treatment of employees includes the right to do so in a public forum. *See Quicken Loans, Inc.*, 361 NLRB No. 94, slip op. at 1 n.1 (Nov. 3, 2014). Accordingly, we determined that the following rules were unlawfully overbroad because they reasonably would be read to require employees to refrain from criticizing the employer in public.

- **"Refrain from any action that would harm persons or property or cause damage to the Company's business or reputation."**

- **"[I]t is important that employees practice caution and discretion when posting content [on social media] that could affect [the Employer's] business operation or reputation."**

- **Do not make "[s]tatements "that damage the company or the company's reputation or that disrupt or damage the company's business relationships."**

- **"Never engage in behavior that would undermine the reputation of [the Employer], your peers or yourself."**

With regard to these examples, we recognize that the Act does not protect employee conduct aimed at disparaging an employer's product, as opposed to conduct critical of an employer's labor policies or working conditions. These rules, however, contained insufficient context or examples to indicate that they were aimed only at unprotected conduct.

<u>Lawful Rules Regulating Employee Conduct towards the Employer</u>

In contrast, when an employer's handbook simply requires employees to be respectful to customers, competitors, and the like, but does not mention the company or its management, employees reasonably would not believe that such a rule prohibits Section 7-protected criticism of the company. The following rules, which we have found lawful, are illustrative:

- No "rudeness or unprofessional behavior toward a customer, or anyone in contact with" the company.

- "Employees will not be discourteous or disrespectful to a customer or any member of the public while in the course and scope of [company] business."

Similarly, rules requiring employees to cooperate with each other and the employer in the performance of their work also usually do not implicate Section 7 rights. *See Copper River of Boiling Springs, LLC*, 360 NLRB No. 60, slip op. at 1 (Feb. 28, 2014). Thus, we found the following rule was lawful because employees would reasonably understand that it is stating the employer's legitimate expectation that employees work together in an atmosphere of civility, and that it is not prohibiting Section 7 activity:

- "Each employee is expected to work in a cooperative manner with management/supervision, coworkers, customers and vendors."

And we concluded that the following rule was lawful, because employees would reasonably interpret it to apply to employer investigations of workplace misconduct rather than investigations of unfair labor practices or preparations for arbitration, when read in context with other provisions:

- "Each employee is expected to abide by Company policies and to cooperate fully in any investigation that the Company may undertake."

As previously discussed, the Board has made clear that it will not read rules in isolation. Even when a rule includes phrases or words that, alone, reasonably would be interpreted to ban protected criticism of the employer, if the context makes plain that only serious misconduct is banned, the rule will be found lawful. *See Tradesmen International*, 338 NLRB 460, 460–62 (2002). For instance, we found the following rule lawful based on a contextual analysis:

- "Being insubordinate, threatening, intimidating, disrespectful or assaulting a manager/supervisor, coworker, customer or vendor will result in" discipline.

Although a ban on being "disrespectful" to management, by itself, would ordinarily be found to unlawfully chill Section 7 criticism of the employer, the term here is contained in a larger provision that is clearly focused on serious misconduct, like insubordination, threats, and assault. Viewed in that context, we concluded that employees would not reasonably believe this rule to ban protected criticism.

C.   Employer Handbook Rules Regulating Conduct Towards Fellow Employees

In addition to employees' Section 7 rights to publicly discuss their terms and conditions of employment and to criticize their employer's labor policies, employees also have a right under the Act to argue and debate with each other about unions, management, and their terms and conditions of employment. These discussions can become contentious, but as the Supreme Court has noted, protected concerted speech will not lose its protection even if it includes "intemperate, abusive and inaccurate statements." *Linn v. United Plant Guards*, 383 U.S. 53 (1966). Thus, when an employer bans "negative" or "inappropriate" discussions among its employees, without further clarification, employees reasonably will read those rules to prohibit discussions and interactions that are protected under Section 7. *See Triple Play Sports Bar & Grille*, 361 NLRB No. 31, slip op. at 7 (Aug. 22, 2014); *Hills & Dales General Hospital*, 360 NLRB No. 70, slip op. at 1 (Apr. 1, 2014). For example, although employers have a legitimate and substantial interest in maintaining a harassment-free workplace, anti-harassment rules cannot be so broad that employees would reasonably read them as prohibiting vigorous debate or intemperate comments regarding Section 7-protected subjects.

Unlawful Employee-Employee Conduct Rules

We concluded that the following rules were unlawfully overbroad because employees would reasonably construe them to restrict protected discussions with their coworkers.

- **"[D]on't pick fights" online.**

We found the above rule unlawful because its broad and ambiguous language would reasonably be construed to encompass protected heated discussion among employees regarding unionization, the employer's labor policies, or the employer's treatment of employees.

- **Do not make "insulting, embarrassing, hurtful or abusive comments about other company employees online," and "avoid the use of offensive, derogatory, or prejudicial comments."**

Because debate about unionization and other protected concerted activity is often contentious and controversial, employees would reasonably read a rule that bans "offensive," "derogatory," "insulting," or "embarrassing" comments as limiting their ability to honestly discuss such subjects. These terms also would reasonably be construed to limit protected criticism of supervisors and managers, since they are also "company employees."

- "[S]how proper consideration for others' privacy and for topics that may be considered objectionable or inflammatory, such as politics and religion."

This rule was found unlawful because Section 7 protects communications about political matters, e.g., proposed right-to-work legislation. Its restriction on communications regarding controversial political matters, without clarifying context or examples, would be reasonably construed to cover these kinds of Section 7 communications. Indeed, discussion of unionization would also be chilled by such a rule because it can be an inflammatory topic similar to politics and religion.

- Do not send "unwanted, offensive, or inappropriate" e-mails.

The above rule is similarly vague and overbroad, in the absence of context or examples to clarify that it does not encompass Section 7 communications.

- "Material that is fraudulent, harassing, embarrassing, sexually explicit, profane, obscene, intimidating, defamatory, or otherwise unlawful or inappropriate may not be sent by e-mail . . . ."

We found the above rule unlawful because several of its terms are ambiguous as to their application to Section 7 activity—"embarrassing," "defamatory," and "otherwise . . . inappropriate." We further concluded that, viewed in context with such language, employees would reasonably construe even the term "intimidating" as covering Section 7 conduct.

<u>Lawful Employee-Employee Conduct Rules</u>

On the other hand, when an employer's professionalism rule simply requires employees to be respectful to customers or competitors, or directs employees not to engage in unprofessional conduct, and does not mention the company or its management, employees would not reasonably believe that such a rule prohibits Section 7-protected criticism of the company. Accordingly, we concluded that the following rules were lawful:

- "Making inappropriate gestures, including visual staring."

- Any logos or graphics worn by employees "must not reflect any form of violent, discriminatory, abusive, offensive, demeaning, or otherwise unprofessional message."

- "[T]hreatening, intimidating, coercing, or otherwise interfering with the job performance of fellow employees or visitors."

- No "harassment of employees, patients or facility visitors."

- No "use of racial slurs, derogatory comments, or insults."

With respect to the last example, we recognized that a blanket ban on "derogatory comments," by itself, would reasonably be read to restrict protected criticism of the employer. However, because this rule was in a section of the handbook that dealt exclusively with unlawful harassment and discrimination, employees reasonably would read it in context as prohibiting those kinds of unprotected comments toward coworkers, rather than protected criticism of the employer.

D. Employer Handbook Rules Regarding Employee Interaction with Third Parties

Another right employees have under Section 7 is the right to communicate with the news media, government agencies, and other third parties about wages, benefits, and other terms and conditions of employment. Handbook rules that reasonably would be read to restrict such communications are unlawfully overbroad. *See Trump Marina Associates*, 354 NLRB 1027, 1027 n.2 (2009), *incorporated by reference*, 355 NLRB 585 (2010), *enforced mem.*, 435 F. App'x 1 (D.C. Cir. 2011). The most frequent offenders in this category are company media policies. While employers may lawfully control who makes official statements for the company, they must be careful to ensure that their rules would not reasonably be read to ban employees from speaking to the media or other third parties on their own (or other employees') behalf.

Unlawful Rules Regulating Third Party Communications

We found the following rules were unlawfully overbroad because employees reasonably would read them to ban protected communications with the media.

- **Employees are not "authorized to speak to any representatives of the print and/or electronic media about company matters" unless designated to do so by HR, and must refer all media inquiries to the company media hotline.**

We determined that the above rule was unlawful because employees would reasonably construe the phrase "company matters" to encompass employment concerns and labor relations, and there was no limiting language or other context in the rule to clarify that the rule applied only to those speaking as official company representatives.

- **"[A]ssociates are not authorized to answer questions from the news media .... When approached for information, you should refer the person to [the Employer's] Media Relations Department."**

- **"[A]ll inquiries from the media must be referred to the Director of Operations in the corporate office, no exceptions."**

These two rules contain blanket restrictions on employees' responses to media inquiries. We therefore concluded that employees would reasonably understand that they apply to *all* media contacts, not only inquiries seeking the employers' official positions.

In addition, we found the following rule to be unlawfully overbroad because employees reasonably would read it to limit protected communications with government agencies.

- **"If you are contacted by any government agency you should contact the Law Department immediately for assistance."**

Although we recognize an employer's right to present its own position regarding the subject of a government inquiry, this rule contains a broader restriction. Employees would reasonably believe that they may not speak to a government agency without management approval, or even provide information in response to a Board investigation.

Lawful Rules Regulating Employee Communications with Outside Parties

In contrast, we found the following media contact rules to be lawful because employees reasonably would interpret them to mean that employees should not speak on behalf of the company, not that employees cannot speak to outsiders on their own (or other employees') behalf.

- **"The company strives to anticipate and manage crisis situations in order to reduce disruption to our employees and to maintain our reputation as a high quality company. To best serve these objectives, the company will respond to the news media in a timely and professional manner *only* through the designated spokespersons."**

We determined that this rule was lawful because it specifically referred to employee contact with the media regarding non-Section 7 related matters, such as crisis situations; sought to ensure a consistent company response or message regarding those matters; and was not a blanket prohibition against all contact with the media. Accordingly, we concluded that employees would not reasonably interpret this rule as interfering with Section 7 communications.

- **"Events may occur at our stores that will draw immediate attention from the news media. *It is imperative that one person speaks for the Company to deliver an appropriate message and to avoid giving misinformation in any media inquiry.* While reporters frequently shop as customers and may ask questions about a matter, good** reporters identify themselves prior to asking questions. Every . . . employee is expected to adhere to the following media policy: . . . 2. Answer all media/reporter questions like this: 'I am not authorized to comment for [the Employer] (or I don't have the information you want). Let me have our public affairs office contact you.'"

We concluded that the prefatory language in this rule would cause employees to reasonably construe the rule as an attempt to control the company's message, rather than to restrict Section 7 communications to the media. Further, the required responses to media inquiries would be non-sequiturs in the context of a discussion about terms and conditions of employment or protected criticism of the company. Accordingly, we found that employees reasonably would not read this rule to restrict conversations with the news media about protected concerted activities.

E.   Employer Handbook Rules Restricting Use of Company Logos, Copyrights, and Trademarks

We have also reviewed handbook rules that restrict employee use of company logos, copyrights, or trademarks. Though copyright holders have a clear interest in protecting their intellectual property, handbook rules cannot prohibit employees' fair protected use of that property. *See Pepsi-Cola Bottling Co.*, 301 NLRB 1008, 1019–20 (1991), *enforced mem.*, 953 F.2d 638 (4th Cir. 1992). For instance, a company's name and logo will usually be protected by intellectual property laws, but employees have a right to use the name and logo on picket signs, leaflets, and other protest material. Employer proprietary interests are not implicated by employees' non-commercial use of a name, logo, or other trademark to identify the employer in the course of Section 7 activity. Thus, a broad ban on such use without any clarification will generally be found unlawfully overbroad.

Unlawful Rules Banning Employee Use of Logos, Copyrights, or Trademarks

We found that the following rules were unlawful because they contain broad restrictions that employees would reasonably read to ban fair use of the employer's intellectual property in the course of protected concerted activity.

- Do "not use any Company logos, trademarks, graphics, or advertising materials" in social media.

- Do not use "other people's property," such as trademarks, without permission in social media.

- "Use of [the Employer's] name, address or other information in your personal profile [is banned]. . . . In addition, it is prohibited to use [the Employer's] logos, trademarks or any other copyrighted material."

- "Company logos and trademarks may not be used without written consent . . . ."

Lawful Rules Protecting Employer Logos, Copyrights, and Trademarks

We found that the following rules were lawful. Unlike the prior examples, which broadly ban employee use of trademarked or copyrighted material, these rules simply require employees to respect such laws, permitting fair use.

- "Respect all copyright and other intellectual property laws. For [the Employer's] protection as well as your own, it is critical that you show proper respect for the laws governing copyright, fair use of copyrighted material owned by others, trademarks and other intellectual property, including [the Employer's] own copyrights, trademarks and brands."

- "DO respect the laws regarding copyrights, trademarks, rights of publicity and other third-party rights. To minimize the risk of a copyright violation, you should provide references to the source(s) of information you use and accurately cite copyrighted works you identify in your online communications. Do not infringe on [Employer] logos, brand names, taglines, slogans, or other trademarks."

F.   Employer Handbook Rules Restricting Photography and Recording

Employees also have a Section 7 right to photograph and make recordings in furtherance of their protected concerted activity, including the right to use personal devices to take such pictures and recordings. *See Hawaii Tribune-Herald*, 356 NLRB No. 63, slip op. at 1 (Feb. 14, 2011), *enforced sub nom. Stephens Media, LLC v. NLRB*, 677 F.3d 1241 (D.C. Cir. 2012); *White Oak Manor*, 353 NLRB 795, 795 (2009), *incorporated by reference*, 355 NLRB 1280 (2010), *enforced mem.*, 452 F. App'x 374 (4th Cir. 2011). Thus, rules placing a total ban on such photography or recordings, or banning the use or possession of personal cameras or recording devices, are unlawfully overbroad where they would reasonably be read to prohibit the taking of pictures or recordings on non-work time.

Unlawful Rules Banning Photography, Recordings, or Personal Electronic Devices

We found the following rules unlawfully overbroad because employees reasonably would interpret them to prohibit the use of personal equipment to engage in Section 7 activity while on breaks or other non-work time.

- "Taking unauthorized pictures or video on company property" is prohibited.

We concluded that employees would reasonably read this rule to prohibit all unauthorized employee use of a camera or video recorder, including attempts to document health and safety violations and other protected concerted activity.

- "No employee shall use any recording device including but not limited to, audio, video, or digital for the purpose of recording any [Employer] employee or [Employer] operation . . . ."

We found this rule unlawful because employees would reasonably construe it to preclude, among other things, documentation of unfair labor practices, which is an essential part of the recognized right under Section 7 to utilize the Board's processes.

- A total ban on use or possession of personal electronic equipment on Employer property.

- A prohibition on personal computers or data storage devices on employer property.

We determined that the two above rules, which contain blanket restrictions on use or possession of recording devices, violated the Act for similar reasons. Although an employer has a legitimate interest in maintaining the confidentiality of business records, these rules were not narrowly tailored to address that concern.

- Prohibition from wearing cell phones, making personal calls or viewing or sending texts "while on duty."

This rule, which limits the restriction on personal recording devices to time "on duty," is nonetheless unlawful, because employees reasonably would understand "on duty" to include breaks and meals during their shifts, as opposed to their actual work time.

<u>Lawful Rules Regulating Pictures and Recording Equipment</u>

Rules regulating employee recording or photography will be found lawful if their scope is appropriately limited. For instance, in cases where a no-photography rule is instituted in response to a breach of patient privacy, where the employer has a well-understood, strong privacy interest, the Board has found that employees would not reasonably understand a no-photography rule to limit pictures for protected concerted purposes. *See Flagstaff Medical Center*, 357 NLRB No. 65, slip op. at 5 (Aug. 26, 2011), *enforced in relevant part*, 715 F.3d 928 (D.C. Cir. 2013). We also found the following rule lawful based on a contextual analysis:

- **No cameras are to be allowed in the store or parking lot without prior approval from the corporate office.**

This rule was embedded in a lawful media policy and immediately followed instructions on how to deal with reporters in the store. We determined that, in such a context, employees would read the rule to ban *news* cameras, not their own cameras.

G.   Employer Handbook Rules Restricting Employees from Leaving Work

One of the most fundamental rights employees have under Section 7 of the Act is the right to go on strike. Accordingly, rules that regulate when employees can leave work are unlawful if employees reasonably would read them to forbid protected strike actions and walkouts. *See Purple Communications, Inc.*, 361 NLRB No. 43, slip op. at 2 (Sept. 24, 2014). If, however, such a rule makes no mention of "strikes," "walkouts," "disruptions," or the like, employees will reasonably understand the rule to pertain to employees leaving their posts for reasons unrelated to protected concerted activity, and the rule will be found lawful. *See 2 Sisters Food Group*, 357 NLRB No. 168, slip op. at 2 (Dec. 29, 2011).

Unlawful Handbook Rules Relating to Restrictions on Leaving Work

We found the following rules were unlawful because they contain broad prohibitions on walking off the job, which reasonably would be read to include protected strikes and walkouts.

- **"Failure to report to your scheduled shift for more than three consecutive days without prior authorization or 'walking off the job' during a scheduled shift" is prohibited.**

- **"Walking off the job . . ." is prohibited.**

Lawful Handbook Rules Relating to Restrictions on Leaving Work

In contrast, the following handbook rule was considered lawful:

- **"Entering or leaving Company property without permission may result in discharge."**

We found this rule was lawful because, in the absence of terms like "work stoppage" or "walking off the job," a rule forbidding employees from leaving the employer's property during work time without permission will not reasonably be read to encompass strikes. However, the portion of the rule that requires employees to obtain permission before *entering the property* was found unlawful because employers may not deny off-duty employees access to parking lots, gates, and other outside nonworking areas except where sufficiently justified by business reasons or pursuant to the kind of narrowly tailored rule approved in *Tri-County Medical Center*, 222 NLRB 1089, 1089 (1976).

- **"Walking off shift, failing to report for a scheduled shift and leaving early without supervisor permission are also grounds for immediate termination."**

Although this rule includes the term "walking off shift," which usually would be considered an overbroad term that employees reasonably would understand to include strikes, we found this rule to be lawful in the context of the employees' health care responsibilities. Where employees are directly responsible for patient care, a broad "no walkout without permission" rule is reasonably read as ensuring that patients are not left without adequate care, not as a complete ban on strikes. *See Wilshire at Lakewood*, 343 NLRB 141, 144 (2004), *vacated in part*, 345 NLRB 1050 (2005), *enforcement denied on other grounds*, *Jochims v. NLRB*, 480 F.3d 1161 (D.C. Cir. 2007). This rule was maintained by an employer that operated a care facility for people with dementia. Thus, we found that employees would reasonably read this rule as being designed to ensure continuity of care, not as a ban on protected job actions.

H.   Employer Conflict-of-Interest Rules

Section 7 of the Act protects employees' right to engage in concerted activity to improve their terms and conditions of employment, even if that activity is in conflict with the employer's interests. For instance, employees may protest in front of the company, organize a boycott, and solicit support for a union while on nonwork time. *See HTH Corp.*, 356 NLRB No. 182, slip op. at 2, 25 (June 14, 2011), *enforced*, 693 F.3d 1051 (9th Cir. 2012). If an employer's conflict-of-interest rule would reasonably be read to prohibit such activities, the rule will be found unlawful. However, where the rule includes examples or otherwise clarifies that it is limited to legitimate business interests, employees will reasonably understand the rule to prohibit only unprotected activity. *See Tradesmen International*, 338 NLRB 460, 461–62 (2002).

Unlawful Conflict-of-Interest Rules

We found the following rule unlawful because it was phrased broadly and did not include any clarifying examples or context that would indicate that it did not apply to Section 7 activities:

- **Employees may not engage in "any action" that is "not in the best interest of [the Employer]."**

Lawful Conflict-of-Interest Rules

In contrast, we found the following rules lawful because they included context and examples that indicated that the rules were not meant to encompass protected concerted activity:

- Do not "give, offer or promise, directly or indirectly, anything of value to any representative of an Outside Business," where "Outside Business" is defined as "any person, firm, corporation, or government agency that sells or provides a service to, purchases from, or competes with [the Employer]." Examples of violations include "holding an ownership or financial interest in an Outside Business" and "accepting gifts, money, or services from an Outside Business."

We concluded that this rule is lawful because employees would reasonably understand that the rule is directed at protecting the employer from employee graft and preventing employees from engaging in a competing business, and that it does not apply to employee interactions with labor organizations or other Section 7 activity that the employer might oppose.

- As an employee, "I will not engage in any activity that might create a conflict of interest for me or the company," where the conflict of interest policy devoted two pages to examples such as "avoid outside employment with a[n Employer] customer, supplier, or competitor, or having a significant financial interest with one of these entities."

The above rule included multiple examples of conflicts of interest such that it would not be interpreted to restrict Section 7 activity.

- Employees must refrain "from any activity or having any financial interest that is inconsistent with the Company's best interest" and also must refrain from "activities, investments or associations that compete with the Company, interferes with one's judgment concerning the Company's best interests, or exploits one's position with the Company for personal gains."

We also found this rule to be lawful based on a contextual analysis. While its requirement that employees refrain from activities or associations that are inconsistent with the company's best interests could, in isolation, be interpreted to include employee participation in unions, the surrounding context and examples ensure that employees would not reasonably read it in that way. Indeed, the rule is in a section of the handbook that deals entirely with business ethics and includes requirements to act with "honesty, fairness and integrity"; comply with "all laws, rules and regulations"; and provide "accurate, complete, fair, timely, and understandable" information in SEC filings.

Part 2: The Settlement with Wendy's International LLC

In 2014, we concluded that many of the employee handbook rules alleged in an unfair labor practice charge against Wendy's International, LLC were unlawfully overbroad under *Lutheran Heritage*'s first prong. Pursuant to an informal, bilateral Board settlement agreement, Wendy's modified its handbook rules. This section of the report presents the rules we found unlawfully overbroad, with brief discussions of our reasoning, followed by the replacement rules, which the Office of the General Counsel considers lawful, contained in the settlement agreement.

A.   Wendy's Unlawful Handbook Rules

The pertinent provisions of Wendy's handbook and our conclusions are outlined below.

Handbook disclosure provision

No part of this handbook may be reproduced or transmitted in any form or by any means, electronic or mechanical, including photocopying, recording, or information storage and retrieval system or otherwise, for any purpose without the express written permission of Wendy's International, Inc. The information contained in this handbook is considered proprietary and confidential information of Wendy's and its intended use is strictly limited to Wendy's and its employees. The disclosure of this handbook to unauthorized parties is prohibited. Making an unauthorized disclosure of this handbook is a serious breach of Wendy's standards of conduct and ethics and shall expose the disclosing party to disciplinary action and other liabilities as permitted under law.

We concluded that this provision was unlawful because it prohibited disclosure of the Wendy's handbook, which contains employment policies, to third parties such as union representatives or the Board. Because employees have a Section 7 right to discuss their wages and other terms and conditions of employment with others, including co-workers, union representatives, and government agencies, such as the Board, a rule that precludes employees from sharing the employee handbook that contains many of their working conditions violates Section 8(a)(1).

Social Media Policy

Refrain from commenting on the company's business, financial performance, strategies, clients, policies, employees or competitors in any

social media, without the advance approval of your supervisor, Human Resources and Communications Departments. Anything you say or post may be construed as representing the Company's opinion or point of view (when it does not), or it may reflect negatively on the Company. If you wish to make a complaint or report a complaint or troubling behavior, please follow the complaint procedure in the applicable Company policy (e.g., Speak Out).**

Although employers have a legitimate interest in ensuring that employee communications are not construed as misrepresenting the employer's official position, we concluded that this rule did not merely prevent employees from speaking on behalf of, or in the name of, Wendy's. Instead, it generally prohibited an employee from commenting about the Company's business, policies, or employees without authorization, particularly when it might reflect negatively on the Company. Accordingly, we found that this part of the rule was overly broad. We also concluded that the rule's instruction that employees should follow the Company's internal complaint mechanism to "make a complaint or report a complaint" chilled employees' Section 7 right to communicate employment-related complaints to persons and entities other than Wendy's.

Respect copyrights and similar laws. Do not use any copyrighted or otherwise protected information or property without the owner's written consent.

We concluded that this rule was unlawfully overbroad because it broadly prohibited *any* employee use of copyrighted or "otherwise protected" information. Employees would reasonably construe that language to prohibit Section 7 communications involving, for example, reference to the copyrighted handbook or Company website for purposes of commentary or criticism, or use of the Wendy's trademark/name and another business's trademark/name in a wage comparison. We determined that such use does not implicate the interests that courts have identified as being protected by trademark and copyright laws.

[You may not p]ost photographs taken at Company events or on Company premises without the advance consent of your supervisor, Human Resources and Communications Departments.
[You may not p]ost photographs of Company employees without their advance consent. Do not attribute or disseminate comments or statements purportedly made by employees or others without their explicit permission.

We concluded that these rules, which included no examples of unprotected conduct or other language to clarify and restrict their scope, would chill employees from engaging in Section 7 activities, such as posting a photo of employees carrying a picket sign in front of a restaurant, documenting a health or safety concern, or discussing or making complaints about statements made by Wendy's or fellow employees.

[You may not u]se the Company's (or any of its affiliated entities) logos, marks or other protected information or property without the Legal Department's express written authorization.

As discussed above, Wendy's had no legitimate basis to prohibit the use of its logo or trademarks in this manner, which would reasonably be construed to restrict a variety of Section 7-protected uses of the Wendy's logo and trademarks. Therefore, we found this rule unlawfully overbroad.

[You may not e]mail, post, comment or blog anonymously. You may think it is anonymous, but it is most likely traceable to you and the Company.

Requiring employees to publicly self-identify in order to participate in protected activity imposes an unwarranted burden on Section 7 rights. Thus, we found this rule banning anonymous comments unlawfully overbroad.

[You may not m]ake false or misleading representations about your credentials or your work.

We found this rule unlawful, because its language clearly encompassed communications relating to working conditions, which do not lose their protection if they are false or misleading as opposed to "maliciously false" (i.e., made with knowledge of falsity or reckless disregard for the truth). A broad rule banning merely false or misleading representations about work can have a chilling effect by causing employees to become hesitant to voice their views and complaints concerning working conditions for fear that later they may be disciplined because someone may determine that those were false or misleading statements.

[You may not c]reate a blog or online group related to your job without the advance approval of the Legal and Communications.

We determined that this no-blogging rule was unlawfully overbroad because employees have a Section 7 right to discuss their terms and conditions of employment with their co-workers and/or the public, including on blogs or online groups, and it is well-settled that such pre-authorization requirements chill Section 7 activity.

Do Not Disparage:
Be thoughtful and respectful in all your communications and dealings with others, including email and social media. Do not harass, threaten, libel, malign, defame, or disparage fellow professionals, employees, clients, competitors or anyone else. Do not make personal insults, use obscenities or engage in any conduct that would be unacceptable in a professional environment.

We found this rule unlawful because its second and third sentences contained broad, sweeping prohibitions against "malign[ing], defam[ing], or disparag[ing]" that, in context, would reasonably be read to go beyond unprotected defamation and encompass concerted communications protesting or criticizing Wendy's treatment of employees, among other Section 7 activities. And, there was nothing in the rule or elsewhere in the handbook that would reasonably assure employees that Section 7 communications were excluded from the rule's broad reach.

Do Not Retaliate:
If you discover negative statements, emails or posts about you or the Company, do not respond. First seek help from the Legal and Communications Departments, who will guide any response.

We concluded that employees would reasonably read this rule as requiring them to seek permission before engaging in Section 7 activity because "negative statements about . . . the Company" would reasonably be construed as encompassing Section 7 activity. For example, employees would reasonably read the rule to require that they obtain permission from Wendy's before responding to a co-worker's complaint about working conditions or a protest of unfair labor practices. We therefore found this rule overly broad.

Conflict-of-Interest Provision

Because you are now working in one of Wendy's restaurants, it is important to realize that you have an up close and personal look at our business every day. With this in mind, you should recognize your responsibility to avoid any conflict between your personal interests and those of the Company. A conflict of interest occurs when our personal interests interfere—or appear to interfere—with our ability to make sound business decisions on behalf of Wendy's.

We determined that the Conflict-of-Interest provision was unlawfully overbroad because its requirement that employees avoid "any conflict between your personal interests and those of the Company" would reasonably be read to encompass Section 7 activity, such as union organizing activity, demanding higher wages, or engaging in boycotts or public demonstrations related to a labor dispute. Unlike rules that provide specific examples of what constitutes a conflict of interest, nothing in this rule confined its scope to legitimate business concerns or clarified that it was not intended to apply to Section 7 activity.

Moreover, we concluded that the Conflict-of-Interest provision was even more likely to chill Section 7 activity when read together with the handbook's third-party representation provision, located about six pages later, which communicated that unions are not beneficial or in the interest of Wendy's: **[b]ecause Wendy's desires to maintain open and direct communications with all of our employees, we do not believe that third party/union involvement in our relationship would benefit our employees or Wendy's.**

Company Confidential Information Provision

During the course of your employment, you may become aware of confidential information about Wendy's business. You must not disclose any confidential information relating to Wendy's business to anyone outside of the Company. Your employee PIN and other personal information should be kept confidential. Please don't share this information with any other employee.

We concluded that the confidentiality provision was facially unlawful because it referenced employees' "personal information," which the Board has found would reasonably be read to encompass discussion of wages, hours, and terms and conditions of employment.

Employee Conduct

The Employee Conduct section of the handbook contained approximately two pages listing examples of "misconduct" and "gross misconduct," which could lead to disciplinary action, up to and including discharge, in the sole discretion of Wendy's. The list included the following:

Soliciting, collecting funds, distributing literature on Company premises without proper approvals or outside the guidelines established in the "No Solicitation/No Distribution" Policy.

The blanket prohibition against soliciting, collecting funds, or distributing literature without proper approvals was unlawfully overbroad because employees have a Section 7 right to solicit on non-work time and distribute literature in non-work areas.

Walking off the job without authorization.

We found that this rule was unlawfully overbroad because employees would reasonably construe it to prohibit Section 7 activity such as a concerted walkout or other strike activity. As discussed in Part 1 of this report, the Board has drawn a fairly bright line regarding how employees would reasonably construe rules about employees leaving work. Rules that contain phrases such as "walking off the job," as here, reasonably would be read to forbid protected strike actions and walkouts.

Threatening, intimidating, foul or inappropriate language.

We found this prohibition to be unlawful because rules that forbid the vague phrase "inappropriate language," without examples or context, would reasonably be construed to prohibit protected communications about or criticism of management, labor policies, or working conditions.

False accusations against the Company and/or against another employee or customer.

We found this rule unlawful because an accusation against an employer does not lose the protection of Section 7 merely because it is false, as opposed to being recklessly or knowingly false. As previously discussed, a rule banning merely false statements can have a chilling effect on protected concerted communications, for instance, because employees reasonably would fear that contradictory information provided by the employer would result in discipline.

<u>No Distribution/No Solicitation Provision</u>

[I]t is our policy to prohibit the distribution of literature in work areas and to prohibit solicitation during employees' working time. "Working time" is the time an employee is engaged, or should be engaged, in performing his/her work tasks for Wendy's. These guidelines also apply to solicitation and/or distribution by electronic means.

We concluded that this rule was unlawful because it restricted distribution by electronic means in work areas. While an employer may restrict distribution of literature in paper form in work areas, it has no legitimate business justification to restrict employees from distributing literature electronically, such as sending an email with a "flyer" attached, while the employees are in work areas during non-working time. Unlike distribution of paper literature, which can create a production hazard even when it occurs on nonworking time, electronic distribution does not produce litter and only impinges on the employer's management interests if it occurs on working time.

<u>Restaurant Telephone; Cell Phone; Camera Phone/Recording Devices Provision</u>

Due to the potential for issues such as invasion of privacy, sexual harassment, and loss of productivity, no Crew Member may operate a camera phone on Company property or while performing work for the Company. The use of tape recorders, Dictaphones, or other types of voice recording devices anywhere on Company property, including to record conversations or activities of other employees or management, or while performing work for the Company, is also strictly prohibited, unless the device was provided to you by the Company and is used solely for legitimate business purposes.

We concluded that this rule, which prohibited employee use of a camera or video recorder "on Company property" at any time, precluded Section 7 activities, such as employees documenting health and safety violations, collective action, or the potential violation of employee rights under the Act. Wendy's had no business justification for such a broad prohibition. Its concerns about privacy, sexual harassment, and loss of productivity did not justify a rule that prohibited all use of a camera phone or audio recording device anywhere on the company's property at any time.

B.   <u>Wendy's Lawful Handbook Rules Pursuant to Settlement Agreement</u>

<u>Handbook Disclosure Provision</u>

This Crew Orientation Handbook . . . is the property of Wendy's International LLC. No part of this handbook may be reproduced or transmitted in any form or by any means, electronic or mechanical, including photocopying, recording, or information storage and retrieval system or otherwise, for any business/commercial venture without the express written permission of Wendy's International, LLC. The information contained in this handbook is strictly limited to use by Wendy's and its employees. The disclosure of this handbook to competitors is prohibited. Making an unauthorized disclosure of this handbook is a serious breach of Wendy's standards of conduct and ethics and shall expose the disclosing party to disciplinary action and other liabilities as permitted under law.

<u>Social Media Provision</u>

- Do not comment on trade secrets and proprietary Company information (business, financial and marketing strategies) without the advance approval of your supervisor, Human Resources and Communications Departments.

- Do not make negative comments about our customers in any social media.

- Use of social media on Company equipment during working time is permitted, if your use is for legitimate, preapproved Company business. Please discuss the nature of your anticipated business use and the content of your message with your supervisor and Human Resources. Obtain their approval prior to such use.

- Respect copyright, trademark and similar laws and use such protected information in compliance with applicable legal standards.

Restrictions:

YOU MAY NOT do any of the following:

- Due to the potential for issues such as invasion of privacy (employee and customer), sexual or other harassment (as defined by our harassment /discrimination policy), protection of proprietary recipes and preparation techniques, Crew Members may not take, distribute, or post pictures, videos, or audio recordings while on working time. Crew Members also may not take pictures or make recordings of work areas. An exception to the rule concerning pictures and recordings of work areas would be to engage in activity protected by the National Labor Relations Act including, for example, taking pictures of health, safety and/or working condition concerns or of strike, protest and work-related issues and/or other protected concerted activities.

- Use the Company's (or any of its affiliated entities) logos, marks or other protected information or property for any business/commercial venture without the Legal Department's express written authorization.

- Make knowingly false representations about your credentials or your work.

- Create a blog or online group related to Wendy's (not including blogs or discussions involving wages, benefits, or other terms and conditions of employment, or protected concerted activity) without the advance approval of the Legal and Communications Departments. If a blog or online group is approved, it must contain a disclaimer approved by the Legal Department.

Do Not Violate the Law and Related Company Policies:

Be thoughtful in all your communications and dealings with others, including email and social media. Never harass (as defined by our anti-harassment policy), threaten, libel or defame fellow professionals, employees, clients, competitors or anyone else. In general, it is always wise to remember that what you say in social media can often be seen by anyone. Accordingly, harassing comments, obscenities or similar conduct that would violate Company policies is discouraged in general and is never allowed while using Wendy's equipment or during your working time.

Discipline:
All employees are expected to know and follow this policy. Nothing in this policy is, however, intended to prevent employees from engaging in concerted activity protected by law. If you have any questions regarding this policy, please ask your supervisor and Human Resources before acting. Any violations of this policy are grounds for disciplinary action, up to and including immediate termination of employment.

Conflict of Interest Provision

Because you are now working in one of Wendy's restaurants, it is important to realize that you have an up close and personal look at our business every day. With this in mind, you should recognize your responsibility to avoid any conflict between your personal interests and those of the Company. A conflict of interest occurs when our personal interests interfere – or appear to interfere – with your ability to make sound business decisions on behalf of Wendy's. There are some common relationships or circumstances that can create, or give the appearance of, a conflict of interest. The situations generally involve gifts and business or financial dealings or investments. Gifts, favors, tickets, entertainment and other such inducements may be attempts to "purchase" favorable treatment. Accepting such inducements could raise doubts about an employee's ability to make independent business judgments and the Company's commitment to treating people fairly. In addition, a conflict of interest exists when employees have a financial or ownership interest in a business or financial venture that may be at variance with the interests of Wendy's. Likewise, when an employee engages in business transactions that benefit family members, it may give an appearance of impropriety.

Company Confidential Information Provision

During the course of your employment, you may become aware of trade secrets and similarly protected proprietary and confidential information about Wendy's business (e.g. recipes, preparation techniques, marketing plans and strategies, financial records). You must not disclose any such information to anyone outside of the Company. Your employee PIN and other similar personal identification information should be kept confidential. Please don't share this information with any other employee.

Employee Conduct Provision

- Soliciting, collecting funds, distributing literature on Company premises outside the guidelines established in the "No Solicitation/No Distribution" Policy.

- Leaving Company premises during working shift without permission of management.

- Threatening, harassing (as defined by our harassment/discrimination policy), intimidating, profane, obscene or similar inappropriate language in violation of Company policy.

- Making knowingly false accusations against the Company and/or against another employee, customer or vendor.

No Distribution/No Solicitation Provision

Providing the most ideal work environment possible is very important to Wendy's. We hope you feel very comfortable and at ease when you're here at work. Therefore, to protect you and our customers from unnecessary interruptions and annoyances, it is our policy to prohibit the distribution of literature in work areas and to prohibit solicitation and distribution of literature during employees' working time. "Working Time" is the time an employee is engaged or should be engaged in performing his/her work tasks for Wendy's. These guidelines also apply to solicitation by electronic means. Solicitation or distribution of any kind by non-employees on Company premises is prohibited at all times. Nothing in this section prohibits employees from discussing terms and conditions of employment.

Restaurant Telephone/ Cell Phone/Camera Phone/Recording Devices Provision

Due to the potential for issues such as invasion of privacy (employee and customer), sexual or other harassment (as defined by our harassment /discrimination policy), protection of proprietary recipes and preparation techniques, Crew Members may not take, distribute, or post pictures, videos, or audio recordings while on working time. Crew Members also may not take pictures or make recordings of work areas. An exception to the rule concerning pictures and recordings of work areas would be to engage in activity protected by the National Labor Relations Act including, for example, taking pictures of health, safety and/or working condition concerns or of strike, protest and work-related issues and/or other protected concerted activities.

HYPOTHETICAL

1.   Organic Green Growers of Colorado (Employer) is in the business of growing and selling organic good and organic edibles in the Denver Metropolitan area. The Employer's owners, Jerry Garcia and Carlos Santa Ana, got into the organic goods business early on and are now multi-millionaires. The Employer has a workforce of 24 individuals who are employees under the National Labor Relations Act (Act). Half of those employees, classified as the green thumbs, work in greenhouses growing and cultivating plants. Another six employees prepare and bake edibles, including brownies, cookies, cupcakes and cakes, for sale to the public. They are referred to as the sweets enhancers. The remaining six employees work directly with the public selling the Employer's products and are classified as the enablers. Three individuals oversee the employees' work. They are Jerry Jones (sales supervisor), Carmen Cracraft (edibles supervisor), and Jennifer Green (greenhouse supervisor). In January of 2013, the Employer signed a collective bargaining agreement with the United Marigold Employees Union (Union) that covers a unit consisting of the green thumbs, sweets enhancers, and enablers. Additionally, the contract provides for a grievance procedure and final and binding arbitration. Employees Stephanie Smith and John Lightly are the Union's shop stewards.

2.   On March 15, 2015, employees Jeff Bridges and Norma Ray, who work in the greenhouse as green thumbs, had a conversation in the Employer's breakroom about supervisor Green. They complained about her mistreating them and scheduling them to work overtime at the last minute. They decided to speak with the other green thumbs to see what, if anything, they could do. On March 18, 2015, about 7 green thumbs met at Ray's home for a barbecue. During the barbecue, the employees discussed their concerns about being scheduled overtime at the last minute and Green's mistreatment. It was agreed that employees Ray and Bridges would meet with owners Garcia and Santa Ana to discuss their concerns about overtime and their supervisor.

3.   When Ray reported to work on March 19, 2015, supervisor Green approached her and said, "I know what you are up to. There will be consequences if you go to the owners and complain about me. I would start looking for another job if I were you because I am going to can you. We cannot have radicals around here." Ray, who was facing Green, threw the shovel she was holding on the ground and told supervisor Green that she was a f--king piece of shit." Ray's voice was loud and she was moving her hands excitedly as she spoke. By then, all the other green thumbs, who had heard the commotion, approached the two women but said nothing. Green became upset and said, "Missy, you did yourself in. You are fired." Ray left the greenhouse and the facility and went to the Union hall where she spoke with Union representative Juan Camarillo

about what happened. Camarillo said he would file a grievance and he did so on March 20, 2015. He also filed a charge with the National Labor Relations Board (the Board), alleging that the Employer had violated Section 8(a)(1) of the Act by terminating Ray for engaging in protected concerted activity. The Board deferred the charge to the grievance procedure outlined in the collective bargaining agreement. The underlying grievance is scheduled to be arbitrated in August.

4.   On May 24, 2015, steward Lightly met with the Employer's owners, Santa Ana and Garcia, who began the meeting by saying "Actually, we wanted to talk with you because a lot of product has disappeared in the greenhouses and we think you may be involved. You know, our rules say that is a basis for termination. I want to know if…" Steward Lightly did not allow Santa Ana to finish his comment before saying, "I want my steward present. The contract states that I am entitled to Union representation when you meet with me to discuss an employee stealing or smoking product at work." Garcia responded, "criminals are not entitled to union representation. If you leave this meeting you will be automatically terminated." He added, "Actually, we want you to submit to a drug test and we do not feel you are entitled to anyone representing you. We may be liberal, but we will not be pushed too far." Lightly responded, "I will not take a drug test without my steward present." Green then said, "You do not get to consult with the Union over your drug test. You are fired, you ingrate." Get out of here and don't ever come back." Lightly left the facility and went to his car. He called Union representative Camarillo on her cell phone and explained what happened. The next day, Camarillo filed a grievance and a Board charge alleging violations of Section 8(a)(1) and (3) of the Act. More specifically, the Union alleged that the Employer: (1) denied Lightly his rights under *Weingarten*; and (2) terminated Lightly in retaliation for exercising his contractual rights. After the investigation of the Board charge, Region 007 made a decision to defer the matter to the grievance procedure under *Collyer*.

5.   On June 16, 2015, enabler Paul Arbusto was working and minding his own business when he was approached by Santa Ana. Santa Ana told Arbusto that Lighthead was not a loyal person and had been terminated for being disloyal and becoming active in the Union. Santa Ana then said that they were running out of employees in the greenhouses so they needed him to go work at that location immediately. Arbusto responded that the contract specifically provided that the enablers could not be required to go work in the greenhouse. Santa Ana responded, "The door is right there buddy. If you do not like your new assignment go ahead and go. You are working in the greenhouse or nowhere". Employees and customers started congregating around the two men as the discussion became more heated. Arbusto pulled out his Union contract from his pocket and in a raised voice as he held the contract in his hand said, "It's right here in black and white, you cannot make me work in the greenhouse." Arbusto was raising his voice by then. Santa Ana shouted in

response, "I do not care what it says in your stupid contract. Go work in the Greenhouse now!" Arbusto also raised his voice and said, "You are one stupid businessman. The only reason your customers keep coming back and buying your rat-poison laced edibles is the other enablers and I have told them it's a special secret formula." Santa Ana said, "You are fired!" The Union filed a grievance over Arbusto's termination. The Union files a charge with the National Labor Relations Board, alleging the Employer discharged Arbusto because he engaged in union activities and "other activities protected under the Act." The Employer maintains it fired Arbusto for being disrespectful, raising his voice during the confrontation in front of customers and employees, and disloyalty. Region 007 has decided to also defer this charge.

6.   Jeff Bridges continued to work for the company, but was approached by a rival grower because he known as one of the best green thumbs in the business. He wanted to learn more about the distribution end of the business, and decided to start hanging around in the shared customer/employee parking lot where he could get a feel for which customers might be willing to change suppliers. After a week of hanging around for three or four hours after work every day, Greenhouse Supervisor Jennifer Green explained to him that he was violating handbook policy 23, which provides "employees may not loiter in the parking lot or other outdoor non-work areas of the company's property more than 20 minutes after shift end time." Bridges replied that he did not like that policy, because he loved his employer and enjoyed the conversation with customers after work, and finding out what their favorite products were. Green issued Bridges a write-up and one day suspension for "violation of handbook policy 23." Bridges filed both a grievance and an unfair labor practice charge with the NLRB. The Region has issued a letter advising the charge will be deferred under *Collyer*.

.

ANSWER KEY

1st Paragraph:

1. Do the protections of the National Labor Relations Act apply to employees of this "organic grower?"

The NLRB's Division of Advice has determined that the Agency will not decline jurisdiction over medical marijuana businesses solely on the basis that it operates within the medical marijuana industry. *A List MMJ*, 19-CA-093389 (Advice Memorandum, December 16, 2013)

2nd Paragraph:

1. Question: Did Bridge's and Ray's discussion in the break room about Green's mistreatment of employees and unfair overtime scheduling constitute concerted activity under the Act?

Answer: Yes. These employees were seeking to initiate, induce, or to prepare for group action by discussing these issues and by deciding to discuss the issues further with coworkers. See *Salon/Spa at Boro, Inc.*, 356 NLRB No. 69, slip op. at 19-20 (2010) (affirming the ALJ's reasoning that employees' conduct of repeatedly raising specific grievances about management's treatment of employees and policies and seeking the support and approval of coworkers is "the type of preliminary groundwork necessary to initiate group activity" and constitutes concerted activity.) See also: *Champion Home Builders Co.*, 343 NLRB 671 fn. 3 (2004), enf. in pertinent part 209 Fed. Appx. 692 (9th Cir. 2006) (finding activity is concerted where the activity consisted of an employee discussing his "concerns about bonuses with coworkers on several occasions" and his statements to management indicating that his coworkers agreed with his complaint). See also *SKD Jonesville Div.*, 340 NLRB 101, 103 (2003) (holding Section 7 protects employees' rights to discuss work-related matters with each other); *Aroostook County Regional*, 317 NLRB 218, 220 (1995), enfd. denied 81 F.3d 209 (D.C. Cir. 1996) (holding that employees' complaints to each other about schedule changes constitutes protected concerted activity).

2. Question: Is the activity "protected" under the Act?

Answer: Yes. The subject matter, overtime and supervisor's mistreatment of employees considered by the Board to be terms and conditions of employment under the Act. See *Salon/Spa at Boro*, and Champion *Home Builders, supra.*

3. Question: Did the employees engage in protected concerted activity at the barbecue?

Answer: Yes. For the same reasons discussed above, the employees' discussions at the barbecue and their decision to raise their concerns about overtime and their supervisor to the owners constitute protected concerted activity.

3rd **Paragraph:**

1. Question: Did Supervisor Green violate the Act by making the following statement to Ray: "I know what you are up to. There will be consequences if you go to the owners and complain about me. I would start looking for another job if I were you because I am going to can you."

Answer: Yes. This statement is an independent violation of Section 8(a)(1) because it constitutes an unlawful threat of discharge for engaging in protected concerted activity. See *Triple Play Sports Bar and Grill*, 361 NLRB No. 31, slip op. (2014) (finding that the employer's threat to discharge employees for protected concerted activity on Facebook violates Section 8(a)(1) of the Act).

2. Question: What framework is applicable to assessing whether the Employer's discharge of Ray was a lawful action given Ray throwing the shovel and telling Green that she is "a f—king piece of shit?"

Answer: The proper framework for analyzing this issue is *Atlantic Steel Co.*, 245 NLRB 814 (1979) because their conversation pertained exclusively to Ray's protected concerted activity of discussing with coworkers concerns about over time and supervisor Green and their group decision to bring those concerns to the owners. Typically, the Board applies the *Atlantic Steel* factors to analyze whether direct communications, face-to-face in the workplace, between an employee and a manager or supervisor constituted conduct so opprobrious that the employee lost the protection of the Act. *Triple Play Sports Bar and Grill*, 361 NLRB No. 31, slip op. (2014).

The Board would likely find that Ray did not lose the protection of the Act. In that regard, the topic of the discussion was Ray's protected concerted activity at the barbeque. In addition, Ray's outburst was provoked by Green's unlawful threat to discharge Ray if she continued to engage in protected concerted activity. See *Consumers Power Co.,* 282 NLRB 130, 132 (1986)("disputes over wages, hours, and working conditions are among the disputes most likely to engender ill feelings and strong responses"); *Plaza Auto Center, Inc.*, 360 NLRB No. 117 (2014)(employee raised his voice, stood up, pushed a chair, called the manager a "fucking crook," "stupid," "asshole," and said manager would "regret it" if he was fired, actions all held protected); *Felix Industries, Inc.*, 339 NLRB 195, 196-197 (2003) adopted by 2004 WL 1498151 (D.C. Cir. 2004) (Board found employee did not lose the protection of the Act during the course of protected concerted activity where the supervisor was hostile to the employees' protected, concerted activity and the employee yelled at the supervisor "You're just a fucking kid. I don't have to listen to a fucking kid. Things were a lot different before you were here").

3. Question for Discussion: Under the new *Babcock* standards, what type of language would the contract need to contain for the arbitrator to decide the statutory issues? If the contract did not contain language about protected concerted activity would the arbitrators decide these statutory issues in the event that the parties entered into an agreement authorizing the arbitrator to do so?

Fourth Paragraph: **LIGHTLY**

Question: Whether the Employer denied Lightly his Weingarten rights in violation
      of Section 8(a)(1) of the Act.

An employer interferes with employees Section 7 rights by requiring an employee
to take part in an investigatory interview without union representation if the employee
requests representation and has a reasonable fear that discipline could occur. *NLRB v.
J. Weingarten, Inc.,* 420 U.S. 251 (1975). The *Weingarten* right to union representation
during the course of an interview arises if the interview is investigatory and a reasonable
person would believe that the interview might result in discipline. Id.

Here, a reasonable person would believe that Lightly would be subject to
discipline if he were to succumb to the questioning by the owners because the owners
told Lightly that they suspected that he was somehow involved in the disappearance of
product from the greenhouse, which is a basis for termination.

An employee's Weingarten right to representation at an investigatory interview
attaches when the employee requests the presence of representative. It is irrelevant
that the employer does not volunteer to provide representation, or that the employee is
frightened and confused during the interview. *Weingarten,* 420 U.S. at 257;
Montgomery Ward & Co., 269 NLRB 904, 904-905 (1984).

Here, Lightly has a right to his *Weingarten* representative because he requested
one.

Once an employee makes a valid request for a union representative, the burden
is on the employer to (1) grant the request, (2) discontinue the interview, or (3) offer the
employee the choice of a meeting without a representative or of no meeting at all.
Postal Service, 241 NLRB 141 (1979).

Here, the owners did not abide by any of these options. The owners did not
grant Lightly's request for union representation nor offered Lightly the choice of meeting
without the representative or no meeting at all; instead, the owners continued the
interview by demanding that Lightly submit to a drug test. Because requiring Lightly to
submit to a drug test was part of the owners' investigation into whether Lightly was
involved in the disappearance of product, the owners continued the investigatory
interview without affording Lightly a union representation in violation of Section 8(a)(1).
See *Manhattan Beer Distributors, LLC,* 362 NLRB No. 192, slip op. at 2 (2015) (where
an employer insists that an employee submit to a drug and/or alcohol test as part of an
investigation into an employee's alleged misconduct, the employee has a right to union
representation before consenting to take the test) (citations omitted).

Question: Whether the Employer discharged Steward Lightly because he engaged in Section 7 activity in violation of Section 8(a)(3) of the Act.

An employer violates both Sections 8(a)(1) and (3) when it disciplines an employee for engaging in protected concerted activity of enforcing the provision of a collective bargaining agreement. *Tillford Contractors*, 317 NLRB 68, 69 (1995).

In assessing whether a discipline is unlawful, the Board applies a mixed motive analysis, which is set out in *Wright Line*, 251 NLRB 1083 (1980), enfd. on other grounds 662 F.2d 899 (1st Cir. 1981), cert. denied 455 U.S. 989 (1982), approved in *NLRB v. Transportation Management Corp.*, 462 U.S. 393 (1983). Under *Wright Line*, the General Counsel must first demonstrate, by a preponderance of the evidence, that the worker's protected conduct was a motivating factor in the adverse action. The General Counsel satisfies this initial burden by showing: (1) the individual's protected activity; (2) employer knowledge of such activity; and (3) animus. If the General Counsel meets his initial burden, the burden shifts to the employer to prove that it would have taken the adverse action, even absent the protected activity. See, e.g., *Mesker Door*, 357 NLRB No. 59, slip op. at 2 (2011). The employer cannot meet its burden, however, merely by showing that it had a legitimate reason for its action; rather, it must demonstrate that it would have taken the same action in the absence of the protected conduct. *Bruce Packing Co.*, 357 NLRB No. 93, slip op. at 3–4 (2011). If the employer's proffered reasons are pretextual (i.e., either false or not actually relied on), the employer fails by definition to show that it would have taken the same action for those reasons regardless of the protected conduct. *Metropolitan Transportation Services*, 351 NLRB 657, 659 (2007).

A.   Whether Lightly Engaged in Section 7 Activity.

Rule: When an employee makes an attempt to enforce a collective-bargaining agreement, he is acting in the interest of all employees covered by the contract. It has long been held that such activity is concerted and protected under the Act. *NLRB v. City Disposal Systems*, 465 U.S. 822, 840 (1984); *Interboro Contractors*, 157 NLRB 1295 (1966). An employee making such a complaint need not specifically refer to the collective-bargaining agreement. As long as the nature of the complaint is reasonably clear to the person to whom it is communicated, and the complaint does, in fact, refer to a reasonably perceived violation of the collective-bargaining agreement, the complaining employee is engaged in the process of enforcing that agreement. *Bechtel Power Corp.*, 277 NLRB 882, 884 (1985); *Roadway Express*, 217 NLRB 278, 279 (1975).

Here, Lightly demanded that the owners provide him with union representation because the contract provides an employee with one when questioned about stealing or smoking pot at work. Accordingly, under *Interboro,* Lightly engaged in protected, Section 7 activity.

B.   Whether the Owners Knew of Lightly Section 7 Activity.

In this case, Lightly's remark that "the contract states that [he] [is] entitled to Union representation when [the owners] meet with [him] to discuss an employee stealing or smoking product at work" is reasonably clear that he is asserting a contractual right.

C.   Whether There Is Sufficient Evidence of Animus

Statements by the employer that are specific as to the consequences of protected activities and are consistent with the actions taken against the employee. (*see*, *e.g.*, *Wells Fargo Armored Services Corp.*, 322 NLRB 616, 616 (1996) (unlawful motivation found where employer unlawfully threatened to discharge employees who were still out in support of a strike, and then disciplined an employee who remained out on strike following the threat).

Here, Santa Ana threatened Lightly with automatic discharge if he left an otherwise unlawful investigatory interview where he protested that the owners denied is contractual (and statutory) right to a union representation. Indeed, when Lightly refused to submit to a drug test in the absence of a union representative, the owners fired him in response to his protected activity.

Statements of animus directed to the employee or about the employee's protected activities. See, e.g., *Austal USA, LLC*, 356 NLRB No. 65, slip op.1 (2010) (unlawful motivation found where HR director directly interrogated and threatened union activist, and supervisors told activist that management was "after her" because of her union activities).

Here, Santa Ana's statement to Paul Arbusto that Lightead was terminated because "he was fake and for being a pinking and because of his involvement with the Union" proves this element.

Fifth Paragraph Arbusto's Discharge

Question: Whether the Employer discharged Arbusto because she engaged in Section 7 activity in violation of Section 8(a)(1) and 8(a)(3) of the Act.

When a respondent-employer defends disciplinary action based on employee misconduct that is part of the res gestae of the employee's protected activity, the Board typically analyzes the case under the four-factor test set forth in *Atlantic Steel Co.*, 245 NLRB 814, 816 (1979), rather than using a *Wright-Line* analysis. *Fresenius USA Mfg., Inc.*, 358 NLRB No. 138, slip op. at 5 (2012); *Aluminum Co. of America*, 338 NLRB 20, 22 (2002); *Atlantic Steel Co.*, 245 NLRB 814 (1979). The rationale behind this is that there is an assumed causal connection between the protected activity of the employee and the discipline, and the pivotal issue is whether the employee's conduct was removed from the Act's protection under the criteria set out in *Atlantic Steel Co.*, above. *Aluminum Co. of America*; see also *Atlantic Scaffolding Co.*, 356 NLRB No. 113, slip op. at 5 (2011); *Phoenix Transit System*, 337 NLRB 510, 510 (2002), enfd. 63 Fed. Appx. 524 (D.C. Cir. 2003).

Here, the General Counsel asserts that Arbusto was discharged in violation of Section 8(a)(3) because he engaged in Section 7 activity. On the other hand, the Employer contends that Arbusto was fired for being disrespectful, aggressive and shouting in front of customers and employees, presumably while engaging in protected Section 7 activity.

The threshold inquiry is whether Arbusto engaged in Section 7 activity. Here, the evidence shows that Arbusto engaged in Section 7 activity by seeking to enforce the provisions of his collective-bargaining agreement dealing with his work assignments and that of the other enablers. *NLRB v. City Disposal Systems*, 465 U.S. 822, 840 (1984); *Interboro Contractors*, 157 NLRB 1295 (1966). In this regard, Arbusto told Santa Ana that the contract provides that he and other enablers cannot be required to work in the greenhouse when Santa Ana told him that he needed to work there immediately. When Santa Ana disregarded his protected protest, Arbusto continued to assert his contractual rights, albeit he was shouting, by pulling out the union contract and telling Santa Ana "It's right here in black and white, you cannot make me work in the greenhouse." Second, there is enough evidence that Santa Ana knew Arbusto was engaging in protected activity. Based on Arbusto's assertion, Santa Ana could reasonably perceive Arbusto's complaint to concern a violation of the collective-bargaining agreement. Furthermore, knowledge is further proven by Santa Ana's statement, "I do not care what it says in your stupid contract." Without question, Arbusto was engaged in protected Section 7 activity.

Now that it has been established that Arbusto engaged in Section 7 activity, we turn to the *Atlantic Steel Co.*, supra, analysis. The following four factors are considered, and weighed in the aggregate: (1) the place of discussion; (2) the subject matter; (3) the nature of the employee's outburst; and (4) whether the outburst was in any way provoked by the employer's unfair labor practice.

As in *Fresenius USA Mfg., Inc.*, 358 NLRB slip op. at 6, if the place of discussion is one that is unlikely to disrupt production, i.e., a nonwork area, it favors continued protection. As another factor here, the Board considers whether the comments were made in the presence of other employees and, if so, the location factor is neutral. Id.; *Beverly Health & Rehabilitation Services*, 346 NLRB 1319, 1322 fn. 20 (2006). Here, because the place of discussion occurred in the presence of customers, we presume that it occurred in the work floor. If so, this factor does not favor continued protection. However, because Arbusto's protected activity was also in the presence of other employees, this weighs in favor of continued protected. At best, this factor is neutral.

As to the subject matter, Arbusto's activity—seeking to enforce a contractual right—went to the heart of collective bargaining. See the cases cited above. This factor weighs strongly in favor of continued protection. *Postal Service*, 360 NLRB No. 74 slip op. (2014).

As to the nature of the employee's outburst, the issue is whether it was "sufficiently egregious" to remove him from the Act's protection. See *Coca Cola Puerto Rico Bottlers*, 358 NLRB No. 129, slip op. at 3 fn. 12 (2012); *Stanford Hotel*, 344 NLRB 558, 558 (2005).

The Board draws a line between "cases where employees engaged in concerted actions that exceeded the bounds of lawful conduct in a moment of animal exuberance or in a manner not motivated by improper motives and those flagrant cases in which the conduct is so violent or of such character to render the employee unfit for further service."' *Kiewit Power Constructors Co.*, 355 NLRB 708, 711 (2010), enfd. 652 F.3d 22 (D.C. Cir. 2011), citing *Prescott Industrial Products Co.*, 205 NLRB 51, 51-52 (1973). In *Kiewit*, the Board found protected remarks that were "intemperate" but simple, brief, and spontaneous reactions, distinguishing them from premeditated, sustained personal threats, or unambiguous or outright threats of personal violence. Id.; see also *Fresenius*, 358 NLRB slip op. at 6-7; *Beverly Health*, 346 NLRB at 1322-1323.

Here, the Employer contends that Arbusto was disrespectful, aggressive and was shouting in front of customers and other employees as the reason for his termination. In the absence of physical threats of violence, Arbusto's shouting and telling Santa Ana that he is "one stupid businessman" in the midst of engaging in protected activity is not sufficiently egregious to lose the Act's protection, especially considering that it was provoked by Santa Ana's unfair labor practice, as discussed below. Compare *Stanford Hotel*, 344 NLRB at 559 (the Board found that an employee calling a supervisor "a f--ing son of a bitch" while angrily pointing a finger at him weighed against protection. Nevertheless, other factors weighed in favor of protection, and the Board concluded that the employee's conduct was protected.)

The last factor is provocation by the employer's unfair labor practices. This does not require that the employer's conduct be explicitly alleged as an **unfair labor practice** so long as the conduct evinces an intent to interfere with protected rights. *Network Dynamics Cabling, Inc.*, 351 NLRB 1423, 1429 (2007) (manager provoked employee by admonishing him to cease engaging in union activity); *Overnite Transportation Co.*, 343 NLRB 1431, 1438 (2004) (supervisor provoked union steward, who was seeking information relevant to possible discharge grievances, by his "complete: and "hostile" refusal to discuss the situation).

Here, Arbusto's shouting and comments towards Santa Ana were provoked by the Employer's unfair labor practice. While is not alleged as an unfair labor practice, Santa Ana's statement to Arbusto that "The Door is right there buddy. If you do not like your new assignment go ahead and go. You are working in the greenhouse or nowhere " amounted to an implied threat of discharge and, thus, an unfair labor practice in violation of Section 8(a)(1).   The Board has held that an employer's invitation to an employee to quit in response to their exercise of protected concerted activity is coercive, the Board approved the administrative law judges' finding that: because it conveys to employees that support for their union or engaging in other coercive activities and their continued employment are not compatible, and implicitly threaten discharge of the employees involved. *McDaniel Ford, Inc.*, 356 NLRB 956, 956 n.1, 962 (1997) (citing *Stoody Co.*, 312 NLRB 1175, 1181 (1993); *Kenrich Petrochemicals,* 291 NLRB 519, 531 (1989); *L.A. Baker Electric, Inc.*, 265 NLRB 1579, 1580 (1983)). See also *Jupiter Medical Ctr. Pavilion*, 346 NLRB 650, 651 (2006) (employer's statement that, if employee was unhappy, "[m]aybe this isn't the place for you . . . there are a lot of jobs out there" was implied threat of discharge); *Chinese Daily News*, 346 NLRB 906, 906 (2006) (Board found that an employer telling an employee to resign if she was not happy with her job in response to protected concerted activity was an implied threat) enfd. 224 Fed.Appx. 6 (D.C. Cir. 2007); (*Paper Mart,* 319 NLRB 9, 9 (1995) (Board found that, in the context of the discussion about an employee soliciting for the union, the president's statement that if employee "was not happy he could seek employment elsewhere" was an implicit threat of discharge); *Intertherm, Inc.*, 235 NLRB 693, 693 n.6 (1978) (Board found that a supervisor's statement that if the employee " 'was not happy with the Company, he should look elsewhere for a job' " made in the context of a reprimand issued to the employee because of his absence to serve as the union observer), enfd. in part, denied in part 596 F.2d 267 (8th Cir. 1979). Accordingly, because Arbusto's shouting and remarks towards Santa Ana were provoked by the latter's unlawful threat of discharge, Arbusto's conduct did not lose the Act's protection.

In summary, all of the four *Atlantic Steel* factors, individually and in the aggregate, weight in Arbusto's favor, and his behavior did not remove his conduct on June 16, 2015 from the protection of the Act. Accordingly, the Employer discharged Arbusto in violation of Section 8(a)(3) and 8(a)(1).

Question: Whether the fact that Abrusto made negative comments about the Employer's product in the presence of customers changes the analysis?

Employee appeals concerning employment conditions made to third-parties, i.e. parties outside the immediate employer-employee relationship· are ·analyzed under the Supreme Court's decision in *Jefferson Standard,* 343 U.S. 464 (1953). Under *Jefferson Standard,* employee communications to third parties in an effort to obtain their support are protected where the communication indicated it is related to an ongoing dispute between the employees and the employer and the communication is not so disloyal, reckless, or maliciously untrue as to lose the Act's protection. *Mountain Shadows Golf Resort,* 330 NLRB 1238 (2000). For example, in *Jefferson Standard,* the Court upheld the discharge of employees who publicly attacked the quality of their employer's product and its business practices without relating their criticisms to a labor controversy. The Court found that the employees' conduct amounted to disloyal disparagement of their employer and, as a result, fell outside the Act's protection. 346 U.S. at 475-477

Here, it could be argued that the *Jefferson Standard* analysis should be applied because the confrontation between Abrusto and Santa Ana took place in the presence of customers. See *Triple Play Sports Bar & Grille*, 361 NLRB No. 31 slip. op at 3 (2014) (analyzing the legality of an employee's protected concerted activity on Facebook under the *Jefferson Standard* framework and specifically holding that *Atlantic Steel* framework is inapplicable to Facebook posts).

The first step in the *Jefferson Standard* analysis is to determine whether Abrusto's comments are related to a labor dispute and conditions of his employment. As discussed above, Abrusto was engaged in protected concerted activity as he was asserting his contractual right that specifically provides that enablers cannot be required to work in the warehouse

Next, it must be determined whether Abrusto lost the protection of the Act because his statements about the Santa Ana and the Employer's product were so disloyal, reckless, or maliciously untrue as to lose the Act's protection. See *Emarco, Inc.*, 284 NLRB 832, 833 (1987). Statements have been found to be unprotected as disloyal where they are made "at a critical time in the initiation of the company's" business and where they constitute "a sharp, public, disparaging attack upon the quality of the company's product and its business policies, in a manner reasonably calculated to harm the company's reputation and reduce its income." *NLRB v. Electrical Workers Local 1229 (Jefferson Standard)*, 346 U.S. 464, 472 (1953); accord: *Endicott Interconnect Technologies, Inc. v. NLRB*, 453 F.3d 532, 537 (D.C. Cir. 2006), denying enforcement of 345 NLRB 448 (2005). The Board is careful, however, "to distinguish between disparagement of an employer's product and the airing of what may be highly sensitive issues." *Professional Porter & Window Cleaning* Co., supra at 139. To lose the Act's protection as an act of disloyalty, an employee's public criticism of an employer must evidence "a malicious motive." *Richboro Community Mental Health Council*, 242 NLRB 1267, 1268 (1979).

Here, Abrusto called Santa Ana "one stupid businessman" and stated that "the only reason your customers keep coming back and buying your rat-poison laced edibles is the other enablers and I have told them it's a special secret formula."

Abrusto's first statement that Santa Ana is a "stupid businessman" is not so disloyal or reckless to lose the Act's protection. See *El San Juan Hotel*, 289 NLRB 1453, 1455 (1988) (leaflet's "references to the trustee as a 'Dictator' and as 'Robin Hood' [were] obvious rhetorical hyperbole"); *NLRB v. Container Corp. of America*, 649 F.2d 1213, 1214, 1215-1216 (6th Cir. 1981) (newsletter criticizing company's grievance process and calling the general manager a "slave driver" was protected rhetoric), enfg. in relevant part 244 NLRB 318 (1979).

Abrusto's second statement that "the only reason your customers keep coming back and buying your rat-poison laced edibles is the other enablers and I have told them it's a special secret formula" is a closer issue. Under the circumstances of this case where Abrusto was not specifically appealing to customers but rather customers happened to be present during the confrontation and Abrusto's comments were provoked by the Employer's unfair labor practices, would militate in favor of the Board would likely find his statement protected. See *Miklin Enterprises Inc.,* 361 NLRB No. 27 (2014) (finding protected posters about the sick leave policy on community bulletin boards in the Respondent's stores. The poster displayed side-by-side pictures of a sandwich, one described as made by a healthy Jimmy John's worker and the other as made by a sick worker. The poster stated, "Can't Tell the Difference? That's too bad because Jimmy John's workers don't get paid sick days. Shoot, we can't even call in sick. We hope your immune system is ready because you are about to take the sandwich test. Help Jimmy John's workers win sick days.") As against that, the employee's exclamation, which he knew customers would hear, that the employer laced its product with rat poison arguably amounts to product disparagement and "maliciousness" beyond the protection of the Act.

6th **Paragraph Jeff Bridges**

Question: Whether Jeff Bridges as suspended pursuant to an unlawful rule in violation of Section 8(a)(1) of the Act.

In *The Continental Group, Inc.,* 357 NLRB No. 39, slip op. at 6 (2011) (citations omitted), the Board held that discipline imposed pursuant to an unlawful rule is invalid under the following circumstances:

Discipline imposed pursuant to an unlawfully overbroad rule violates the Act in those situations in which an employee violated ·the rule by (1) engaging in protected conduct or (2) engaging in conduct that otherwise implicates the concerns underlying Section 7 of the Act. Nevertheless, an employer will avoid liability for discipline imposed pursuant to an overbroad rule if it can establish that the employee's conduct actually interfered with the employee's own work or that of other employees or otherwise actually interfered with the employer's operations, and that the interference, rather than the violation of the rule, was the reason for the discipline. It is the employer's burden, not only to assert this affirmative defense, but also to establish that the employee's interference with production or operations was the actual reason for the discipline. In this regard, an employer's mere citation of the overbroad rule as the basis for discipline will not suffice to meet its burden. Rather, ·assuming that the employer provides the employee with a reason (either written or oral) for its imposition of discipline, the employer must demonstrate that it cited the employee's interference with production and not. simply the violation of the overbroad rule.

A. Whether the Employer's "Handbook Policy 23 "No Loitering Rule" is Unlawfully Overbroad.

In determining whether the maintenance of a work rule violates Section 8(a)(1), the appropriate inquiry is whether it reasonably tends to chill employees in the exercise of their Section 7 rights. *Lafayette Park Hotel,* 326 NLRB 824, 825 (1998), enfd. 203 F.3d 52 (D.C. Cir. 1999). Under the test enunciated in *Lutheran Heritage Village-Livonia,* 343 NLRB 646 (2004)', if the rule explicitly restricts Section 7 rights, it is unlawful. If it does not, "the violation is dependent upon a showing of one of the following: (1) employees would reasonably construe the language to prohibit Section 7 activity; (2) the rule was promulgated in response to union activity; or (3) the rule has been applied to restrict the exercise of Section 7 rights." Id. at 647 A rule does not violate the Act if a reasonable employee merely *could* conceivably read it as barring Section 7 activity. Rather, the inquiry is whether a reasonable employee *would* read the rule as prohibiting Section 7 activity. Id.

The Employer's Handbook Policy 23 states that "[E]mployees may not loiter in the parking lot or other outdoor non-work areas of the company's property more than 20 minutes after shift end time." Applying the *Lafayette Park Hotel* test, the Employer's no-loitering rule does not explicitly restrict Section 7 activity, was not promulgated in response to Section 7 activity, nor has been applied to prohibit Section 7 activity. Thus, the relevant inquiry is whether employees would reasonably construe the rule to prohibit Section 7 activity.

The legality of off-duty employee access rules is governed by the Board's test, set forth in *Tri-County Medical Center,* 222 NLRB 1089, 1089 (1976). Therein, the Board held that "except where justified by business concerns, a rule which denies off-duty employees entry to parking lots, gates, and other outside, nonworking areas will be found unlawful. The Board also found that a no-access rule, concerning off-duty employees, will be found valid only if it (1) limits access solely with respect to the interior of the plant and other working areas; (2) is clearly disseminated to all employees; and (3) applies to off-duty employees seeking access to the plant for any purpose and not just to those employees engaging in union activities. In short, a rule which denies off-duty employees entry to outside nonworking areas is invalid unless justified by valid business considerations. *The Presbyterian Medical Center,* 227 NLRB 904, 905 (1977); *Eastern Maine Medical Center,* 253 NLRB 224, 241 (1980).

Here, the Employer's no-loitering rule is unlawfully overbroad because it is not limited to the interior areas of the plant. Instead, the rule restricts off-duty employee access to the Employer's parking lot and other outdoor non-work areas of the company's property. Indeed, the Board has found similar rules unlawful. E.g., *Lutheran Heritage Village-Livonia,* 343 NLRB 646, 655 (2004) (a rule prohibiting "[l]oitering on company property (the premises) without permission from the Administrator" violated Section 8(a)(1));Tecumseh *Packaging Solutions, Inc.,* 352 NLRB 694, 694··(2008) (a work rule. prohibiting "[l]oitering on Company property after working hours" was unlawful). In so finding, the Board has explained that "employees could reasonably interpret the rule to prohibit-them from lingering on the [r]espondent's premises after the end of a shift in order to engage in Sec[tion] 7 activities, such as the discussion of workplace concerns." *Lutheran Heritage,* 343 NLRB at 649 fn. 16. While employers may raise various concerns to ban after-hours loitering, such as prevention of violence and avoidance of liability for accidents and injuries, nothing in the Board's decisions prevent employers from maintaining rules and policies tailored to those concerns, so long as it does not maintain overbroad no-loitering rules. *Tecumseh Packaging Solutions, Inc.,* 352 NLRB at 694. For these reasons, the Employer's has maintained an unlawfully overbroad "no-loitering" rule in violation of Section 8(a)(1) of the Act.

B.   Now That We Found the No-Loitering Rule to Be Unlawfully Overbroad, The Issue Remains Whether Jeff Bridges' Suspension is Unlawful under *The Continental Group, Inc.*

Here, the Employer, by supervisor Green, admittedly suspended Jeff Bridges because he violated handbook policy 23, which we have determined is unlawfully overbroad in violation of Section 8(a)(1) of the Act. Under *The Continental Group* test, discipline imposed pursuant to an unlawfully overbroad rule violates the Act in those situations in which an employee violated the rule by (1) engaging in protected conduct or (2) engaging in conduct that otherwise implicates the concerns underlying Section 7 of the Act. 357 NLRB slip op. at 6. Here, Jeff Bridges was not engaged in protected concerted conduct, such as discussing wages, hours or other terms and conditions of employment with his coworkers or other individuals. Instead, Jeff Bridges was disciplined for talking to the Employer's customers after work and finding out what their favorite products were, as he told his supervisor. Accordingly, his suspension is not unlawful under the first prong of the *Continental Group* test.

His suspension, however, might be found unlawful under the second prong of the test because engaging in discussions with the Employer's customers is conduct that otherwise implicates concerns underlying Section 7 of the Act. In this regard, employees have a right to talk about their wages, hours, and other terms and conditions of employment with their coworkers and other individuals, such as the Employer's clients. *Eastex v. NLRB,* 437 U.S. 556, 565 (1978) (The protections under Section 7 of the Act extends to employee efforts to improve their terms and conditions of employment, or their "lot as employees," through channels outside the immediate employee-employer relationship.); *Handicabs, Inc.,* 318 NLRB 890 (1995) (employees have a protected right to raise concerns about their terms and conditions of employment to the employer's clients), enfd. 95 F.3d 681 (8th Cir. 1996), cert. denied 521 U.S. 1118 (1997). Here, because the Employer disciplined Jeff Bridges because he was in the parking lot talking to customers while off-duty, the suspension has the effect of discouraging him and other employees from engaging in further discussions with Employer's client that could one day develop into full blown protected Section 7 conduct, such as the discussion of wages, hours, and terms and conditions of employment. Accordingly, the discipline may have been unlawful under the second prong of *The Continental Group* test, a new area of the law in which there is not yet a wide body of experience.

Under *The Continental Group,* in order to avoid liability for the discipline imposed pursuant to an overbroad rule, the Employer must establish that the employee's conduct actually interfered with the employee's own work or that of other employees or otherwise actually interfered with the employer's operations. The Employer cannot meet is burden because Jeff Bridges was not on-the-clock when he engaged in conversations with the customers nor was he conversing with other employees who were working. For these reasons, Bridges' suspension is unlawful under Section 8(a)(1) of the Act because it was issued pursuant to an unlawfully overbroad no-loitering rule if the second prong of *The Continental Group* is satisfied.

CPSIA information can be obtained
at www.ICGtesting.com
Printed in the USA
LVHW050423191122
733530LV00006B/584